10
Steps to
Fashion
Freedom

10
Steps to
Fashion
Freedom

Discover Your Personal Style from the Inside Out

Malcolm Levene
& Kate Mayfield

Crown Publishers
New York

Copyright © 2001 by Malcolm Levene and Kate Mayfield

Published by Crown Publishers, New York, New York.
Member of the Crown Publishing Group.

Random House, Inc. New York, Toronto, London, Sydney, Auckland
www.randomhouse.com

Crown is a trademark and the Crown colophon is a registered trademark of Random House, Inc.

Printed in the United States of America

Design by Debbie Glasserman

Library of Congress Cataloging-in-Publication Data

Levene, Malcolm.
    10 steps to fashion freedom : discover your personal style from the inside out / by Malcolm Levene and Kate Mayfield.
        1. Clothing and dress.   2. Fashion.   3. Grooming for men.
    4. Identity (Psychology).   I. Title: Ten steps to fashion freedom
    II. Mayfield, Kate.   III. Title.
    TT507.L447 2001
    646'3—dc21   00-065615

ISBN 0-609-60645-X

10 9 8 7 6 5 4 3 2 1

First Edition

For the clients and customers

who placed their confidence in us.

Their courage and trust made

this book possible.

ACKNOWLEDGMENTS

We gratefully acknowledge and express deep appreciation to the many wonderful people who have made this book a reality:

To our agent, David Vigliano, for his unfailing commitment and belief in our book and our ability to write it ourselves. And to the staff at Vigliano Associates, for their help and guidance.

To Kristin Kiser, our gifted editor at Crown, whose encouragement, insight, and skill in editing helped to produce the best book possible. We are also grateful for her solid expression of exuberance for the work in *10 Steps*.

To Janet Biehl, we thank you for your talent for being an eloquent streamliner and your ability to juggle sensitively. Thank you for understanding.

To Susan Leon, whose tenacious act of retrieving our knowledge taught us how to proceed for the duration of the writing process.

To Alex Smithline, who is largely responsible for converting the 10 Sessions to book form.

To Gus Campbell, for not changing your telephone number! Thank you, Gus, for sharing your unmatched talent. Your understanding of visual balance, incredible sense of color, and visual harmony are gorgeous. Mind the gap and ta ever so.

To Denise Stewart, whose valuable suggestions, literary prowess, and the generous gift of her time equaled her unwavering support.

To the heads of companies, who have had foresight and confidence in us in allowing us to work with their employees.

To Jim Kakalik, our own personal computer wizard, who brought us into the 2000s. His expertise, patience, and good humor with our computer panics were steadfast and generous. We literally could not have done it without him.

A huge thank-you to family members in Kentucky, who both received and placed many phone calls and e-mails laced with love to break up the long days of writing. We love you and appreciate your support.

To the Learning Annex, which provided a place for us to teach *and* learn in our workshops and seminars for many months.

To Roberto, Tom, and Lonnie, who generously provided great coffee with a smile at a time of morning when almost no one smiles.

To the many people who have served as our teachers over the years, who don't necessarily go by that title.

To Dean English, who always knew which button to keep pushed. Immeasurable thanks!

We have found the writing process to be immensely rewarding, but at times it has been isolating and frustrating. It is with profound love and respect that we thank each other for employing a great deal of humor and the three *D*'s—desire, discipline, and determination to keep writing.

CONTENTS

	Introduction	1
Session 1	PASSIONATE BEGINNINGS	25
Session 2	CREATING YOUR PERSONAL STYLE STATEMENT	42
Session 3	HEALING YOUR IMAGE WOUNDS	61
Session 4	YOUR INNER STYLE INVENTORY	97
Session 5	THE AESTHETIC FIELD TRIP	139
Session 6	THE SPIRIT OF CLOTHES	148
Session 7	COLOR	190
Session 8	YOUR PERSONAL STYLE PROFILE	217
Session 9	CLOSET ANALYSIS	229
Session 10	SHOPPING	265
	A Final Word	299
	Index	301

10
Steps to Fashion Freedom

INTRODUCTION

"I have a closet overflowing with clothes—but nothing I put on feels right for me. Every morning when I go to my closet to get dressed I just stand there and stare. I feel I have nothing to wear and I get upset. It's a terrible start to my day."

—JANET

"I know that my image is not up to par with the position I hold at my job. I want to look more successful."

—ALAN

"A few days ago I wore my favorite jeans, and I felt and looked great in them. Only a couple of days later I put them on and they made me feel fat and I thought I looked terrible in them. What happened? What's going on?"

—CHRISTINE

"My husband and I fight about his clothes every weekend. He always looks like he doesn't care."

—VICKY

"I hate shopping. I've gained some weight and nothing fits me anymore, and I feel self-conscious when I go shopping."

—JAKE

"My children are no longer living at home, and I'm starting a new career. All of a sudden I have absolutely nothing to wear and no idea where to start."

—ANNA

"I have a pretty conservative dress code for business. How can I put my own stamp on my wardrobe without rocking the boat?"
—ANDREW

"I'm too old to wear trendy and certainly not old enough to wear matronly. How can I look stylish and current on a reasonable budget?"
—FRAN

How do you feel when you look in your closet every morning? Do you feel confident that your clothing choices allow you to present yourself most effectively in business? When you are in social and casual environments, do you feel self-assured and comfortable with the way you look? Or do you find it a challenge to get yourself dressed for the day? Do you constantly worry about the way you look, never quite satisfied with your overall appearance? Do the clothes you wear express who you really are?

Everyone we've met—clients, associates, friends, ourselves included—has experienced some form of insecurity, confusion, or dissatisfaction about his or her image. Our clients have included celebrities, politicians, world leaders, business executives, homemakers, models, teachers, and people from all walks of life. Although the scope of their image concerns have varied widely, all of them have had one thing in common—they had not yet discovered their own personal style.

You have a personal style. You have specific and unique tastes. You have your own sensibilities, values, passions, and dislikes, as well as your own sense of what image you would like to project. But self-doubt, conditioning, and the desire to please others often combine to prevent authentic self-expression. Being concerned about other people's opinions of us becomes a habit, so much a part of ourselves that we lose our true identity.

You may simply be unaware of what kind of image you are projecting. You may deny or ignore your own desire to cultivate your image. Perhaps, as you grew into adulthood, you left behind your personal style because of conditioning from family and friends or the demands of your business or career. Perhaps your mother repeatedly told you when you were younger that you could never wear a certain color. Or maybe the demands of your business restrict your image. Have you been running after an image you want to project but are now becoming worn out from the race?

Many of you are projecting *a style* that is not your own personal style but a composite of others' interpretations of a particular style. And some of you who think you are projecting your personal style may not actually be doing so. Your desire to look a certain way—cute, manly, sexy, strong, younger, fill in the blank—has camouflaged the most interesting aspect of your image—you. That's right, the real you is so much more interesting than the "you" that you attempt to project.

Each and every day we have to present ourselves to the world, and like it or not, other people judge us based on the way we look. Social scientists tell us that our personal image can affect the way we are treated, even our credibility in certain situations. Within the first fifteen seconds of our meeting someone, a subconscious impact is made. Simply by the clothes we choose to wear and the image we project, others may judge our class, imagination, state of mind, sexuality, financial status, self-esteem, personality, politics, and individuality.

Think of how many times you have read a novel, newspaper article, or magazine story in which someone's clothes were described in detail. Authors use the way a person is dressed to tell readers something about his or her personality. Clothing choices are a window into the person's character, into who he or she really is.

Solving the question of identity is something we all have to do eventually. Your identity speaks to your individuality and the characteristics that manifest as your personality. Ideally your identity, your uniqueness, is something that you project in your image.

The word *image* is usually associated with public manipulation and an emphasis on appearance over substance. But when we talk about image in this book, we mean something deeper, something more serious and vital than that casual shorthand. Your image is the totality of how you present yourself to the world—your visual presentation of your inner and outer self. It is the manifestation of your personal style. When we teach you how to define your personal style, we will be helping you to project an image that is authentic. When people use image to camouflage the truth about themselves, it is often called "trendy" or even "fashionable."

The subject of image and personal style has never been taken seriously. We have all been conditioned to believe that caring about the way we look is vain, self-indulgent, shallow, and in the grand scheme of things, unimportant. But image is integral and relevant within that grand scheme. It is a serious matter, because it affects how we live, our self-confidence, and the way we feel about ourselves in the world. What could be more serious than that?

Perhaps you are thinking, "I don't care how I look—I'm fine the way I am." We're not saying that you're not fine the way you are—but we firmly believe that everyone has a desire to improve, no matter how deeply buried that desire may be. What people usually really mean when they say "I don't care" is "I don't know what to do. I don't know where to begin, or who to ask. I feel as if I should know." When they tell themselves that image is not important, they really mean, "I'm not important enough."

Or you may be thinking, "If people are going to judge me by my appearance, then those are the wrong people for me." Of course we don't want to be judged by our appearance, but the fact remains we are and will continue to be. *You cannot avoid being judged, but you can encourage people to make judgments that will serve you rather than detract from you.* By taking care of yourself and your image, you will build more self-confidence. When you acquire more self-confidence, others will mirror that behavior by respecting you too. The ten sessions in this book were created by our work in helping people to recognize the value of discovering their personal style so that they could get on with their lives.

For eighteen years, the former Malcolm Levene retail store in London, England, played host to men and women from all walks of life. This well-known store had an excellent reputation for providing much more than beautifully designed clothes: it became renowned for its exemplary service, in which people could buy a piece of clothing and at the same time receive an image education. Customers who normally would have been intimidated by fashion learned how to make choices for themselves. Although they were informed about what was current in the world of fashion, they learned how to interpret it so that it became *their* look. The result was that the customers always felt confident about their image.

The combination of a Savile Row–trained designer and retailer (Malcolm) and an American teacher of self-development methods (Kate) proved a compatible and effective mix. We learned from each other and traded each other's experiences and expertise to create a more holistic approach to style and image.

Soon business executives who had been our very satisfied customers asked us if we could do for their employees what we had done for them. Our personal style and image-development consultancy thus was a natural outgrowth of the retail business. In addition, we were asked to conduct workshops and seminars on how to present a successful image. Over the years our work became a tried and tested method for discovering personal style—the ten sessions that you will find in this book. Although we are now based in the United States, we continue to work regularly with our corporate and private clients in Europe.

On both sides of the Atlantic, we have come to recognize, many people find change to be a challenge. The people who inhabit the world of fashion, celebrities from all fields, public figures, and the like are all *expected* to stand out and be different. They are allowed—even required—to agonize over the minutest decisions about their image. But when the woman who works in the telephone sales department of a computer company enters her workspace and is seen to be gradually changing her image, she may receive unwanted attention. Generally speaking, people are frightened by change, especially by changes that have a visual impact. They worry about what else might change, and how these changes will ultimately affect them. It all comes down to this: How is *your* change going to affect *me?*

Don't let other people's insecurities or fears get in your way. As our clients have made improvements in their image, they have been promoted, formed better relationships, and made successful career moves. Some experienced a short period of adjustment while they and the other people in their lives adapted to the progress they were making. This is quite normal.

We encourage you to remain focused on your goals. If, during the course of your work with these ten sessions, you find that someone is pressuring you to quit or is not supporting you as you might expect, communication is the most important remedy. Our clients who have communicated honestly to their family, friends, and business colleagues about this work have found that the skeptics become much more positive when they saw the wonderful changes it produced.

Most of our clients tell us that the observations and comments they have received have been encouraging and complimentary. One reason is that progress is made gradually and carefully. Slight changes in appearance or manner over time are much easier for clients to assimilate into their lifestyle than large, abrupt changes. When one of our clients attended her annual review meeting with her employer, she saw an appreciative look on his face as she entered the room. He clearly noticed a positive difference in her, in an unspoken moment of recognition and approval.

The fashion world is home to a food chain of image experts, color consultants, wardrobe consultants, personal shoppers, and clothing stylists. These savvy shoppers have eyes in the back of their heads, and they are quick to translate what they see into a look. They will tell you what to wear and how to wear it. That is not what we do. We do not want you to be dependent on our style choices, or to look for outside approval for what you are wearing. *What we do instead is teach people how to improve their image and discover their own personal style.* We provide a therapeutic road that enables and empowers people to successfully find their true style and make positive changes in the image they present.

You can buy someone else's taste; you can buy the services of a personal shopper; you can buy beautiful clothes; you can even buy beauty. But you can't buy your personal style.

THE PROBLEM WITH CATEGORIES

Unlike most books about style, *10 Steps to Fashion Freedom* contains no diagrams, beautiful pictures, or color charts. That is because this is not a conventional "style" book or a "beauty" book, and it is certainly not a fashion book. It is *a self-help book about how to discover your own personal style.*

For many fashion experts, "process" means identifying a client's category: "Phew, that's done. I'm a Winter!" or "Oh, I've got it now— I'm 'Sporty.' Now can we please go shopping?" Trouble is, what does a "Romantic" do who happens to work on Wall Street, or a "Gamine" who lifts weights? All of these ways of fingerprinting people— whether by seasons, colors, or personality types—are different versions of the quick fix.

Those who use these categories do not ask you to look inside yourself to explore who you are. They are looking at groups. *You are not a group. You are an individual.* Our approach is about self-awareness— we ask you to use what you have learned to determine your own categories.

Your image also reflects your *inner style,* through very specific messages about who you are and what you represent: your attitudes, your behavior, and the way you communicate. Do your business associates find you personable? Do you remember your manners, even when you have a bad day? Sometimes your inner style messages are so strong that elements of your outer style—your clothes, your hair—become almost invisible. Knowing what your inner assets are, and communicating well both verbally and physically, are just a few of the elements that make up your inner style. When you have defined your inner and outer style, you will be able to integrate them seamlessly to create your true personal style.

But if your image is incongruent, untruthful, and inappropriate for your inner style, it causes distractions and misrepresents who you really are. One "creative" whom we met was trying to express the fact that he lived and worked in a creative field. He wore all-black clothing, with chunky black boots, and he sported a goatee, which had become the hip trend in men's facial hair. He was sending out the message *I am creative* loud and clear. The problem was that that wasn't the message people were receiving.

His black clothing was worn and faded. His jeans had been washed so many times, they were now gray. His trendy facial hair did not complement the shape of his face, and his black boots interfered with the way he carried himself. He thought his image represented his creativity, but in reality it had swallowed his personality and made him look shabby. Those who met him might well have wondered: *If he is that uncaring about himself and his image, then why would we want to be around him or trust him as a "creative"?*

Most people do care about their appearance and want to improve it by finding their unique style. But most people don't know how to go about achieving it. They try quick fixes and superficial ways to feel good about themselves in the form of one-day makeovers and shopping sprees. But as soon as the shopping high wears off, they become discouraged and are once again dissatisfied with how they look. And they no longer feel confident participating in their own transformation.

At this point many people turn to prefabricated style, in the form of well-marketed logos and mass-produced looks. This is an abdication of responsibility, a surrender to the Big Brother of Clothes. Like joining a club, it creates not personal style but conformity, safety, mediocrity, and a false sense of security.

We are often asked to consult on the clothing aspect of makeovers for television shows. One daytime talk show was working on a tight schedule and gave us very little time even to do the makeovers, let alone anything more meaningful. The participants were herded around to different stores and were left standing like mannequins while we rushed around to find the best clothing items for them. For the taping, as instructed by the show's producers, the participants arrived at the studio in their "worst" clothing, with no makeup and messy hair; the men were unshaven. Obviously, the worse people look in the beginning, the more dramatic their changes will appear to be.

Then later the participants appeared with their new hairstyles, new makeup, and new clothing. The makeovers were a success for the audience, the show, and the producers. There were lots of ooh's and ahh's from the audience. The participants truly enjoyed the whole experience. They had received two days of everyone's undivided attention. They were on national television. They liked the way they looked. They felt great for those few hours.

But they did not participate in their own transformations, because they had been handed over to the capable hands of experts. On the way home from the show, we talked about what would happen to those people the next day. The makeup would be washed off; the clothes, jewelry, and accessories would be returned to the stores (that's right, most times you can't even keep the clothes!), the hair extensions would be removed, the hairstyles would droop and flatten, and eventually even the hair color would wash out. Maybe the participants had the time of their lives, but *they did not learn anything* from their makeovers, except that they couldn't afford the services they had received or the clothes that they had been asked to wear for an hour. We had no time to teach them why we chose a particular color for them, or why a certain jacket style was flattering, or why the fabric of a blouse felt good.

TV shows feature makeovers solely for their entertainment value. They engineer them for the audience's benefit, so that viewers will be amazed with the transformations. One TV producer exclaimed to us in horror that a woman we'd chosen as a makeover subject for her show was unacceptable because she wasn't a "mess" and the transformation would not be dramatic enough. That was true: like most people, while neither beautiful nor glamorous, the woman *we* chose was simply open to making improvements in certain aspects of her appearance. Unfortunately, the audience never experienced the everyday reality of her needs and desires. And here is the crux of the problem.

True transformations are not dramatic overnight successes. They are journeys of discovery. The journey is one of fulfillment and a comforting progression toward discovering and revealing your true self.

OUR INTENTIONS

We have no intention of converting you into a fashion maven, a trend watcher, or a follower of any kind. When it comes to personal style, our clients want to be leaders, not followers. We do, however, hope to lead you into the direction of self-empowerment. We want to teach you how to make choices that better represent who you are.

We have also worked in stage and film production creating identities for characters, sometimes based on only a thread of information. For a BBC television movie, we received a brief for a character that was to be played by Albert Finney: it was to speak of his shyness, his shabby chic taste, and his mild eccentricities.

Because the character was shy, he would avoid any clothing item, fabric, or color that would have brought attention to him. The color taupe was chosen for his suits because although it was discreet, it was also flattering on Mr. Finney. To create the "shabby" in shabby chic, the fabric for the suits underwent a special wash process that gave them an older, "worn many times" effect. The fabric was a soft-to-the-hand but resilient winter-weight brushed cotton, a very good-quality fabric because the character knew how good-quality clothing should feel, which communicated the "chic" in shabby chic. Accessories were used to subtly suggest that even though he was shy, he sometimes expressed his eccentricities in the form of a witty pair of socks or cufflinks.

Much like that of a stage or film character, your identity can be brought to life by a combination of guided introspection and education. If a single statement about a man's character can create a recognizable identity, think how, by gathering enough information, you can experience your image potential and express your personal style.

YOUR COMMITMENT

Your image is serious business. International financial institutions and other corporations take image so seriously that they often call upon us to address the image issues of their employees. These companies recognize the importance of having their executives come across well to clients. Since first impressions can make the difference in winning an account or closing a deal, companies want to make their best effort. Companies like these are saying to their employees, *You're worth the trouble*—and we agree. So while a portion of this work will be fun and interesting, a level of commitment is imperative for your success. If you use this book to discover your personal style and reflect it in your clothing and in the way you present yourself, you will be more successful in your personal and professional lives. We've seen this happen with our clients, as you will see in their stories.

WHAT YOU CAN EXPECT FROM THIS BOOK

Learning who you are in relation to your style and image is the key to finding your personal style and expressing it. Only then will you be able to present yourself authentically. This is the crucial difference between a quick fix and a solution that is permanent and long lasting. Simply put, before you go shopping, find out who you are shopping for.

Some people seem to have been born with good taste or a knack for creating their own unique look, but they too are usually projecting the results of hard work and a desire to learn. The earliest photographs of the late Princess Diana, for example, portrayed her as a somewhat awkward-looking country schoolgirl. Even after she stepped into the limelight and acquired the means to "purchase her style," it took her several years to develop into a graceful and stylish woman.

She made a few harmless mistakes along the way. As she traded in the cotton flower-print dresses for her new look, the colors she chose, her hats, and the style of her suits and dresses were sometimes a bit too grown-up-looking and spoke of trying to fit in. But as she experimented and grew as a person, she settled into sophisticated, flattering colors. She developed a reputation for preferring daring, glamorous evening wear, yet when times called for seriousness, compassion, and advocacy, she dressed more demurely. Yes, she was a woman of privilege, but she still worked at developing her look and learned how best to accentuate her assets. Princess Diana was a student of her own personal style.

Through the years she had ample opportunity to study her image. She compared vast amounts of videotape and photographs to identify the most flattering poses and clothing. From the tilt of her head to the enigmatic look in her eyes, we may never know how much of her public persona was consciously manipulated. But the public was allowed to see every aspect of her image. Fans were as excited to see her in dressed-down jeans as in glamorous gowns—a true testament to the development of her inner style. To catch a glimpse of her in a bathing suit was a coup; a royal in a bikini was unheard of! And through it all, we watched the way she handled stress, pressure, and indecisiveness. We witnessed her growth. The development of her image was ours to study.

Jacqueline Onassis is another example of someone who seemed to have been born with a natural talent for knowing exactly what to do. She did know—but she also took a great deal of advice from fashion editors. She talked with designers about how to make their clothes her own. She studied what she wanted to project and then learned how to do it.

These two women had unusual life stories: they learned and grew under a tremendous microscope. Fortunately, developing your personal style does not require a journey of iconic proportions. Many people have taken their journey privately, yet with the same good, solid results. They have found that expressing their identity through their personal style has affected every aspect of their lives.

CLIENT PROFILES

We will use case histories and client profiles throughout this book to help you recognize your own image and personal style issues. Our clients have been our best teachers, and we are confident that you too will enjoy learning from them. For some of these people, we will follow their progress throughout the book. Others will appear only briefly, so that we may demonstrate a specific point.

You will notice that our clients are both male and female. If you are female, do not skip over the male profiles, and vice versa. You will be surprised by what the opposite sex can teach you. True style knows no gender—the work is the same, and so is the message.

First we will introduce Julia, so you can see how we help our clients discover their inner style.

MEET JULIA

Julia was an attractive woman in her early thirties. When we first met her, she was wearing her corporate uniform, which made her look ten years older than she was. Her dark navy blue suit was designed for a more mature-looking and older woman. Her white shirt was very stiff, and the collar was too large. The shirt seemed to have a life of its own: whenever she tried to put the collar under her jacket, it would spring back to its awkward position. She had no specific hairstyle and wore her long hair pulled back in a loose and low ponytail. She wore no makeup. When she shook hands with us, her handshake was too forceful and almost intrusive. She made glaring and yet guarded eye contact. Her stiffly upright posture made her appear tense. But the image of the woman who walked into the room was a shadow compared to the woman who later revealed herself to us and eventually to her co-workers, friends, and family.

Some of our most interesting work takes place in the corporate arena, which is where we met Julia. Her employer had asked her to attend a pre-meeting and then to decide if she would be willing to work with us. He felt that she had great potential in the company but that her lack of a strong identity—an underdeveloped image—was holding her back. She wasn't doing anything wrong, her performance at work was good—she was loyal and hardworking. What she lacked was that extra polish.

Amazingly, clients who begin this process "kicking and screaming" and are skeptical and insecure are often the ones who make the most astounding changes. Julia didn't arrive kicking and screaming, but she was somewhat nervous and unsure about meeting with us. Her body language was a bit defensive; she was polite but very standoffish and minimally communicative. This is very understandable and not uncommon: image and personal style are intimate subjects. Even when an employer explains that we are there to teach them how to make the best of their personal presentation, some clients naturally react with "But what's wrong with me?" *This work is not about being wrong; it is simply about making discoveries and improvements.*

Initially, Julia was under the impression that the first thing we were going to do was to take her shopping. She thought we would choose clothes for her to buy, tell her what colors to wear, suggest how she should wear her hair, and generally provide a quick-fix makeover. But we didn't do that. Instead, we asked her to talk to us about the things in her life that meant a great deal to her. We asked her what kind of visual impression she felt she was making. We asked her when she felt confident and when she did not. We addressed some important issues about who she was as a person, not as an employee or a client. The point of our questioning was to draw her out—to have Julia tell us who she was.

We discovered that Julia had a great passion for nature, animals, scuba diving, and snow skiing. She also loved black-and-white movies from the 1930s and 1940s. Quite a unique combination! These things ignited her imagination and made her feel special. Connecting to her passions, she told us, made her feel comfortable and satisfied and put her in a "good mood."

Julia was also burdened with expectations from others and was trying desperately hard to live up to them. Her parents expected her to be at the top of her game in business and to be a supermom, wife, and daughter. Her husband expected her to be more attentive to him, even though they had a three-year-old who was also in need of attention. Not surprisingly, when Julia finally had the opportunity to talk freely about herself, she had some difficulty doing so. She hadn't thought about herself outside of business and family for so long that addressing her self-image was extremely challenging for her. Regular visits to the hairdresser, shopping excursions, and her weekly yoga class, she explained, had been postponed indefinitely because of her other commitments. Due to the needs and demands of others, Julia was neglecting herself, but it wasn't only neglect that defined her behavior; she lived in a state of *unawareness* with regard to her image.

By becoming aware of her tastes and values, Julia learned how to incorporate them into her personal style. Not only did she actually do the homework we gave her, she told us that she enjoyed it and was able to assimilate it into her lifestyle. She did most of it on [in fact, we live in a different country from Julia and were person to guide her only a few times, just as we will guide you through each of the ten sessions.

The most helpful part of this process, she told us later, was the creation of her goal statement, what we call a Personal Style Statement. Julia's Personal Style Statement was "I present a unique, accessible, and professional image." This statement kept her on track, calmed her when she became confused, and inspired her.

Julia's *assets* included beautiful auburn hair, a peaches-and-cream complexion, and vivid blue eyes. She was tall and had a potentially elegant physicality and a naturally still, compelling presence. We worked with Julia to identify and enhance her assets by using the exercises you will find in the Inner Style Inventory (Session 4). She had no clue as to what her assets were (though they were apparent to us!) or how to make them work for her. She was completely unaware, for example, that the combination of her hair color, her skin tone, and her blue eyes held great potential.

The reason Julia was unaware of these assets was that she had what we call an "image wound." When she was young, other children, both girls and boys, had teased her about her red hair and freckles. She happened to be the only child in her class who had this coloring, and she felt she stood out negatively because of it. Even when the freckles had long since faded, her memory and embarrassment had not. To an outside observer, what Julia found negative as a child made for a unique and compelling look today. But Julia couldn't get beyond her earlier pain until we stepped into the picture.

Julia had never worn makeup; her personal belief was that wearing makeup would make her appear false, as if she were wearing a mask. Also, working in a predominantly man's world, she was afraid that wearing makeup would present her as too feminine and therefore vulnerable and weak. This fear is shared by many of our female clients whose careers are in male-dominated business arenas. In our experience, when women celebrate their femininity naturally—without flaunting it or using it as a manipulative tool—they become more empowered, not less.

We asked Julia if she was willing to try some makeup. If she had been unwilling, we would not have pursued it with her. But she made her own decision to experience one makeup lesson. We introduced her to a makeup artist who specializes in low-key, natural-looking makeup, and she taught Julia how to use it to obtain the best effect naturally.

When Julia applied a small amount of this natural-looking and professionally chosen makeup to enhance her coloring, she saw immediately how her eyes stood out and her skin glowed. It took her a little time to get used to it, but the compliments she received helped to ease her uncertainty. As a businessperson, she realized that wearing makeup was a polished and sophisticated addition to her image.

Julia was not ready to make any significant changes to her current hairstyle immediately. Like many people, she was partial to one particular hairstyle and had difficulty seeing herself in any other. She had an emotional attachment to her long hair; she said it made her feel feminine and youthful. Yet Julia *was* very feminine and youthful—she had no cause to worry about being perceived as too mature or anything but feminine. She also said that if she wore a more current-looking hairstyle, she might appear trendy, and that wouldn't be appropriate for business. Ironically, her lack of hairstyle and her matronly suit gave her exactly the opposite image of the one she wanted: they made her look older and frumpy.

Finally Julia decided that she was ready to "deal with" her hair, but she admitted that she was fearful of change. We guided her to do a bit of research and homework. She looked through magazines and started to notice the hairstyles of other employees and business associates. She didn't see anything she liked and asked us if she was being too picky. We told her absolutely not! We encouraged her to be picky—it was important for her to take her time and to wait until she felt inspired. This helped her to relax about the whole thing, and as soon as she did, she ran right into her inspiration.

One weekend night she was sitting in a theater with her husband—a rare thing in her busy life—when she saw the hairstyle she wanted, on an actress performing onstage. She knew she looked nothing like the actress, but the actress's hair looked close to the coloring and texture of her own. Seeing it in person onstage was a bonus; she loved the way the actress's hair moved and appreciated its healthy, shiny look. We suggested she take her inspiration to a hairstylist and talk to him about how to realistically achieve the same affect. The result was a hairstyle that was shorter, slightly cut into, and textured and styled with a few subtle bangs. She learned how to take care of it, style it herself, and use the right products for her hair type, which made it shiny and current looking. These few small and subtle changes took minimal time but made all the difference to her self-image. She began to see herself more realistically and clearly—as the young, attractive woman that she really was.

Based on the results of her Inner Style Inventory, Julia realized that there were aspects of her physicality that she wanted to improve. Although we had experienced an almost military atmosphere in Julia's physicality, we could also see a calm and elegant physical presence. Julia herself knew it existed, due to her years of yoga practice. She just needed reminding that she had a potential gracefulness in her physical presence.

Julia practiced shaking hands, entering a room, and making good eye contact with the idea of *flexibility, calmness,* and *softness*—words she associated with her yoga practice. She came to know the difference between assertive behavior and aggressive behavior, work she initially found challenging. She particularly struggled with the concept of "graceful assertiveness": she said it seemed as though gracefulness and assertiveness were a contradiction. And she had always considered aggressiveness and assertiveness to be one and the same. We explained that being assertive is related to being effective—not to being bombastic. We asked her to perform a mock confrontation with a business associate, and a new-client presentation. She enlisted the help of her husband, who had become very supportive of the work she was doing. She practiced with him on nights before important meetings. She compared the experience with learning to ride a bike. First she felt fear and uncertainty and wobbled a bit. But she quickly overcame the fear and wobbled only a tiny bit—then wondered what all the fuss had been about. Being assertive soon became as comfortable as riding a bike.

Julia's other assets included loyalty, integrity, and a surprisingly wicked sense of humor. We added these qualities to her clothing and to her way of communicating and expressing herself. For example, on days when she knew that work would be particularly challenging, she would wear a new, somewhat foppish blouse, one that remained within the protocol of her business yet made her laugh when she thought of it. We don't really know why she found it so amusing, we just know it looked wonderful on her—but that is the point of this work. *It was unique and personal to her.*

We helped Julia use her deeply felt passions as a guide to making better decisions about her clothing, interpreting those passions in ways that would be meaningful for her personal style. Her love of nature, animals, and somewhat high-risk outdoor activities indicated a desire for freedom of movement, which calls for a freedom of movement in both style and fabrics. Wearing natural fibers would give her a sense of comfort and harmony. She related to the elegant, witty, totally feminine, yet strong women of the 1930s and 1940s movies.

Julia learned how to choose clothes that connected with her tastes, complemented her lifestyle, flattered her body shape, and worked within her budget. "I began to experience clothing as much more than just items that covered my body," she said. "I began to see that I could use it to say what is best about me." She upgraded the quality of what she bought and became a little more imaginative regarding the colors she chose. When she carefully chose a different blue—an "air force blue"—to wear instead of her regular dark navy blue, the result was quite striking against her skin and hair. The dark navy had drained her of color, but the new blue enhanced her features and coloring. Not only did Julia look better, she *felt* better. The softer blue made her feel softer, less stiff in her manner and demeanor—it was a *friendly* color for her.

Because Julia was so feminine, she could easily wear more masculine-looking clothing items—as long as they were made of soft and malleable fabrics that moved freely, unlike that stiff, ill-fitting white shirt. Although she was tall, she was pear shaped and benefited from wearing items of clothing that brought visual balance to her body shape. She needed to accentuate her waist, so she paid attention to the shoulders of her jackets—choosing a shape that was complementary to her silhouette, with shoulders that were just a tiny bit bigger than her own. Fitted jackets that accentuated her small waist, sat comfortably on her hips, and were a little bit longer than average flattered her body shape and represented a strong authoritive look. Deep-pleated pants that were high in the waist and full cut in the leg, yet not baggy, gave her the casual elegance in which she felt comfortable. This kind of clothing resembles the style that Katharine Hepburn might have worn and more recently Diane Keaton. At the same time these clothes appealed to her outdoor sensibilities and her desire for elegance.

Julia became much fussier about the fit of her clothes, demanding comfort and clean-cut lines. After a number of educational shopping experiences, she realized the big difference between a good fit and a not-so-good fit! She was more aware of her comfort level and confidence level and felt more attractive in clothes that fit well. She steered away from anything that needed complicated tailoring adjustments. One of the keys to her personal style in clothes was that they should be classic yet contemporary, with a nod to that which is current. This key eliminated high fashion because it was too complicated and too demanding and did not complement her professional life.

Julia learned how to take better care of her clothing, to extend its life and maintain a fresh look. Adding these details made her feel and look more confident and gave her polish.

Julia had previously shopped only when she was in desperate need of something. It took her a great deal of time, because she was never entirely sure of where to go or even what she needed. She would spend whole weekends searching for a suit or a dress for a special occasion, only to go back later because she had no shoes or sweater or blouse to wear with it. She used our Closet Analysis exercise to learn about not only what she needed but also who she was buying it for!

The Closet Analysis exercise—a favorite of all of our clients—took a great deal of stress out of Julia's life. She created her own personal categories for her clothing, enabling her to avoid the "what am I going to wear today" syndrome. She organized her closet so as to group together items that she could count on for her business, personal, and social lives. Her husband was grateful, because he and their daughter were able to spend more time with her on the weekends!

Julia's boss began to notice the changes immediately. First he noticed that her physical guard had begun to come down. She was more engaging and looked less matronly and much more urbane—which was right for the business as well. He was impressed with her commitment to herself and the fact that it reflected in her job performance. She appeared and sounded more confident and generally made a better impression. He began sending her to various international cities to represent the company. She told us that she was so relieved that she had done this work, for when she met with the sophisticated and savvy women from companies in other countries, she felt confident that she was representing herself at her best and therefore the business at its best.

During our time together, Julia took several small steps and a few giant leaps. We encouraged her to pace herself in accordance with her lifestyle. Some days she was too tired or busy to even think about her image, and other times she spent an evening at her yoga class, or a whole weekend doing the Closet Analysis. She is a great example of how a desire to grow and develop one's style and image can overcome time limitations and life's daily demands.

Julia is still learning, making improvements and facing challenges, not because she needs to but because she enjoys it. One thing is for certain: if you were to meet Julia today, you would meet a woman who has a definitive personal style, one that truly represents who she is.

LEARNING ABOUT CLOTHES
FROM THE INSIDE OUT

In our sessions, we remove the veneer from "fashion" and make it real so that you can begin to feel included in what many feel is an exclusive world. The practical information offered here will educate you about the nuts and bolts of clothing. We answer the most-frequently-asked questions about fabrics, fit, colors, shopping, and more. We teach you how to detect the best and the worst, the subtleties and nuances of what makes a garment well designed versus just fashionable. And you will learn about these aspects of clothing as they relate to you, not by being told that pink and cashmere are "in" this month.

By learning about quality, you will learn how to get the best for your money, about which items to spend the most on (and which not to)—and why having quality does not mean having quantity. We have worked with people from extremely different income brackets, and we firmly believe that it costs no more to present oneself with style than without style. Armed with this information and more, you will become your own authority.

Finally, we will discuss the "insecure" topic of trends—how to avoid having an ephemeral wardrobe, and how to stay current without succumbing to trends.

THE EXERCISES

Each chapter represents a different session. It contains exercises, tasks, and information that will surprise you, educate you, and ultimately reveal *you.*

The exercises have been developed over a lifetime of work in the fields of fashion, design, retail, and lifestyle improvements. They incorporate aspects of psychology and creativity and have been designed to help you open the door to your inner style. We have used these exercises with scores of clients through the years, and you will benefit from being able to do the exercises at your leisure, in your own time.

Over the years they have been fine-tuned and simplified so that they produce the most effective combination of introspection, discovery, and education—the greatest changes and the most lasting effects.

HOW TO OBTAIN THE MOST FROM THIS BOOK

Although you could thumb through this book and on any given page find useful and enlightening information, in its entirety it describes a *process.* Each of the ten sessions builds on the ones before until, with the last one, the foundation is laid for a successful personal style. You will probably have much more success in Session 10's shopping excursion if you have created a goal for your image (Session 2) and analyzed your closet (Session 9). So we strongly suggest that you begin with Session 1, taking your time to do each session without a time limit or pressure of any kind.

YOUR PERSONAL STYLE JOURNAL

The road to your authenticity is your Personal Style Journal.

The exercises in this book are not difficult, but they will challenge you to reveal yourself. In essence, obtaining the *most* from this book really means discovering the *most* about you. The more you are willing to be ruthlessly honest with yourself about yourself, the more material you will have to work with. A special and safe place to do that work will be your own private journal.

A journal is crucial for many reasons. Your own writings from the exercises and tasks, your observations, thoughts, and feelings, will be the basis upon which you form a picture of yourself and your new-found personal style. It will help you to keep things in order chronologically and keep you connected to the process. At times we will ask you to go back to something you have written to be sure you are on track, so that the discovery process is consistent and coherent. Practically, it will be much easier for you to refer to one journal rather than to pieces of paper strewn in different places.

If for some reason you do not wish to write in longhand and prefer to use your computer, that is fine. Do, however, print out your work and keep it in order in some kind of notebook, as you will need to refer to it later.

The work you do in your Personal Style Journal bears no resemblance to "journal writing." There is no daily requirement or time period for you to follow. Do all the work in your own time, when you feel inspired and ready.

Session Contents

The following is an overview of the ten sessions. As you will see, performing introspective exercises will gradually help you to identify your uniqueness and lead you to discover your image.

■ SESSION 1. PASSIONATE BEGINNINGS

You will begin by learning how your passions can open the door to your personal style. You will learn to establish and recognize your tastes by using one simple yet effective exercise.

■ SESSION 2. CREATING YOUR PERSONAL STYLE STATEMENT

Not only is it helpful to define your goals relating to your image—it is imperative!! What do you want for your image? Who are you, and what do you want to become? You will create a goal-oriented statement for yourself that will define your aspirations. We will help you to do this with an exercise that unveils your desires for your image. And we will give you examples of how others have created this Personal Style Statement for themselves.

■ SESSION 3. HEALING YOUR IMAGE WOUNDS

Body images and image wounds are topics that cause most of us to wince. Yes, it is a delicate area, but in order to get past it and move on, we must look at the way we perceive our bodies and how this perception affects our personal style decisions. Although we all wish it weren't so, our self-esteem and the way we feel about ourselves in our clothes is directly related to our body image.

■ SESSION 4. INNER STYLE INVENTORY

The Inner Style Inventory will help you take stock of where you are right now in regard to all aspects of your personal style that are not related to clothing or grooming. We help you to define and recognize your assets so that you can learn how to enhance them and make the most of them.

■ SESSION 5. AESTHETIC FIELD TRIP

It's time to get out of the house with the Aesthetic Field Trip. It's a great deal of fun and a great learning experience. And we're not telling you any more right now!

■ SESSION 6. THE SPIRIT OF CLOTHES

This is an insider's guide to a new way of thinking about clothes. We get down to the business of clothes—how fashion happens, how trends happen (and how not to succumb to them!), the media's impact on us, the spirit of a garment, quality, fit, design—and all about how those things relate to you. We will help you to determine what *your* essentials are, not someone else's.

■ SESSION 7. COLOR

The Color session will open your eyes and your creativity. We will do away with tired and inappropriate color myths and discuss why color is crucial to your personal style and often hard to pin down. The psychological aspects of color will be addressed and how color relates to you personally.

■ SESSION 8. YOUR PERSONAL STYLE PROFILE

Your Personal Style Profile will be unique to you. You will review the work you have done so far and highlight the events, feelings, and impressions that mean the most to you. These things will be personal and specific to you, and a picture of your own personal style will begin to emerge.

■ SESSION 9. CLOSET ANALYSIS

Time to get into your closet. This is not just a clean-out—it is time to analyze and edit your wardrobe armed with all the new information you have about yourself and your image. This exercise is immensely cathartic. We offer a detailed, scientific, and even fun way to approach this task.

■ SESSION 10. SHOPPING

Finally! The culmination of this process is your first shopping trip in which you are armed with the ability to make better choices. The Shopping session is a guide and an emotional support system. We tell you how to shop effectively, what to do when you become confused, upset, or overwhelmed, and insiders' tips on how to shop successfully—even if that means not buying a thing! And so that you will not be left in the lurch, we include "shopping aftercare"—tips on how to assess your experience and clarify any emotional tugs and pulls you may have had.

■ FINISHING TOUCHES

Many times our clients are anxious to get started right away with a new hairstyle and a new makeup regime. These outer changes in your physical appearance involve serious decisions that must be made carefully. Hair and makeup are very important aspects of your personal style, but we have intentionally placed these topics at the end of the book for the same reason that your shopping trip is at the end of the book.

This is a guide to making more informed and considered decisions about your hair and makeup. We have enlisted the help of highly skilled and experienced experts to share their valuable information with you. We strongly suggest that before you make any important decisions about these two aspects of your image, you complete the ten sessions in this book. The choices you make about your hair and makeup will be significantly different from anything you would have chosen without having done the sessions.

Feeling empowered, making a memorable first impression, being more successful in the workplace, having better relationships, shopping successfully for yourself, liking what you see in the mirror—these are the results our clients have experienced from this process. And these results and others yet to be discovered can be yours as you begin your journey toward discovering your personal style.

Passionate Beginnings

Early one evening we were in our former London shop practically buried beneath a new season's arrival of clothing. As usual, the collection had been designed well over a year in advance, and it was exciting to finally see it displayed in the shop. Into this very energized atmosphere entered a distinguished-looking yet somewhat imposing man. He walked in as if he were on a mission to buy something, but we could tell he did not want to be pounced upon by an overly exuberant salesperson. He looked as though he needed some space to feel his way through. As we watched him, we decided to approach him because we could not take our eyes off his beautiful shoes. We complimented him on them and asked him where he had purchased them. His whole demeanor changed. He smiled sheepishly and admitted that he had a passion for beautiful shoes. He even spent Sunday afternoons in his country cottage with his family performing his most-loved occupation—polishing each pair of his family members' shoes. This gentleman's family consisted of his wife and four children!

He enjoyed this chore because he took great pleasure in making the shoes look cared for, and he knew his efforts helped to make the shoes last longer. Finishing the job was important for him, for he loved seeing each pair of shoes lined up against the wall shining and ready for the coming week. And finally, he enjoyed presenting them to his family; the gesture was emotionally satisfying to him.

Within those few moments, he told us everything about his personal style that we needed to know to get started. He was a man of tradition, yet slightly quirky. He appreciated good, lasting quality. Getting value for his money was very important to him. He loved simplicity in design and made considered decisions about his clothing and grooming. Respect and discipline entered his wardrobe as well. The colors and fabrics he would choose would always be subtle, with the minutest hint of eccentricity.

Our years of experience with thousands of clients and customers enabled us to shortcut our process with this man's dialogue on shoe polishing. But with all the information you will discover about yourself, you too can create a specific, unique, and *personal* image.

PASSION EXERCISE

Initially we used this simple exercise as a starting point with our clients, a kind of "getting to know you" tool. But we quickly realized that it touches upon something much more powerful than just introductions. We continue to be amazed at how revealing our clients' answers are, how open, honest, and generous most people are, and therefore how ready they are for our program.

We now ask you to do the exercise. Please write your answers to the following questions:

- What things do you love and feel passionately about?
- What things do you dislike and feel passionately about?

We suggest that you spend some time thinking about your answers to these two questions. They will become the foundation for your personal style.

Write about your passions in some detail. If your list sounds something like this—"Love my car, love to travel, love my dog"—then you have not dug deeply enough. You must emotionally connect to the things you feel passionately about. Your passions may stimulate your mind or emotions to such a high level that they prompt you to take action. You may love something so much that you sacrifice your time, your money, or even your relationships for the sake of that which moves you! One of your passions may be so excruciatingly beautiful that you have difficulty just writing about it. These are the kinds of passions we'd like you to identify.

Writing about your passions may elicit strong opinions. This is positive—we want you to be aware of your opinions. But a person's true passions are not always obvious. You may feel that yours are private and keep them secret, even from those to whom you feel closest. For those of you who'd rather not shout your passions and hidden desires from an open window, please be assured that it is certainly not necessary to do so. When you eventually incorporate your passions into your personal style, many of your choices will be based upon your own little secrets.

One of our clients, Eric, had a reputation for being a ruthless businessman. Harvard Business School educated and having interned in Manhattan, he now had his own internationally based company. Eric believed that if his business associates ever knew what his first and foremost passion was, he would never seem the same to them. He had a secret passion for Darth Vader. He wasn't particularly interested in any other aspects of the *Star Wars* movies; he just wanted to be Darth Vader. He fantasized about dressing in the costume and speaking with the voice. Most of all, he was attracted to the power and skill of this bigger-than-life character.

Eric was concerned about what we might think of him; he assumed we would think him eccentric or even bizarre. We assured him that unless it was something illegal or harmful to himself or others, we really don't place judgments on what people are drawn to. It took a while for him to finally let go and admit this secret passion. He was very brave and now trusts that no one who reads this will ever know it is he. But his Darth Vader passion became an interesting tool for him to work with. When he experienced how his passion could be used in a sound and discriminating way, he became deeply satisfied with the results.

Eric confided in us that he was very happy with his performance in his business except for one area—meetings with two or more people. Something about his presentation of himself, he felt, did not make an impact. We suggested that he think of Darth Vader as he prepared his presentations and practiced his speeches. He did so, without actually pretending to be Darth Vader, or mimicking his voice or walking like him. But his demeanor actually changed. *He took what he felt to be the essence of how Darth Vader would handle the meeting and made it his own.* He spoke more slowly, which put the tone of his voice on a deeper level and made him more compelling to listen to.

People felt he had something important to say, something that they *should* be listening to. He bought a pair of very-good-quality shoes of excellent taste that were chunkier and heavier than his usual penny loafers. When he walked or stood in them, he felt more solid. When he stood firmly on the ground, his physical presence filled more of the room. He moved around the room only when it felt natural but yet was strategically important. He practiced this at home so that it became natural and easy for him. Of course, no one knew or would ever guess that Eric's passion for Darth Vader helped him to take command of his meetings.

TWO TOOLS TO HELP

TOOL 1—WHY?

Two tools can help you get the most from the Passion exercise. The first tool is used to expand upon a passion that you have identified and acknowledged: asking *why?* Probing the reasons for your preferences can help you to go beneath the surface of what you *think* is a passion and find that an even deeper, truer passion is hiding underneath. Many clients who finally acknowledge their passions also have secret desires for their image. Asking *why?* brings these desires to light.

Harry was a perfect example of a client who needed a little more probing when it came to his passions. He was superconservative. A typical Harry outfit would have been a navy blue blazer, gray wool pants, a white cotton Oxford shirt, and a polka-dot tie, all of very good quality. His hairstyle was short in the back and on the sides; he was neatly groomed and wore an expensive watch and pricey glasses and shoes. There's nothing wrong with that, right? But did his clothes say anything about who Harry really was? Absolutely not.

When we asked Harry about his passions we could tell by his one-word answers that he was not connecting to what he felt strongly about. But whenever he talked about selling, his eyes lit up and he became animated. He exclaimed that he loved to sell. And so we employed our first tool and asked him—*why?* The conversation went like this:

Why do you love selling, Harry?
I love to win.

Why do you love to win?

I love the challenge.

Why do you love the challenge?

Because it allows me to be creative. And I love being creative; I love being onstage.

Oh, have you ever been onstage?

Oh yes, I'm an actor in our little community theater company on the weekends. [Harry is a real estate developer by day!]

Could this be a passion, Harry?

Well yes, actually it is.

Is there anything else in this creative area that you would consider sharing with us?

Well, I am a *feng shui* student. I also play classical guitar, and I really love painting portraits.

Why would a man like Harry, a man who is quite worldly and very clever, a successful businessman, not list these very creative passions when asked? They weren't exactly a secret. Maybe he was embarrassed to admit just how much he loved acting and painting, or maybe he had never been asked those kinds of questions before. Or perhaps he was just unaware that he had been leaving behind a vital part of who he is when he stepped into his everyday world.

It never occurred to Harry that we would really want to know about his true passions, ones that had nothing to do with business. He intellectualized his passions and placed them in a business framework. He neglected to acknowledge his true feelings. But even with all this heavy filtering, Harry's highly creative passions still emerged when we asked the simple *why* question.

Harry's revelations told us that he was a very creative person, that he loved the arts. Did his passion for *feng shui* (the ancient art of placement), which represents a specific aesthetic sensibility, appear anywhere in his image? No, it did not. Did he want it to? Yes, desperately. Why? Because he knew and felt a disconnect between who he was and how he presented himself to the world.

A Word of Caution

If you are wondering how Harry incorporated his colorful and creative passions into his personal style—don't. It is much too early for that. But know that his discovery of his personal style did not lead him to become a beret-wearing, hip aesthete. The ways in which a person's passions relate to his or her personal style are more subtle, and they are only part of the picture.

Similarly, Eric did not go on a shopping spree to buy various black outfits in order to feel closer to his Darth Vader passion. The fact that you feel passionately about East Asian art and love science fiction movies does not mean that your personal style should include mandarin-collared clothing and that you should use a *Star Trek* character as a prototype for a new hairstyle. The Passion exercise is only the first step; it is designed to shift your awareness away from stereotypical and predictable ways of thinking about your image. Try not to be too analytical right now. The idea is to be as big and passionate on your journal pages as you dare to be, but do not try to connect your passions to clothing at this point. In fact, unless you have a true passion for clothing or fashion itself, your answers should have nothing whatsoever to do with clothes. They will be based on a more subtle and informed perspective. You will have plenty of time to think about clothes and shopping later. Enjoy the freedom of your imagination right now. Enjoy not thinking about your wardrobe! Let yourself go.

There is no need to filter, intellectualize, or judge in this or any other exercise in this book. No one is standing over you, no employer is waiting for an outcome. At this point take the mind-set that anything goes—and we mean *anything*.

No one is going to read your work without your permission, and unlike our private clients you won't even have to show it to us. But we do want you to question your answers. Ask yourself the *why* questions. Keep asking them until you are sure that you have tapped into your true loves and hates. You may even uncover a forgotten passion days or weeks after you think you have completed this exercise. That's great—it means that your thoughts are brewing and your awareness has already begun to change.

TOOL 2—WHAT DOES MY PASSION SAY ABOUT ME? IS IT REFLECTED IN MY PERSONAL STYLE?

This second tool is an effective way to approach the connection between your passions and your desires for your image. It consists of a set of two questions.

The first question is: **What does my passion say about me?** Passions may say different things about different people. Many people, for example, have a passion for modern art. One of our clients specifically loved modern art because, she said, she hated "old things." Old things for her meant used, secondhand junk. She felt physically uncomfortable around antiques, no matter what their quality. Her passion for modern art calmed her. She could spend hours in museums just staring at modern paintings and sculpture. On the other hand, another client had a passion for modern art not only because he preferred it to other types of art but because of the excitement he experienced when he purchased a piece. He loved the research, the deal, the ownership. What a contrast in styles! One was calm, almost detached, while the other was aggressive and possessive. Knowing the bases of their passions was important to these people as they defined their personal style.

The second question is: **Is my passion reflected in my personal style?** The answer to this question will most likely be no. It is too soon for you to think of *how* your passions translate into your personal style—just think about the possibility. Without exception, all of our clients' passions are eventually expressed, even in very subtle and small ways, but in ways that are unique to them. But you would not run into one of them on the street and say, "Wow, look at that man's suit. He sure has a passion for fly-fishing!"

MARY: DISCOVERING PASSIONS

Mary was a fortyish homemaker who had lost herself in the needs of other people. By the time she came to us, she was confused about her image because of the many roles she played in her life. She had decided that she wanted to project just one image, whether she was picking up her kids from school or going to a fancy party with her husband. She wanted to be one of those people others walked up to and said, "Oh, that outfit is so you." But she looked nothing like that—in fact, she looked the opposite.

Mary was tall, with a large frame, and she was slightly overweight. She had beautiful blond hair, but it was disheveled and a bit unkempt looking. She had pretty green eyes, a feature that was lost behind her glasses frames, whose shape was also not flattering to her attractive face. She had an endearing smile that was very warm and genuine.

The clothes she wore the day we met her were oversized and distractingly mismatched. The beige chenille sweater and the loose, cream-colored cargo trousers were "coverup" clothes. The colors blended in with her skin tone and hair color to give an impression of blandness—making her look as though she were hiding. Mary considered her clothing to be current, if not fashionable. By her own admission, however, she hadn't given her appearance any attention for a long time. The overall impression that she made could best be described as "rumpled." You would never have known from her image that she cared greatly about her appearance.

We first started to talk with Mary during a break at one of our seminars, when she seemed to appear out of nowhere. As she introduced herself to us, the first thing we noticed about her was her graciousness. She told us she was enthusiastic about our approach, and she communicated it both verbally and through her posture, in a way that was clear and open. She wanted to work with us privately, and she said she was excited about the possibility of being taught by people who believe that real style begins on the inside.

In just these few moments, we were able to recognize Mary's inner style assets. She was sincere and animated, determined and delightful, someone nice to be around. After the break, she disappeared again, sitting quietly for the rest of the evening, asking no questions and offering no comments.

Before we began working with Mary, we asked her to complete the Passion exercise. Initially she wrote about her passions in a free-style, stream-of-consciousness way. We asked her to expand on several of them, and eventually we asked her to think about the two questions in relation to each of her passions. Taking the time to answer these questions made it easier for her to put it all together, and it all made better sense to her later as she continued the process.

MARY'S PASSIONS

Passion: One of Mary's passions was travel. She loved learning about other cultures and soaking up more than just the superficial. She enjoyed getting out of her own "restricted existence," as she called it, and entering into other people's lives, which were so unlike hers. She chose her destinations carefully, selecting places she felt she and her family would not only enjoy but be affected and even changed by.

What this passion said about her: Mary felt her passion for other cultures denoted her inquisitiveness, an invaluable quality for cultivating one's personal style. When she was traveling, especially to exotic or distant locations, she didn't allow her ego to get in the way of the learning. Admitting that she didn't "know everything" left her free to enjoy the adventure of discovery. She was willing to take the blinkers off. Her experiences, she believed, gave her a colorful background that enhanced her personality and boosted her confidence level.

Reflecting the passion: Mary's worldly experiences were not reflected in her personal style, but she wanted them to be. She wanted to appear and be more sophisticated. She wanted to expand her tastes, learn another language, and incorporate and express her somewhat eccentric humor into her personal style. When she traveled, even just for a short weekend trip, she experienced a freedom that allowed her to be creative and inspired her to explore her potential.

Passion: Mary had loved professional figure skating for as long as she could remember. The funny thing was that she didn't know how to ice-skate and had no desire to learn. She loved watching figure skaters soar across the ice with what she interpreted as a total freedom of physical expression. She often imagined herself spinning across the ice with them. This gave her a vicarious pleasure, and she found herself imagining what kind of costume she would wear.

What this passion said about her: Mary connected her passion for figure skating to her desire to be more physically expressive. A less obvious connection, one that she had to dig a bit deeper to identify, was her ability to fantasize and regularly exercise her imagination. She acknowledged that her imagination was a valuable tool that she could call upon when she felt stuck or limited.

Reflecting the passion: Mary was gracious in the way she spoke and made eye contact. As she told us about the ice-skaters' bodies and movement, she expressed her desire to incorporate some of that freedom into her own body language and physical appearance. Mary began to connect her passion for ice-skating with her need to appear and feel physically elegant; she felt this would be integral to her personal style.

Passion: Jewel colors were another passion of Mary's. She was very drawn to them in art, home furnishings, clothes, and basically whenever she saw them. Jewel colors are sapphire blue, amber, and garnet; they are deep, rich, luxurious shades. We asked Mary to expand upon her feelings about these colors: color is such an integral part of personal style that we were quite intrigued. Emotionally, Mary was both intimidated by and attracted to these colors. When she saw them, she stopped what she was doing, sometimes consciously and sometimes unconsciously, and was almost mesmerized by them. She wanted to incorporate them into her personal style but was afraid of looking garish and inappropriate. She saw other people wearing these rich colors, or she saw them in her friends' home decorating, and she was aware that when rich jewel colors are used well, they can be striking, but when they are not, they are distracting. She was afraid of making a mistake.

What this passion said about her: Mary said she wanted to know how it would feel to attract attention with her presence. She wanted to feel the power and vibrancy that she associated with jewel colors. She felt compelled to include them in her wardrobe but knew that it would take a certain amount of confidence to wear them successfully, and her fear about them was linked to her lack of confidence. She had a desire to feel inner confidence.

Reflecting the passion: Mary was dead right about her feelings and attraction to these colors. Her bland appearance—she was wearing cream and beige when we first met her!—and her passion for vibrant colors were at opposite ends of the spectrum. She had begun to make a connection to something that she loved and felt strongly about, and she learned that her passion could be something that she could express in her personal style.

In addition to the passions we have just mentioned, two more passions of Mary's are important to share with you. One was her desire to know and learn about the benefits of good quality, be it in clothing, food, home items, or service. Mary was passionate about learning in general, but when pinned down to choose what she most wanted to learn about her personal style, she came up with a desire to learn about what constitutes and represents good quality. This was an excellent choice for Mary.

The second passion was floral design, which Mary practiced as a hobby. The peace and tranquillity that came over her while she was working with flowers was very emotionally satisfying for her. We found this extremely interesting—and a big clue that would help

Mary to create a better relationship with her clothes and personal style.

Floral design had taught her about line, form, color, texture, and balance. Unless these things are considered, flowers haphazardly placed in a container remain a bunch of flowers. The pleasure she derived from seeing beautifully arranged flowers came from love of clarity, coordination of colors, harmony, and balance.

There was a direct correlation between Mary's appearance and floral design. When she looked at herself in the mirror, she did not feel or see balance, harmony, or complementary colors, and it upset her terribly. She became emotionally dissatisfied, frustrated, and deflated. Certainly many people, when looking at themselves in a mirror, are less than satisfied, and many lack balance and harmony with their appearance. *But Mary needed a direct visual, physical, and emotional connection to her passions in order to really relate to her image desires.* So do most people.

Much like a tapestry, intricately woven with colors, designs, and images, each of us has within us our own image of how we would like to look. At first glance a well-executed tapestry is a beautiful, harmonious, and clear image, but a complex pattern of threads and nuances of color and design creates the initial effect. Similarly, your personal style consists of various threads that, once identified and carefully selected, can be woven together to form a complete image—one that is unique to you.

Mary's very first session showed that she had within her all of the essential threads to create her own tapestry—her personal style. She could not see the image on her tapestry yet. She had yet to learn how to identify and choose the threads she wished to use. Nor had she chosen the colors, patterns, and designs that would constitute the image she would create. But she was certainly off to an exciting start, and in the remaining sessions Mary would learn how to piece together an image that would represent her personal style.

Everyone has their own particular threads, their own scenery, their own profiles that have great potential in relation to their image. A tapestry exists within each of you and is waiting to be created.

THINGS YOU INTENSELY DISLIKE

Rory, one of our seminar participants, was a very pleasant, likable, and ambitious young woman. She had a budding career in a very successful financial institution. One of her image goals was to exude charisma. This goal fit right in with her boss's wish for her to improve her PR skills, as he wrote in her year-end review.

When asked to share with us the things she felt passionately about, Rory had no trouble describing and talking about her passions. But when we asked about her dislikes, she smiled and said there were probably things she didn't like, but there was really nothing she felt an intense dislike for. Even with some gentle prodding and solicitous questioning, Rory still sat silently smiling, shaking her head. No, there wasn't anything she strongly disliked. What was happening? Everyone has things in their lives that they intensely dislike. It is not possible to live without intensely disliking something—even if it is just one thing. Why couldn't Rory respond?

Rory's image challenge was one that we have seen others face many times. She did not want to be seen having "negative opinions." She didn't want to be thought of as having a bad attitude. She also felt more secure when she didn't "rock the boat." She thought that if she stayed "nice" and silent, she would create a better impression.

But by not voicing her opinion, Rory created an effect for her image that was opposite from the one she said she wanted.

The things that you dislike help to make up your personality and evoke strong opinions. And it is your opinions that we are after. Having an opinion engages people. Engaging people is one of the key elements to exuding charisma. One of the ways you participate in creating your own personal style is to be fully aware of your own opinions.

Rory was eased into the suggestion that she might not have been entirely honest with herself. She finally admitted to absolutely hating slovenliness and cold, rainy afternoons. She stated this in public, in front of her peers and us. What might seem to some of us like an insignificant admission was for Rory a moment of liberation.

The beauty of having an opinion is that you can change it. There is a big difference between having an opinion and being opinionated. We're sure you're aware of the kind of effects that extremely opinionated people can have. When opinions border on fanaticism, they cause exclusion and push people away.

Rory had been playing it safe, as most people do. She needed to take some calculated risks. Risk taking is an enjoyable part of learning about your personal style. Some of the best results are attained when people struggle with their opinions and take risks. The following story is a clear testament to how intense dislikes and opinions are entwined with image choices.

A STORY FROM MALCOLM

"One of my longtime male clients is a Grammy Award winner. He writes and sings his own unique brand of popular music, appears in movies, and is considered to be one of the 'in' people in Hollywood. I have designed clothes for his stage performances and his personal wear since the beginning of his career.

"Although he respects my views, my taste, and my interpretation of style, he has very strong opinions of his own and is not shy about voicing them. I recall on one occasion, I had designed a suit he was to wear for a performance he was giving in London. Just before a suit is completed, there is a final fitting, at which time I attend to small details and apply the finishing touches. Because this client is so specific about the requirements for his image and because of his unrelenting eye for detail, the final fitting is all-important to him. That is why he participates in this final process considerably more than most clients do.

"I was very happy with the end product. The suit looked excellent, and with the exception of some minor details—one in particular—I was proud of it. Without too much ado, the smaller items that were in need of adjustment were taken care of, such as the buttons on the cuff and the final pressing. But there was still the question of one particular detail: my client insisted that he wear his trousers so long that they would actually crumple over his shoe. In my opinion this interfered with the elegant image he was trying to create. In his opinion the excessive length made his legs appear longer. His legs were not particularly short, but to his eye they needed to look longer. He had convinced himself that by wearing an overly long trouser, his legs would indeed look longer. I might add that even the most visually adroit of us fail to see the reality of how our body looks as a whole. He had steadfastly expressed this opinion about the length of his trousers for as long as I had known him.

"The fact of the matter was that wearing his trousers so long did exactly the reverse of what he wanted. It drew unnecessary attention to his legs and kept them and the overall line of his frame from looking lean and elegant. I found this particularly interesting, as elegance and leanness were things he wanted to project.

"I broached the subject with great care and subtlety; I was well aware of how sensitive he was about this part of his body. I asked if 'we' might make the length of the trouser a little shorter. He responded with a gracious yet emphatic no. I explained that to project an elegant, unfussy look (which had been achieved in every other aspect of the outfit), the trousers needed to just touch his shoes, not hug them. I asked if I might illustrate this before we sent the suit away for completion. He paused, looked at his watch, and agreed, subject to its not taking too long. I asked our alteration tailor to adjust one leg of the trousers to a length I felt was appropriate: sitting on the shoe, with just the hint of a crease.

"When the tailor finished, I asked my client what he thought of the adjusted leg length. Without too much hesitation, he looked at me, nodded, and gently smiled. He agreed that the length I proposed had greatly improved the overall look of the suit and achieved a far more elegant image. The point is that he took a risk. He changed a lifetime opinion and habit, one to which he was emotionally and visually attached. But if he had not had the opinion in the first place, this important improvement in his image would never have taken place."

Standing up for what you believe in, revealing a part of yourself that might not always seem "nice," is being yourself. By allowing your opinions to emerge, you begin to define your personality and show it to yourself and the world. It's not about being right or wrong, well-informed or ill informed—it's about being yourself, your true self. When you have opinions, colorful or not, you are opening up to learn and grow; you can inspire others and expand the way you communicate with them.

Malcolm's celebrity client is known for his big opinions, but he is also known for his desire to learn about the opinions of others. This quality enables him to feed himself more knowledge and to express his humility. As far as we know, no one who knows him thinks any less of him for the opinions that he has. Whether we agree with them or not, if he changes his opinions or not, they are just opinions.

Ideally, opinions are formed based on knowledge and experience—not from seeking attention and wanting to make a noise. If your opinions are not motivated by your ego, they have a relevance to others as well as to yourself; they are inclusive rather than exclusive. Your opinions can serve you well as you learn about yourself and therefore, your personal style.

We end this session with the story of William, who had one of the most common image dilemmas of both men and women. Countless television makeover shows have addressed this universal enigma. Husbands and wives, daughters and sons, sisters and brothers, mothers and fathers have all offered their loved ones as subjects with this particular problem. Read on to see if William's story relates to you or someone you know.

WILLIAM AND HIS PASSIONS

There are times in many people's lives when they become disconnected visually from their environment and from themselves. Their vision becomes distorted and fragmented, and they see themselves and their environment only selectively. They no longer see themselves as a whole—the whole becomes almost impossible to take in. They miss things that outsiders often recognize immediately—a crooked picture on a wall, or jacket sleeves that are too long.

William was a tall, slim, handsome man with a full head of slightly graying hair. His personal style was stuck in the early 1980s, a period when men's designer clothes had exaggerated proportions. His pants were typical of that era—very, very full cut at the top, with deep front pleats, wide through the leg, and deep-cuffed, floppy bottoms. William was so tall and big that when he walked toward us, all we could see were his pants coming at us. He wore a jacket with huge oversized shoulders, far too short for his body shape and his height. Ties in the 1980s were more graphic and zanier than they are today, designed to be a talking point before a meeting started, an attention grabber. His certainly grabbed ours.

William was a New York oncologist in his late forties. Even though he was well respected and aspired to be the best in his field, his competition was doing better business than he was in the world of managed care. He was frustrated because he couldn't understand what they were doing that he wasn't.

We first met him at his office, which looked much as he presented himself—out of time. It was filled with unlikely 1970s furniture and decor, right down to the brown shag carpet. There were plastic plants, geometrically designed wallpaper, and Muzak. It was 1998, and we felt we were in a time warp. For the work space of someone who was on the cutting edge of medicine and whose clients were understandably seeking the most advanced and up-to-date treatments available, his reception room and office were sending a different message. Patients interviewing the specialist there were coming away with a feeling of uncertainty, something no one wants when his or her life is on the line. The office gave them an impression of negligence and that of an unfocused atmosphere. When you don't project clarity, you cannot elicit confidence.

William's manner was polite, but he was all business and even slightly aloof. He seemed distracted as he spoke with us, as if he would rather have been somewhere else. We wondered if his potential clients got this impression as well.

Would William have to play tag-team with the GQ fashion coterie in order to become stylish and repair his business image? No, but he would need to better understand who he was. And as he began to work with us, he did so with a sincerity and enthusiasm that surprised us. At the very beginning we asked him what he loved and what he disliked. Despite all appearances, he had many sophisticated and worldly tastes.

For one thing, William had a passion for Old World charm and sophistication. He loved the architecture, which to him represented grandness and opulence. He enjoyed strolling down the great boulevards of Paris and equally reveled in roaming the colorful outdoor markets of Florence's narrow cobblestone streets. He identified with the older generation of Europeans who carry a certain charm and civility and live in a world of tradition and ritual. He had a passion for long-established cultures and environments.

Never in a million years did William dream that he would be able to integrate these interests into his own personal style. As he told us about his heartfelt passions, he revealed a vulnerability and sensitivity that were undetectable in his appearance. When he told us about his vacations in Europe, the rough edges of his persona seemed to smooth themselves out. He became more communicative; his body language became friendlier and more relaxed. He was noticeably more approachable and engaging—qualities you want in a doctor! We felt that he was finally "with us," present and relating to us in a dynamic and natural way.

WILLIAM'S DISCOVERY

William had lost sight of all of the images in his life. Visual harmony was lacking in his appearance, in his office, and even in his image of himself as a professional. By bringing this problem to his attention, we gave him a wake-up call. The first step for William was thus awareness. He opened his eyes and fully realized that he had to pay attention to the way he and his business were perceived. When William was made aware of his environment and reminded of his love of sophisticated European charm and civility, he made a connection. He realized that his tastes and interests were not reflected in any aspect of his business or his personal style.

As you follow William through the course of the book, you will see how he made a transition from projecting too many different styles to building one style with a strong identity. Interestingly, only a handful of patients later remarked on his newly refurbished office and his sophisticated appearance. But William knew that this somewhat quiet reaction was exactly the right response. It aligned perfectly with his goal for his image and ultimately for his business.

Creating Your Personal Style Statement

Your Personal Style Statement is a goal-oriented statement of what you desire for your image and how you would like to be perceived.

"I project a substantial and meaningful presence."   —MARY

"I make an elegant and sophisticated impression."   —WILLIAM

"I project a charismatic and unique image."   —JULIA

"My personal style exudes quality and individuality."   —ANNA

"I present an image of clarity, confidence, and comfort."   —PAUL

How important is it for you to construct a Personal Style Statement? When you enter a room, when you have an important interview, when you are choosing your clothes for the day, when you are meeting someone for the first time, when you are going shopping—these are only a few scenarios in which you can call upon this valuable statement.

Your Personal Style Statement is your anchor. It is motivational and supportive, especially when it comes time to make decisions about clothing. When you are standing in front of your closet deciding what to do with the clothes you already have, your Personal Style Statement can guide you. You may love your 1977 baseball jacket, but not only has it seen better days, it no longer relates to the image you want, which you have articulated in your Personal Style Statement.

Let's say you're in a sticky situation at work. You've been thrown into a business lunch with clients whom you've never met but who have a reputation for being very difficult. Maybe they are rude or crude (or both!). Your Personal Style Statement expresses your values and the things you really care about. By repeating your statement to yourself, you will know how to behave. *And behavior is a large part of image!* If your statement contains the word *confident* or *sophisticated,* then you will want to remember those goals when faced with the rude lunch companions. Ask yourself: *How would a confident person handle this situation? How would a sophisticated person behave right now?* When you hone in on your goals for your image and translate them into one personal statement, it will rescue you, calm you, and offer you clarity when you are confused.

Goal setting has become the norm for almost every aspect of life, from business and career to personal matters. The goal-oriented statement that you create for your image will help you to achieve your other goals, both in your professional and personal lives—provided you are honest and realistic.

We use two steps in creating a Personal Style Statement. The first one is another simple yet revealing exercise.

STEP 1: ICON EXERCISE

In Session 1 you turned your attention inward to discover the things you feel passionately about and the things you dislike. Now look outside of yourself and think of the people whom you most admire. Think of people in the public eye, perhaps from the worlds of film, television, business, and politics. They may be living or not. They may be figures from history or people you see in the media on a daily basis. Of course, they don't have to be in the public eye at all—you may greatly admire a friend or relative or former teacher.

You may choose more than one person, even ones who aren't the same gender as you. Write about why you admire these people. What you are looking for are the *qualities* that you admire in these people.

Write about them in as much detail as you wish. It doesn't matter if your account of these people's qualities is accurate—just record your impressions and what you think they might be like if you were to meet them.

If one of your icons is a fashion or glamour icon, it's fine to include him or her. But do not include people who are widely known as "style icons" unless you truly admire them. Don't try to think of someone you would like to look like, dress like, or act like. Simply think of people about whom you have good feelings.

Mary's Icon exercise taught us something very important about her.

EXCERPTS FROM MARY'S ICON EXERCISE

I feel that **Grace Kelly** *embodies her name. When I think of her, I am reminded of grace, dignity, and elegance. How fitting it was for her to become a princess! I always got the impression that she was a person of substance. I admired her move from Hollywood to taking on the responsibilities of wife, mother, and royalty.*

I know it is a predictable and typical choice, but **Audrey Hepburn** *will always be one of my most admired and respected icons. Here is a woman who seemed to make her life meaningful, and she did it with oodles of style and sophistication. Was she born that way? I was hopelessly mesmerized as a young adult by her movies and love to watch them still today. But as we both grew older, my main attraction to her became the work she did for UNICEF. Her work outside the limelight really moved me. She didn't have to do that. And I guess on a style note, I am still in awe of how she was always appropriately dressed. Whether she was in Africa visiting children, or whether she was wearing her Givenchy gowns, she was always Audrey.*

Mother Teresa *should be given sainthood. She lived her life in a way that mattered. She contributed. She wore the equivalent of a uniform, but she performed remarkable acts of courage with a selflessness that is practically obsolete these days. In my opinion, Mother Teresa had what you guys call "consummate inner style." I just admire so much her no-nonsense approach to life and her work. For such a tiny little lady, she had great strength and conviction.*

Mary's personal choices of icons were neither right nor wrong, but they also could not have been more perfect. The reason is that Mary's essence contained small degrees of the qualities of all of the icons she wrote about. She was not yet fully aware of them, but she had the potential to express the same qualities that she admired in her icons. **Mary was just beginning to tap into her own special qualities, which were similar to if not the same as those of the people she admired.**

STEP 2: IDENTIFYING QUALITIES

The second step in creating your Personal Style Statement is to read over the work you have done so far and highlight the words that stand out to you. Please include your writings from Session 1 on your passions, as well as your descriptions of your icons. As you revisit the material, pay close attention to your feelings, your intuition, and your emotions.

You may come across a phrase or even an idea that you feel strongly about—highlight it. A certain word, idea, or group of words may be repeated throughout your material—highlight it. Be honest and open. The rational part of your mind may not quite understand why you are experiencing a strong feeling about a particular word or phrase, but just go with it—don't dismiss any feelings!

After you have highlighted the most significant words, list them separately on the next clean page in your notebook. If you have chosen several words that basically mean the same thing, choose one that most closely represents the meaning of all those words. For example, if you chose the words *unique, individual, different,* and *special,* choose the one that gives you the biggest emotional charge or the one you like the most.

Spend some time with these words, and then come back to them later to gauge any additional feelings you may have about them. These are the words from which you will construct your Personal Style Statement.

Depending on how many words are in your list, choose two or three words at the most to form a sentence. Insert these words into a sentence in the present tense. The most often used sentences are:

I present an image that is . . .
I project . . .
My personal style is one of . . .

My image . . .
I leave an impression of . . .

If you're having trouble converting an idea or a group of words into a concise, clear message, take the time to come up with the words that you feel are right for you and your image. You may not get it right the first time. This is a very important statement you are making; wait until you are inspired by the words that mean the most to you. They should express the message you most wish to convey. Remember where these words came from: your passions, your desires, and your choices of enduring symbols.

One of our clients, Gordon, was mulling over the phrases "a life full of color" and "exciting to be around." These phrases had appeared several times in both of his sessions. While they were clearly important for him and his personal style, he just couldn't put his finger on the one word that said it all for him. A few days after he had done this work, we received a message from him. He said, "Hi, this is Gordon. Vibrant, vibrant, vibrant." And he hung up.

Let's look now at the words Mary chose from her work in the first two sessions:

Substance
Meaningful
Sophistication
Appropriate
Attractive
Learning
Inner Confidence
[And she told us the idea of philanthropy is very important to her.]

Mary wanted to make a difference in the world and to leave her mark. To do so, she felt it was vital to be a person of substance and to have meaning to her life. In this way she felt she could share, teach, and learn.

Mary's Personal Style Statement was: **"I project a substantial and meaningful presence."**

Mary had no idea how *substantial* and *meaningful* would manifest in her appearance and image decisions. It felt like a big statement to make, and she wondered if and how she would live up to it. She even questioned its authenticity. It made her a little nervous. But these were very healthy reactions. They meant that Mary cared and was taking responsibility for a decision that she could live with and live up to. Finally she trusted that the statement felt right to her.

THE DICTIONARY: A HIGHLY RECOMMENDED TOOL

We have discovered an incredible learning tool that has helped to give voice, clarity, and understanding to many Personal Style Statements—the dictionary! When you have created your Personal Style Statement, get out your dictionary and look at the definitions of the words you have chosen.

The definitions of words are open to interpretation—make sure you are fully aware of their true meanings. If you are in doubt, go to the dictionary. The dictionary's definitions are almost always accurate and pure. They will inspire you and motivate you.

Mary's Personal Style Statement contained the words *substantial* and *meaningful*. Here is the *American Heritage College Dictionary*'s definition of those two words:

> **Substantial—solid and practical in character, quality, or importance; to be present.**
>
> **Meaningful—having meaning, function, or purpose; inner significance.**

There were a few other definitions for both of these words, but these were the ones that resonated for Mary. Defined in this way, Mary's words brought a sense of calm to her. She felt confident that she could bring solidity and a practicalness to her image. Quality was indeed important to her, as were function and purpose. She began to relax and soon became excited that these words and their meanings would eventually be part of a statement that would say everything about her personal style.

Mary's choices were very good ones for who she was. Later she discovered, for example, that she was hanging on to clothes, relationships, and lifestyle habits that were not *substantial* and that no longer had *meaning* in her life.

You may find, during the course of this book, that you need to change your statement. This most often happens when people set their goals too high or are unrealistic in what they are committed to accomplishing. And sometimes people have a change of heart, or they become more clear about what is important to them and their image later in the process. It doesn't matter if your Personal Style Statement is not completed immediately—what does matter is that you create it and eventually become comfortable with it. Remember, it is a goal statement—something to work toward.

EVE'S UNREALISTIC GOALS

One of the many benefits that we derive from our clients, customers, and seminar students is knowledge. Not only do we learn about a wide variety of people, we also learn about others' interpretations of personal style. The story of our client Eve, whom we worked with several years ago, is not a typical one. The physical changes she was willing to undergo were almost unlimited, as was the amount of money she was prepared to spend. Most of the clients we work with want to make improvements, increase self-esteem, and create a personalized, individual style. But Eve's quest was for consummate beauty—nothing less would do. As Eve was to learn, physical changes alone and the ability to spend large sums of money do not buy personal style. Hers is also the story of a strong desire for complete transformation. But as she learned, strong desire must be tempered with a grounded reality.

Eve began her career working out of her home, with just a telephone and a computer. Gradually her asset-management enterprise grew into a highly successful brokerage business. While her business was growing, Eve chose to keep a low profile. She rarely met with clients in person, often leaving that job to an account manager.

Eve spent so much time working in an environment that was essentially sealed off from the rest of the world that she eventually felt out of touch with everything, including her image. Now Eve was embarking on a brand-new road—she wanted to be an actress. Her intentions were to use her hard-earned money to facilitate her major career change.

Eve had heard about us from a friend. When we first spoke with her, she explained that she was about to undergo cosmetic surgery.

She had always felt uncomfortable with the shape of her nose and had always felt like an ugly duckling. The biggest treat of her life, she said, would be to physically change her appearance. During the next weeks, in addition to having cosmetic surgery on her nose, Eve underwent laser surgery, liposuction, and breast augmentation. She did all this surgery before she met with us, as she strongly wanted our first meeting to be with the "new her."

(Eve had already made up her mind and did not consult us about her surgery, but our clients have asked us many times about cosmetic surgery. Should they or shouldn't they? How do we feel about it with them specifically and in general? The decision to change a physical aspect of oneself through surgery is a deeply personal one. It needs to be made with great care and personal responsibility. It would be inappropriate for us to assume that responsibility. We do recommend, however, that anyone considering such a change have the best possible understanding of the psychological limitations and ramifications. Have complete knowledge of what you are doing. Read as much as you can about the particular procedure you are considering. Speak to as many people as you can, and interview as many experts as possible. Speak to therapists and former patients—both those who are pleased and those who are not.)

When Eve phoned us to set up her first session, she told us how pleased she was with the results of her surgery and how she felt this was going to change her life. She was excited to see such a great improvement so quickly, and she was eager to keep the momentum going. We were happy that Eve felt better about herself and were pleased that the surgery had gone well.

We knew Eve had already interviewed a number of different image and style consultants, and we felt this was the perfect time to explain how we work with private clients. We work differently from other consultants, we told her, and we stressed that what we really do is teach. Once again we emphasized how important it was for her to participate and collaborate so that maximum results could be achieved. This process would not produce an overnight image transformation, we warned her, as her surgery had seemed to. She reiterated that she was intrigued by our approach and understood that creating a personal style was a process that would develop over time.

We shared her excitement about working together and looked forward to meeting her for the first time. When the day arrived, a friendly, hospitable woman who had a very attractive face greeted us. Individually, each of Eve's features was pleasing; she had large blue eyes, beautiful skin, and a full mouth that relinquished a very pretty smile. Her facial features were natural looking, and they showed absolutely no sign of cosmetic surgery. She had acquired the physical facial attributes of a classic beauty.

But Eve was an incomplete tapestry. Her vibrant features and her bubbly personality were not matched by certain other aspects of her image. Remember that historically Eve had never bothered with any aspect of her appearance and had not even been in the public eye for quite some time. So when she "came out of her office," she wasn't quite prepared for the modern world she found. This was reflected in the clothes she wore. Her long, dark green rayon skirt and matching tunic top were matronly looking. Her long, straight brown hair, which she parted in the middle and wore very flat to her head, was not flattering to her attractive face.

The way Eve carried herself, walked, and communicated physically and verbally made her seem older than she was. She could have been described as dowdy. Essentially, her visual message was disorienting. Her assets were very strong, but the image improvements she wished to make as they related to her Personal Style Statement were equally pronounced.

Eve was well aware that she presented a confusing image and that she needed to work toward completing her startling transformation. She needed to create a personal style that would be integrated into her new physical image. Curiously, we were never to see any pictures of Eve from before her surgery; we would never know how different her image had been from that of the woman who stood before us.

Eve created the Personal Style Statement **"I present a head-turning, glamorous image."** It would have been easy for us to question her right away about how exactly she had created her statement—but it would also have been denying her the right to empower herself, learn about herself, and fine-tune her goals. It wasn't wrong for Eve to desire these things for her image, but it was also not yet realistic. Our job was to help her to become more aware of what she would have to do to achieve her goal.

Soon after we began working with Eve, she became antsy. She was anxious to buy new clothes and to see herself wearing them as soon as possible. When we tried to discuss the issues not specifically related to buying clothes, which were important ones for her—working on her posture, voice, exercise, and nutrition—we were met with "I'll take care of that later." Likewise, in the early stage we wanted to talk to her about her hair. She agreed that it was an important change to make. We introduced her to our tried and tested methods that would enable her to make the best choices about color and style. As you shall see in our later sessions, this is a step-by-step discovery process that requires the client to go out and gather information in order to act effectively later. It is a building process and entails some homework.

Impatient with the process of creating a style that truly represented her personality, and wanting to replicate the high she had experienced following her cosmetic surgery, Eve impulsively chose to skip the work. On a whim she went to the nearest salon and turned herself completely over to the stylist. The next morning Eve was on the phone to us, upset and crying. Her new hairstyle, with its tight and unflattering body wave, was far from an improvement, and she told us it looked worse than it had before.

Hoping to redirect Eve's focus, we asked her to take an Aesthetic Field Trip—Session 5 in our program. We were trying to encourage Eve to explore her own opinions as they related to her tastes. Again, we were met with resistance. When we asked her what she had learned from her field trip, she admitted she hadn't gone.

Once more it was time to reassess what we were doing. We were there to teach Eve to embody her Personal Style Statement, not to just say it. We asked her to think again about her statement and her desire to present a head-turning and glamorous image. If she felt insecure about being among new people, then how was she going to "turn heads"? If she didn't take the time to cultivate and learn about her tastes, how could she become glamorous?

What Eve really wanted was what so many other people want—to buy her image and style and take it home. She wanted to go shopping. This is very, very normal—we all like to eat the icing on the cake first. But it takes discipline, patience, and self-restraint to save at least some of the icing for last—qualities that were challenging for Eve.

We asked her if she would like to change her Personal Style Statement. Gently we explained that what she was doing was not helping her to attain her goal, that she was working against her goal, and that it was okay for her to change it. Did she want to? The question clearly rattled her. She realized that she had been missing out on some of the most important elements of this work. She wasn't experiencing self-empowerment. She wasn't learning anything.

We described to her the dreary and sometimes tedious things that so-called glamorous people have to do to maintain their status. The forethought, demands, and time-consuming efforts necessary in order to be "glamorous" began to lose their appeal for her. We asked her to think about how realistic it was for her to jump from where she was now to an uninformed idea of glamour.

THE REALITY OF GLAMOUR

Glamour—an air of compelling charm and excitement, especially when delusively alluring.

This definition of glamour is an interesting one. While it is possible to possess a natural charm and to leave a charming impression, it is nearly impossible to maintain an "exciting presence" in the face of everyday life. And what does it mean to be "delusively alluring"? Well, it means to be deceivingly enticing. Which is exactly what glamour is—beautifully made, desirable illusions.

In a way, creating glamour is easy, provided you have the resources. The individual professionals who create glamour are talented and skillful enough to create it for anyone—and we do mean literally anyone. Being glamorous does not depend on being beautiful, or having a perfect body, or being a particular age, social status, race, or gender. Glamour is a fleeting moment in time. Least of all does it have anything to do with personal style and a lasting feeling of self-confidence. Unless your career depends on it, glamour has no place in most people's daily lifestyle.

Still, glamour can play a role in our lives from time to time. Opening nights, awards ceremonies, weddings, and other special events are all occasions for which we spend extra time, money, and energy to look as special as we can. But in reality, most of us don't make those efforts often.

The public is constantly deluged with images of glamorous men and women in the media. When people see a glamorous photograph in a magazine or an image on television, they often have an emotional response: "She is so beautiful—I want to look like that." And then, "Why don't I look like that?" And for some, "I'm going to look like that." (And for others, "I'll never be able to look like that.")

Those who respond this way often forget that many people are involved in creating that glamorous illusion. They forget the reality and rush out to buy an element of what they have interpreted as glamour.

Not since Farrah Fawcett's golden *Charlie's Angels* mane in 1976–77 has a hairstyle been copied so frequently as *Friends* star Jennifer Aniston's. In 1994–95 this phenomenon was far-reaching— we received many tearful late-night calls from female clients here and in Europe, telling us that their *Friends* haircuts had been disastrous and disappointing. Hoping to look more glamorous, softer, and more current, they had believed that a new hairstyle alone would achieve that goal. Instead, as one of them said, her hair hung down her face in flat, numerous layers, and she looked like a hag.

In truth, what each of these women wanted to achieve was something more than just a new hairstyle, though most of them would agree their goals had absolutely nothing in common with Jennifer Aniston's lifestyle, hair type, personality, or physical appearance. They were largely professional women who held responsible positions in the worlds of finance and other corporate businesses. Going for the look without having done their homework, they discovered after the fact that this high-maintenance hairstyle (requiring gels, volume enhancers, and at least forty-five minutes of very tricky blow-drying) was totally incompatible with their busy lives.

If these women had done the work outlined in this book, they would not have made this mistake. They would have arrived at a new hairstyle that was uniquely theirs. They would have learned how to cultivate a complete personal style by working from the inside out, based on who they were as individuals. As our clients know, by knowing all about yourself, you become self-referred. You would know how to go about considering—and implementing—such a change; and you would be pleased with the results. Yes, pleased. Relying on the latest trends or on celebrities or the media or even fashion consultants to express your personal style is like playing tag-team with your image.

Glamour can be entertaining and fun, and it may give your confidence a huge, if brief, boost. Sometimes it can inspire and motivate you to take positive steps regarding your image that you would have otherwise neglected. But remember, in reality glamour is acquired only for a limited time.

Some people do have an air about them that may be called glamorous. But more often than not, they have simply cultivated a very highly developed personal style.

EVE'S NEW STATEMENT: REALISTIC GOALS

As we worked together, Eve began to understand that glamour is a sometime thing. She recognized that glamour would make impossible demands on her already busy life. She agreed that in the excitement of all of the many changes she was making, she had overzealously created an unrealistic goal. We asked her if she might be interested in finding out what made her unique and incorporating that into her personal style. She agreed.

Eve now understood that her active involvement in the development of her personal style was fundamental to the transformation she said she wanted. She went back to the work in Sessions 1 and 2 and created a new, realistic Personal Style Statement. She composed her list of passions, and the result included much that we could build from. Eve's list of passions included: the silence of scuba diving; the paintings of Richard Diebenkorn; red maple leaves in the autumn; aromatherapy and shiatsu massage; the comfort of summer rain; and the science of life.

Her icons were the late Princess Diana, Jacques Cousteau, and Meryl Streep.

Her new Personal Style Statement was "I present a confident and sophisticated image."

Eve assured us she was committed to her new goals, and to the program. She was ready now to restart and work deliberately through the process.

Eve's story is an important and emblematic one. You can't cheat the experience— if you wish to attain a true personal style, you must do the work and you must create realistic goals that are in keeping with the amount of work you are prepared to do. Like Eve, you will come to understand that style isn't for sale and that true style consists of many more components than just clothes, hair, and makeup. As Eve realized, everyone learns at their own pace, in their own time, when they are ready.

WILLIAM'S PERSONAL STYLE STATEMENT

William, our competitive doctor, identified his icons relatively easily. Charles Boyer, William Holden, Harrison Ford, and Prince Rainier of Monaco—he chose them quickly and wrote about them with ease. He created what he considered to be a Personal Style Statement with a strong foundation. He felt as if he were on a roll—at least until we asked him to define the words he had chosen!

William felt that Charles Boyer represented the essence of European sophistication and elegance. William greatly admired Boyer's voice and found it distinguished yet friendly. He also loved the way Boyer looked and felt sure that he had great taste and wasn't a snob.

William was attracted to William Holden's "all man" appeal coupled with his handsome features and imposing frame. This conjured up a vision of strength and an all-American sophistication that William admired. He also saw a soft side to the actor's character that represented vulnerability, which William also identified with.

Harrison Ford represented to him assuredness, humor, and a strong presence. William admired the frugality of Ford's speech and the quiet yet meaningful way he communicates. Although William considered Ford to be a man's man, he felt sure that Ford would be very comfortable in the company of women. In spite of Ford's ruggedness, William thought he looked elegant and comfortable whether he was wearing a flannel shirt and jeans or a tuxedo. William found this unique among modern-day male celebrities.

William felt that everything he loved about European elegance, culture, and good breeding was represented by Prince Rainier of Monaco. William also loved the fact that Prince Rainier had been married to Grace Kelly. The combination was almost perfect in William's eyes, a melding of two powers, a beautiful all-American icon and a "real" European prince. This combination of cultures was both visually and intellectually appealing.

The word *elegance* was obviously very important to William, as was *sophistication*. He considered all of his icons to be elegant and sophisticated in their unique ways. His passions kept leading him to the same words. William's Personal Style Statement was: **"I make an elegant and sophisticated impression."**

You may imagine that the new William walks around his home mirroring an English land baron with a glass of Pimm's in hand or a

French aristocrat wearing a silk cravat and monogrammed silk shirts. This is not the case. In fact, for anyone except an actual English land baron or aristocrat, behaving in this way would be ridiculous.

But William's passions are very real, honest, and heartfelt. We asked him what he thought the words *elegant* and *sophisticated* meant. He wasn't quite sure, but he thought they might have something to do with lots of money, a stately home, grand social occasions, embassy dinners, five-star international travel, and frequent indulgencies of foie gras and champagne. He laughed shyly and said, "Isn't that what elegance is all about?" We then asked him how he thought a person who lived that way might look. He told us that he didn't know, he wasn't really sure. Would such a person wear a smoking jacket? Or custom-made riding boots or a handmade suit from Savile Row?

Unlike Eve, who set a demanding and unrealistic goal for herself, William created a statement that was very much in keeping with an untapped, deeply personal desire. We asked him if he would like to explore a deeper, more satisfying meaning of the words he had chosen.

We brought out the dictionary and read to William its definition of elegance.

THE REALITY OF ELEGANCE

Elegance—refinement, grace, and beauty in movement, appearance, or manners; tasteful opulence in form, decoration, or presentation; restraint and grace of style; scientific precision.

William was not alone in wanting to be elegant. A very high percentage of our clients use the word. In fact, it is at the top of the list of what people desire most. Many times its meaning crosses over into other words in Personal Style Statements, such as *tasteful, refined,* and *gracious.* We have listed below several words related to the word *elegant* that are used frequently by our clients. These words may appear in your Personal Style Statement. They are:

Sophistication
Confident
Simplicity
Focused

Reliable
Enigmatic
Compelling
Vibrant

Your Personal Style Statement and your image goals may not contain any of these words. But we are sure that the words you are using are related in some way. The remaining sessions of this book will teach you about the words you have chosen and how to use them to achieve your image goals. First, we'd like to share with you some of our own definitions of the words we listed above, which may help you fine-tune your Personal Style Statement.

Your perception of what true elegance is may not be entirely accurate. You may also feel slightly intimidated by the very thought of elegance! Or maybe you think it is irrelevant to your lifestyle and your down-to-earth existence. If you are someone who shuns or struggles with the idea of incorporating elegance into your personal style because you think you cannot achieve it, know that you absolutely can. Even if you add only one aspect of elegance to your personal style, you are enhancing your image in ways you cannot imagine.

Many people we work with are under the impression that elegance somehow has a shallow and insubstantial connotation. They usually associate elegance with money and social standing, as William did. This couldn't be further from the truth. Elegance is sturdy and dependable. It has structure and form and is pleasing to the eye. A truly elegant person is a person of substance with an unshakable core. Elegance is a way of being; you can wear jeans or sweats and still be an elegant person!

Elegance is not self-conscious and often goes unnoticed. It is filled with subtleties. One small change of a detail in a hairstyle may represent the difference between an elegant look and one that is not. Elegant people respect themselves and look as though they do. They pursue the best quality they can afford and would rather do without than compromise. They take care of the details within the details; they are exact, whether they are writing a thank-you note or buying a clothing item. They leave an impression of clarity—they do not send mixed messages in appearance or manner. Their grooming and manners are immaculate, yet never ostentatious. They revel in the journey—they update themselves and take pleasure in reviewing where they are. They are humble—for they always have a desire to learn more and to continue to improve. Elegance is all about the details—and paying attention to *your* specific details.

The terrain of clothing is specific and highly detailed. If indeed one of your goals is to incorporate an element of elegance into your personal style, you will need to investigate how to create your own version of elegance and place your own personal stamp on it. The following is a short preview of information you will find later in the sessions that pertains to elegance in clothing. It is in no way meant to guide your decisions about clothing. It is meant to ignite your imagination so that you can begin to make a connection to clothing and what it can say about you.

• **Street-savvy elegance**—Combines a number of different current-looking and hip clothing items and accessories of a wide range of prices.

• **Simple elegance**—Is uncluttered, well defined, and always of good quality, with an emphasis on fabric, cut, and style.

• **Tasteful opulent elegance**—Allows the person to shine through and transcend the opulence of couture, costume (royal attire, uniforms), or evening attire.

• **Old World elegance**—Presents a charming image of timelessness and dependability, evoking a sense of history and culture; suggests a resistance to being dictated to.

• **Urban elegance**—Involves a concoction of understated, scientifically selected outfits that are completely interchangeable and fit for any occasion; is current but not necessarily hip or trendy.

• **Retro elegance**—Knows how to choose and put together a thrift shop sweater with an expensive pair of designer pants.

• **Classic elegance**—Is very highly developed and cultivated and very, very controlled; has strong boundaries but is reliable and dependable.

All these versions of elegance have a very important common thread: they convey ease and effortless appearance. They may look as if they just "somehow happened," or were "thrown together," but in fact the reverse is true. Each of them is highly thought out so as to appear as if no thought or effort had been made.

THE REALITY OF SOPHISTICATION

William's reaction to all of this information was endearing. An established professional in the medical field, highly respected by his peers, he looked at us in bewilderment. He was confused, a bit overwhelmed, and slightly intimidated. He thought that if elegance was the goal, then the words in the definition were the ingredients, and he assumed he needed every ingredient in order to achieve the goal. We assured him that his was a normal reaction and that in working toward his desire to leave an impression of elegance, he in no way needed to embody all of these qualities.

We also reminded him that there was certainly no deadline to adhere to—he hadn't learned the many skills of his craft overnight; nor should he expect to achieve his image goals overnight. Creating a new aspect to your image, learning how to bring out the attractive qualities of yourself that are hidden, is also a craft.

Most people do not consider that becoming elegant, chic, or sophisticated requires education, let alone a scientific approach. But even those people who seem born to elegance and sophistication had to undergo training! People are not born sophisticated; it is not a gift. In fact, to prove this point let's go back to the dictionary to see what the word sophisticated really means:

> **Sophisticated—having acquired worldly knowledge or refinement; lacking natural simplicity or naïveté; very complex or complicated.**

This definition caused William another little hiccup. He looked at us with "Well, what does *that* mean?" written all over his face. Being worldly and refined is related to accumulating knowledge and experiences. Sophisticates educate their taste; they learn how to discern what is tasteful and what is not. Sophistication *is* complex, because what makes something or someone sophisticated is determined by many factors. Sophisticated people make edgy and intelligent decisions about behavior, dress, and lifestyle—sometimes in a blink of an eye.

David Michaelis wrote a beautiful article about John F. Kennedy, Jr., in *Vanity Fair* magazine in September 1999, just after his tragic death. The author told of how on the evening of Kennedy's mother's death several years before, he was in her New York apartment telling family members the sad news. A few minutes later he heard a wailing sound from one of the women. Was she a cousin whom he didn't recognize? It turned out she was an older woman whom no one knew. He apologized to her for not knowing her, and she proceeded to give him one false name after another. At that point, he realized that in reality she had come in off the street and somehow made her way into the apartment. How many different ways could he have reacted? What do you say to an intruder at your mother's deathbed? His choice in that moment was to say gently, "Madam, you don't belong here."

Sophisticates have an unrelenting desire, discipline, and determination to be the best they can be, no matter their circumstances. You will learn more about what makes clothing and behavior sophisticated in later sessions.

We asked William to commit to becoming serious about his Personal Style Statement. We felt it was right for him, something he had created out of a great passion and desire. We also felt that he was open and willing to learn. Admitting that he "didn't know" what elegance and sophistication were did not mean that he couldn't work toward experiencing them.

Healing Your Image Wounds

To achieve your image goals, you need to develop a realistic, sympathetic body image. That does not mean losing weight or gaining weight. It does not mean making any physical changes at all. It means changing a negative body image into a more positive one. It means taking an honest look at yourself, accepting yourself, and liking yourself the way you are now. If you can take just one step toward improving your body image, you will be better able to project a personal style that accurately sums up who you really are.

This session offers you an alternative perspective from the one you have now. You will begin to see yourself differently, with more compassion and a new appreciation for your body and yourself.

Our clients usually find Session 3 to be moving and very satisfying. For the first time they are able to better accept themselves without having to worry about changing their bodies to meet someone else's standards. Many of the people we work with feel liberated and able to express themselves in ways that truly represent who they are—their personal style. What you learn in this session will help you to feel better about yourself. We will teach you how to improve your body image—which is possible for each and every one of you.

WHAT IS BODY IMAGE?

Remember the last time you accidentally caught a glimpse of yourself in a plate-glass window or mirror. The person you saw probably seemed unfamiliar to you. On this rare occasion, you saw yourself as others see you.

Perhaps you noticed that your reflection's posture wasn't quite as upright and elegant as you thought it was. Or maybe you looked slimmer or heavier than you thought. Perhaps your shoulders appeared astonishingly broader than you had been imagining. And maybe you realized that it really is time to change your hairstyle. What you were seeing and experiencing was, for a moment, a more accurate view of yourself. Your mental image of yourself was challenged by a bit of reality.

Your *body image* is different from your *image*. In the introduction, we stated that your image is the totality of how you present yourself to the world—it is the presentation of both your inner self and your outer self. Your body image, however, is the picture you have formed in your mind of how you think your body looks. It is your internal self-portrait. Your body image affects the very core of who you are.

Your clothing sits right next to your skin—a very intimate place to reside! As you move your body, your clothes move with you. Your body image has everything to do with how you choose your clothes, how you wear them, and how you feel about yourself in them. Your body image also affects the way people see you—for example, the way you make eye contact, the way you walk, and the way you communicate.

Most often the way you think you look is not really how others perceive you—or how you really are! Many of the things you feel about your body are probably inaccurate. Has someone ever given you a compliment about a certain aspect of your body and you were shocked to hear it? You almost jump to the mirror looking for confirmation. But what you see instead is a mental picture of your body that is compromised by old emotions, image wounds, and unfair comparisons with others' bodies. *Your* perception is off, not the perception of the person who complimented you. He or she does not see the baggage that inhibits your self-view.

BODY IMAGE IS IMPORTANT BECAUSE A POOR BODY IMAGE:
- Can affect your self-esteem.
- Can affect your behavior with others.

These are two very important reasons to take a closer look at your body image.

INTERFERING BEHAVIORS

Over time everyone develops behaviors that are specifically related to his or her image. Some of these behaviors may be mild and harmless, but others habitually undermine that image.

Do you have any behaviors relating to your body image that interfere with the development of your personal style?

If you are uncertain of the answer, the following questions may help you. They are for you to contemplate, an awareness check. It is not necessary to write down your answers, but if you come across something that particularly moves you, we do encourage you to note it.

More than likely you will be able to identify your behavior in one of the following two categories.

ARE YOU AN AVOIDER?

- Do you avoid wearing certain clothes, styles, and colors?
- Do you avoid a physical activity such as dancing, exercising, or a sports activity that might put your body on display?
- Do you avoid looking into the mirror?
- Do you avoid clothing stores?
- Do you avoid people you are attracted to because you feel insecure?
- Do you avoid people who you think look better than you?
- Do you avoid people who you think dress better than you?
- As an act of defiance, do you put as little thought as possible into your appearance?
- Do you avoid using your body in certain ways? Do you avoid sitting or standing in a certain way?

ARE YOU A CHECKER?

- Do you try not to mess up your appearance even when you are physically active? For instance, must you look perfect at the gym?
- Do you spend a great deal of time getting dressed? Do you regularly change your clothes and hair *several* times before you go out?
- Do you become upset or angry when someone complains about how much time you spend getting dressed?
- Do you spend a lot of time checking yourself in the mirror? Whenever you pass by a mirror, a shop window, or a car window—

any place you can find a reflection of yourself—do you check to make sure you look okay?

- Do you constantly compare your looks with others?
- Do you frequently check other people's opinions about your appearance? "Do you think I look okay? Are you sure? Really? You're positive? You can tell me the truth. I really want to know. Are you sure?"
- Do you have grooming rules and rituals that you cannot stop even though you want to? For example, you may constantly refix something that is not really out of place, like your hair or lipstick. Perhaps you are "addicted" to a certain product like hair gel or mascara and become distraught without it.
- Do you spend a great deal of money on your appearance but are never satisfied?

Everyone, to some degree, performs either the avoiding or the checking behaviors. And many people perform both. What are your reactions to these questions? What are your emotions? Have you become defensive, angry, worried? Are you amused? What are you feeling right now?

It is likely you will discover some of the reasons for these behaviors by working through this session. In addition, you will be given the opportunity to make small, gradual changes.

DISSATISFACTION IS UNIVERSAL

By doing creative work in the design studio, spending time with people in various states of undress, and helping people with several forms of bodywork, the two of us have had many diverse experiences with people's relationships with their bodies. Neither of us can recall one single person who has had a completely healthy body image. The varying degrees of dissatisfaction and vulnerability are based on a wide range of complaints and painful experiences.

People are often very intrigued when we explain to them that we include body image as part of the process of revealing our clients' personal style. They are under the impression that most people don't want to address their feelings about their bodies. But we have found the reverse to be true. Our clients are very eager to talk with us about their image wounds and how they perceive themselves. They often say what a great relief it is to finally get their unspoken burdens off of their chests.

One client always stifled his laugh, because he had been repeatedly told he had a big mouth. Many clients feel they are unable to wear certain clothes or colors because of a hurtful remark made to them when they were young. Whatever it is that hurts them or makes them feel uncomfortable about their body is private and personal. Many people become frustrated because they feel they cannot see themselves in an accurate, realistic light.

Not even "beautiful" people necessarily have a favorable body image, yet those considered "plain" do not necessarily have a negative body image. A story from Kate demonstrates this point.

THE IMPORTANCE OF COMPASSION

"A portion of my experience over the years has been in different forms of bodywork. I have always been drawn to the nontraditional. My first yoga class, over twenty years ago, was taught very meditatively and quietly by an unpretentious Yoda-looking man in a small room in an apartment building on West Eighty-third Street in New York City. There were never more than five or six students in class. It was certainly a different atmosphere from that of the large-studio, music-driven classes taught by some of today's teachers, who are becoming celebrities in their own right.

"I have most recently studied for two and a half years the Feldenkrais method, a sophisticated form of body-awareness work. I predict that its benefits will be shared by more and more people, although it is really not new at all. I have been delighted to witness the growth of this and other nontraditional ways to exercise, relax, and develop awareness of one's body.

"My work entailed a direct hands-on relationship with people. In the beginning days of my education and experience, when I was meeting someone for the first time, I would have a preconceived notion about him or her. I would automatically predetermine how the person felt about their body based on the way he or she looked. I was wrong almost every time. I will always remember the day a famous female singer-songwriter walked into the studio for her first lesson. I was startled by the image of her traditionally beautiful body. She was tall, long-limbed, and very well proportioned, and she possessed an elegant body language. I was amazed when she voiced complaints and insecurities about her body!

"The people who I thought looked great and had positive body images turned out to have numerous complaints and intense dislikes about their bodies. And the ones I thought might have a problem were much more comfortable with themselves than I imagined. Even New York City professional dancers, both male and female, who have the most athletically magnificent bodies I have ever worked with, had torturous relationships with their body image.

"One actress I worked with had an extremely petite body shape. She felt like a feather in my hands. In fact, as she was lying on the equipment, she felt so light that I asked her to relax and just give me the weight of her body. Slightly annoyed, she replied that she was giving me her weight. I apologized and explained that she felt so light. (This was early in my career, when I was too naïve and inexperienced to know that silence is golden!) She sat up and looked me straight in the eye and explained to me that she really needed to lose at least fifteen more pounds because the 'camera puts fifteen pounds on you, you know.' I attempted to hide my shock at her comment because I truly didn't know where the fifteen pounds that she wanted to lose were going to come from.

"I had heard about it and read about it—but not until that moment had I seen it. Her baggy clothes, which covered every inch of her body, including her socks, which she refused to take off, and her reaction to my comment explained everything: this woman was suffering from anorexia nervosa.

"My experience with her taught me powerful lessons about compassion and respect for others. I became more sensitive to people's image of themselves. We never know what someone has been through or what he or she might be going through now. To respond with compassion helps to keep criticism, misunderstandings, and judgments at bay.

"I value the lessons that this actress taught me: to have compassion for others in the area where we all have at some time fallen short—our images of ourselves."

WHAT CREATES A NEGATIVE BODY IMAGE?

Your body image was not created overnight; it began during your childhood and has been gradually developing ever since. It is influenced by many factors. Psychologist Dr. Thomas Cash, who has conducted extensive and detailed scientific research on body image, divides these influences into two categories. The first is "historical influences," which are related directly to a person's past. (We call some of these influences "image wounds.") The second category is "current influences," especially those of the media on body image.

IMAGE WOUNDS

Most of us have been criticized about some aspect of our looks at some time. Perhaps you experienced an unkind word, a stony silence, or blatant stares at your body, your clothes, or some other aspect of your appearance. Some of our clients have been humiliated by verbal abuse about their looks, while others were physically intruded upon by classmates or grown-ups. Whatever your degree of suffering, your body image remembers. The effects of name-calling, teasing, and criticism during childhood and adolescence can remain long into adulthood. These deeply uncomfortable moments continue to affect you in ways that you are not aware of. We call these psychic injuries *image wounds*.

Image wounds profoundly damage your relationship with your body, your clothing, and your personal style.

Somehow we all live through these childhood emotional punches. As you grew into adulthood, many aspects of your physical body changed. Some of these were natural developmental changes, while others were changes for which you were responsible. The color and length of your hair, your level of health and fitness, the condition of your skin and teeth are all the result of choices and decisions that you make regarding your body. Even in this age of unprecedented cosmetic surgery, which can produce astounding and sometimes unnatural results, some things about the human body cannot be changed: your height, for example, or the length of your neck or arms.

No image wound is too small to notice—anytime we are criticized for the way we look, it hurts us. Often people don't even mean to hurt or criticize us, but their comments still produce a hurt. Our bodies react in different ways to compensate. If you are told over and over again "You really are tall!" you may begin to think there is something wrong with being tall, or that it is the only thing people will ever notice about you. Perhaps over time you develop a slight stoop in your posture. You might even begin wearing baggy clothes in an effort to somehow "hide your height."

We would like you now to take stock of your body image, using the exercises in this session. The first exercise will help you to identify your image wounds, some of which may be buried so deeply you are not aware of them.

RECOGNIZING YOUR IMAGE WOUNDS

Usually, very specific image wounds are imprinted in the memory. One female client told us of the first time she wore a bra to school. She was wearing it under a sweater that was neither tight nor baggy; it was close fitting enough to give a subtle impression of her shape, but not tight enough to accentuate her breasts very much. A young, immature boy in her class pointed at her chest, giggled, and yelled, "Look, look at Daphne's boobs!" It was, in a word, devastating. She went home crying, declaring she would never wear a bra again, and covered herself with baggy shirts and sweaters. She has since grown up and moved on, but she told us that she has never forgotten that event. On days when she is feeling vulnerable, it is her chest that she protects, by wearing a jacket or a thick sweater that makes her feel secure. She also avoids wearing bright, bold colors that draw attention to her upper body.

Ask yourself:

- Did other children ever taunt you when you were a child?
- Were you teased for being skinny, fat, or ugly, or for something else?
- Did others criticize one of your body parts?
- Did a parent repeatedly tell you to lose or gain weight?
- Did you have a brother or sister who was constantly admired for his or her good looks while you were not?
- Did you have a parent or sibling who complained or was obsessed about his or her own looks?

- Do you recall a specific incident that was particularly traumatic?
- Did your family or classmates give you a hurtful nickname that was related to your appearance?

Your answers to these questions will tell you what your image wounds are.

WHAT ARE YOUR IMAGE WOUNDS?

In answer to this question, write in your journal in as much detail as your memory allows. What were the circumstances of the hurtful incident? Who was involved? How did you feel? Did it feel like a big deal at the time, or did it become more hurtful as time passed? Was the instance repeated? Please limit yourself to image wounds that are related specifically to your physical body.

When you feel you have described your image wounds to your satisfaction, go back and answer the following questions:

- What would you like to say in your adult voice to the people who teased or hurt you?
- Objectively and honestly, has there ever been any truth in the hurtful comments you received?
- How do you feel about that?
- How do you think that has affected your body image?
- Are there any issues relating to your image wounds that you would like to put to rest? If so, what are they?
- How has your relationship with your body changed over the years? For example, are you more or less shy? Do you think about your body image more or less than you used to? Why?
- Which of your image wounds are based on things you cannot change, such as the shape of your head or your height? What would it take for you to be able to accept these aspects of yourself?
- Are there any issues relating to your image wounds that you would like to change if realistically possible? If you were always ridiculed for being fat, or for having curly hair, or for biting your nails, ask yourself in all honesty: "Do I really want to change this aspect of my physical appearance?" Do not worry about how right now. This should be a time for honesty.

ROB'S IMAGE WOUND

Rob, an advertising executive, had been taunted about his big nose for as long as he could remember. As he grew older, he became more desensitized about it—or so he thought. When he worked with us, he said he wanted an image that projected low-key sophistication with subtle nuances of wit. His passions and icons were in alignment with this image, yet he was having trouble creating his Personal Style Statement. He admitted that his efforts were being stifled by his perception of his "big nose." Rob surprised himself with this admission. He had had no idea that his childhood critics were still affecting him.

We asked Rob how he perceived his nose now. He said he realized that his nose was larger than many other people's noses, but that it was also smaller than many others'. We then gave him a homework assignment: to go out and find a successful person who had what he considered to be a large nose. It could be a photograph of someone famous or someone he knew personally. He quickly got the point— he found many successful people with large noses! We asked him if he had ever considered cosmetic surgery. (We were not recommending it—we were fishing to see how seriously the wound had affected him.) He said that he had thought about it but only for an instant. Finally, we asked him if he honestly thought that the size of his nose had anything to do with his sophistication or his sharp wit. No, he admitted, it did not. Rob thus was able to take a realistic, honest view of what he once considered a physical flaw.

MARTHA'S IMAGE WOUND

Martha could represent many people with the pain of her image wound. She was overweight and had been most of her life. She dreaded this part of her work with us—until one day she stood up for herself, made some decisions, and literally got on with her life.

Martha first told us that she really wanted to lose weight. We gave her many choices about how she might proceed. She could research a healthy lifestyle change—not a diet. She could look into nutritionists and fitness trainers. She could join a gym or take up walking. But when we next met with her, approximately a month later, Martha had gained more weight. We didn't make any comments about it and carried on with the work for that day. She seemed slightly distant, as if she were sitting on anger. We asked her what was wrong, and when we did, the floodgates opened: she was upset that we had not asked her about her weight. We asked her to write about all her feelings in that moment about her weight. We left the room to give her a few moments of privacy.

Martha was under a great deal of pressure. Her job was very demanding and competitive. She was financially responsible not only for her own family but for her extended family as well. Her weight, she told us in all honesty, was just not her top priority right now. Yet she was also fearful that if she didn't lose weight, we would not be able to help her with her image (which is why she was upset when we didn't mention it!). What a revelation it was to her to admit that she just did not want to lose weight right now!

We assured Martha that losing weight was not something we would push her into or insist that she do. We do not stand around with our arms folded waiting for people to change. People must be ready for change; they must strongly desire it, without being pressured. Martha was not ready for that particular change, and we placed no judgment on that. There were many different aspects of Martha's personal style that she would indeed address. She did so with commitment and enthusiasm.

In this session, we do not ask the impossible of you. It would be impossible to completely change your negative body image or to heal all of your image wounds in one effort. Many people find the simple act of writing about their image wounds to be a great help to them. But if, for any reason, your image wounds are too overwhelming or too painful to deal with on your own, we encourage you to seek assistance. This session is by no means a replacement for counseling, nutritional guidance, or other related professional services, where they are needed. Everyone deserves to feel better about his or her body.

ANNA'S IMAGE WOUND

Some image wounds are not related specifically to the physical body. Before we ask you more questions to get you to think about them, we'd like to tell you about someone else. We are not going to begin Anna's story with a description of her clothing or her physical looks. We would like you to form your own image of her based on the information we give you. Let your imagination, along with her story, give you a mental picture of how she looks and dresses.

Anna was at the end of a sabbatical from her job as a print journalist—she had taken two years off to reconnect with her family and was now going back to work. Practicing journalism made her conscious of being in the public eye again. She came to us because she wanted to learn how to make a substantial impact in presenting herself, so as to complement her talent and experience.

When we sat down together in Session 1 to begin discussing the things she felt passionately about, she had difficulty in coming up with a response. It was almost as though this marvelously vital and articulate young woman had lost her voice. We were surprised because in her work she was confident and opinionated; at home she was secure and comfortable with her children and husband. But when it came to making decisions about her personal taste, she had little or no confidence.

All of her life, Anna told us, she had turned to others for advice about what she should be wearing—her mother, her sisters, her roommates at school, her husband, her friends, and even her children. It was so much easier, she said, to invite their opinions rather than suffer their criticism. Even on the rare occasions when she went shopping alone, she relied on shop assistants or other customers to validate her selections.

We could only conclude that somewhere along the way, Anna had shut down. People who lack confidence often find it much easier to just agree with other people—even when they are being guided down paths that are inappropriate and that deny their true natures.

Over the course of our next meetings, Anna started to thaw, slowly reacquainting herself with the things she loved and felt passionately about. She recalled her college-girl love for art-house movies and poetry. She enjoyed preparing gourmet food and had a special interest in English cottage furniture. She loved great stone fireplaces and kilim rugs, velvet-covered pillows and tea-stained linens. Her dream house would mix wicker with art nouveau, and she'd adorn her walls with her collection of black-and-white photographs from the beatnik era, which were now somewhere in storage. Her taste was eclectic and tolerated great idiosyncrasy.

Using the information we have given you, take a moment to imagine what Anna looked like. Don't try to guess—just let an image of Anna come to you, if it hasn't already. How do you think she dressed? What colors would she wear? What style and quality of clothing can you see her in? This little exercise will help you later, as you begin to decipher your own profile.

Do you think that Anna looked like a refined, elegantly eccentric bohemian, whose independent nature always spoke of good taste? Did she piece together her outfits cleverly, creatively selecting from an array of clothes or styles? Would she choose an outfit reflecting a colorful imagination one day and the next choose an original black-and-white combination?

Not at all. At our first meeting Anna wore a tight-fitting pale pink cotton T-shirt and a pair of nondescript white cotton trousers. This outfit was followed by a yellowy cream pair of trousers coupled with a white long-sleeved knit shirt. When we eventually found ourselves in her closet, we would discover more variations on the pastel twinsets and flats she wore whenever we met—the same clothing items over and over, in a kind of uniform. The strength and interest of the woman we were getting to know was completely submerged under the uniform of safe suburban chic.

During one of our first meetings, we asked Anna if she would like to use the things she felt passionately about to help create her personal style. She gulped. With this simple question, unknowingly, we had exposed a nerve. Finally Anna started talking about her childhood and how by age ten she had developed opinions and tastes that were very different from those of her family and friends. At first the differences were very exciting, because they made her feel special.

Then one day when she stepped up into the school bus, several of the other students pointed at her and snickered. She was wearing a pair of gray capri pants, her older sister's mohair sweater, a bright red beret, and a pair of ballet slippers. (This outfit would be more in step with today's fashions than those of the late 1950s, when little girls were wearing starched cotton dresses and shiny black shoes with tiny buckles.)

This wasn't the first time Anna had been ridiculed for wearing unusual clothes. But it was the last time. After that day Anna's confidence level dropped to a place that made her change her behavior. She started to observe the way her schoolmates dressed so that she could copy them.

Anna's experience created an image wound. Because of it, she stopped being creative with her clothes and appearance. She lost confidence in experimenting with her uniqueness. As an adult, she chose a profession that put her into the world again, but in a position where all eyes would be focused on her subjects, not on her. As a print journalist she could draw less attention to herself. At first she thought this position would let her off the hook with regard to her image. But she still came face-to-face with having to get dressed every morning to go to work. When she met us, she was still asking others what they thought she should wear and relying on their decisions.

IMAGE WOUNDS CONCERNING CLOTHING

By recognizing her image wound, Anna was on her way to reclaiming her personal style. Now we'd like you to address any lingering image wounds that, like Anna's, are not directly related to your physical body.

Please write your answers to the following questions in your journal:

• Were you ever forbidden to wear a certain color or a specific clothing item? What were they?

• Were you ever made fun of for wearing a clothing item of a particular color or style? Describe which item, color, or style.

• Were your circumstances such that you wore hand-me-downs from siblings or other previously owned clothing? If so, how has this affected your current attitude and relationship toward clothing? Do you only buy expensive clothing now? Do you own a great quantity of clothes? Or do you spend as little money as possible on clothing? Do you buy clothes only when it is absolutely necessary?

• Do you copy someone else's taste because you feel insecure about your own? (Please note that copying is different from being inspired and giving a certain style your own hallmark.)

• Do you feel the need to dress to impress people rather than for your own comfort?

• Are you still dressing rebelliously to "get back at your parents"?

• Do you think wearing stylish clothing is egotistical and superficial?

- Are you afraid to take creative risks with your wardrobe?
- Do you dress conservatively in order to feel safe and secure?
- Do you dress eccentrically or wildly to show people how creative and interesting you are?

Recognizing how image wounds have affected your personal style, and then moving on, is very empowering. Rather than being led by your conditioning and by other people's comments, entertain the concept of becoming self-referred. This does not mean, if you are male and a parent told you that you should never wear pink, that you should rush out now to buy your first pink shirt. Your task still is to gather information about yourself. You may find out in Session 7, on color, that pink really is not a good color for you. The important thing is *how* you decide whether to wear pink. Your decision will not be based on an emotional backlash from your childhood; it will be based on an educated adult decision.

YOUR BODY TALK

We talk to ourselves all the time. Probably you're chatting away to yourself first thing in the morning about your appearance, and the conversation continues throughout the day. Most often this inner monologue is negative: *My nose is too big; my breasts are too small; I'm fat; I'm out of proportion.* The list goes on. Your body talk is a very big clue to how you feel about your body.

Please write down your own private body talk, as much of it as you can remember. If you are not aware of having any constant thoughts about your body, just write about how you feel about your body in general. Don't worry if you can't think of anything positive to say— we'll address that later. Right now just unload, get it all out of your system. Pay special attention to body talk while you are dressing and undressing. Also include any comments about your body that you are aware of regularly saying to family members or friends. For instance, do you complain to your wife or partner every day that you're losing your hair? Do you make remarks out loud to him or her about your body when you're dressing?

After you have written all the dialogue that you can remember and any other thoughts and feelings, please answer the following questions. You may want to do this over a period of time if you prefer, especially if you are not used to being aware of your body conversations.

- Does your inner dialogue relate in any way to your image wounds? If so, how?
- Are you repeating the same negative comments that you have heard all of your life?
- Have you added any new criticisms?

OPTIONAL EXERCISE: YOUR VISUAL HISTORY

If you have trouble remembering your childhood image—or if you'd just like to take a nostalgic trip back to childhood—we have devised an optional exercise for you to use. It is not necessary to do it, but even the busiest of our clients have thoroughly enjoyed it.

This exercise will help you to recall your visual history. You may use photographs, newspaper clippings, school yearbooks, videotapes, your memory—anything that provides valuable visual information about yourself. Some of our clients put their favorite pictures in their journals. Some have made collages of them on poster board and brought them in for us to see.

Here are a few questions that may help to jar your memory.

- When you were a child, what feelings did you have about your body or the way you looked?
- Do you have or remember a favorite photograph of yourself when you were younger? Why is it your favorite?
- During your teenage years, did anything particularly stand out about your appearance?
- Do you recall how you felt about your body as you entered puberty? Did it affect the way you wore your clothes or what you wore? How?
- Were you seduced by the trends of the decades? If so, how?
- Have you noticed anything unique about your visual material? If so, what?
- Do you consider yourself improved as time has passed? In what ways?

We have given you a great deal to think about—this is very important work. When you are ready, please do the following reliable and well-grounded exercise on identifying your physical assets. There is immense satisfaction and value in completing this next exercise because it is essential to healing your image wounds.

IDENTIFYING YOUR PHYSICAL ASSETS

Everyone has physical assets beyond those that are conventionally considered beautiful or attractive. Our dictionary defines an *asset* as "a useful or valuable quality; an advantage or a resource." This definition says absolutely nothing about beauty. Even if you are conventionally beautiful, please look for other qualities to define your physical assets.

We encourage you to acknowledge all of what makes you who you are. This can include the effect your heritage has on the way you look. Search for an emotional connection to your physical attributes. Often people consider their assets to be flaws. People always think that they want something that another person possesses. The perfect example is the straight hair–curly hair syndrome. Invariably, you want the opposite of what you have. Stop pining after an image that you think you want, and instead get to know your physical assets. Try to see your whole self from a more objective perspective.

To help you get started, here is a list of some of our clients' physical assets. They are not "typical" assets—we're sure you can figure those out for yourself!

PHYSICAL ASSETS
Intelligent eyes
Healthy hair
Healthy skin
Warm smile
Unconventional hair and skin coloring
Expressive hands, eyes, mouth
Graceful physical movement
Moves with intention
Compelling physicality
Inviting, open physicality

Expresses himself or herself well physically
Good body awareness
Good posture
Well-proportioned body
Good teeth
Inviting facial expressions

We'd like to help you identify some of your physical assets that you may take for granted or be unaware of.
Do not take for granted what you have inherited physically. You can use your cultural background to enhance your image and express your uniqueness. This does not mean, of course, that you should adopt a national costume or parade your ethnicity in bold and incongruent ways.

ANNA'S ASSETS

Our client Anna had several physical assets, such as good, healthy, thick hair, beautiful skin, and a rich-sounding voice. She also carried herself well. She possessed elegant fingers and hands and used them well to express herself. She had a slightly exotic look and coloring, which exuded sensuality. Her cultural background was American, Israeli, and Iranian. Yet Anna was not aware that her image was naturally sensual and exotic. She undervalued her assets and did not give them the credit they deserved. She needed help identifying something that she was already unconsciously projecting in her image.

Unlike Anna, our client Dhani was very conscious and aware that his ethnicity—his Eastern Indian good looks—could be an asset. He used the coloring of his skin, eyes, and hair to his advantage by learning what colors and fabrics flattered these specific features. He felt an emotional connection to his heritage and liked to express it in subtle and meaningful ways, through both his clothing and his manner.

For example, because he represented his very conservative company in all parts of the world, his suits were hand tailored, classically European in design and fabric; but he had the linings of his jackets made from subtle Indian silk prints that he chose himself. When he took his jacket off at a meeting and placed it on the back of his chair, a flash of color and design would whisk through the air. His colleagues might or might not notice, but it did not matter, for he knew it was there. His identification and conscious awareness of his physical assets *preceded* this manifestation in his wardrobe.

When Anna acknowledged and understood the value of her assets, she did not do anything dramatically different. She certainly did not dress or behave in a more provocative fashion. Instead, she introduced two relatively small additions to her image. One day she found herself in an antique mall killing time when her eyes went straight to a pair of 1940s sunglasses. They were in very good condition and very unusual. The frames were made of vanilla-colored Bakelite, and the shape was perfect for her face. Creatively, she took the glasses to her optician and requested new lenses that were a shade darker, with less green in them. The effect was striking: mysterious and unique.

Anna also came upon a pile of old magazines, and on the cover of one was a South American woman whose lips and lipstick caught Anna's attention. Anna had beautiful lips, which she did not list in her physical assets. But she had a feeling about the photograph, so she bought the magazine. When she next met with us, she showed it to us and said she was thinking of trying to find the same color of lipstick. It could not have been a better choice. Her new shade of crimson, which was a bit adventurous for her, melded well with her exotic good looks.

These are assets for Anna to be aware of and enjoy—they *bring her closer to herself.* She now brings more of herself into how she engages and interacts in the world.

MARY'S ASSETS

We have already discussed Mary's assets, but we would like to go into more detail about how she discovered what they could mean to her. As we stated, she was tall with a large and well-proportioned frame. She had pretty green eyes, thick and silky blond hair, an attractive face, and a warm, genuine, and endearing smile. She was physically communicative, with an open and clear manner. These were assets that Mary readily recognized, and we certainly agreed with her. But Mary also had two very important assets that she had some resistance to acknowledging.

Sometimes clients actually do resemble the icons they have chosen. Mary was one of those people. She didn't know it, but her cool blond looks resembled those of Grace Kelly—she had the definite air of an aristocratic beauty. And although Audrey Hepburn had a slight frame compared to Mary's, they shared the same physical poise and "aliveness" within their bodies. Mary's beauty and her physicality were her unidentified physical assets. But they remained unknown to Mary because of her image wound.

Mary told us that her image wound was a feeling of always being different, an outcast, not knowing where she fit in. We wanted to know where this feeling came from, and how it began. She answered us by sharing that the feeling began at home.

Mary came from an extremely poor, working-class background. Sometimes this kind of background is glamorized, and the parents are often characterized as loving, hardworking adults who do everything they can to better their circumstances. This was not the case with Mary. It was Mary, not her parents, who was loving and hardworking. It was Mary who wished to better her life—her parents were happy to just "get by." Visually, she was like a jewel surrounded by rubble. She was a very beautiful child with a healthy curiosity and desire to learn. She often asked herself why she looked and felt the way she did, when everything around her looked the opposite.

Not surprisingly, as she was developing as a person, Mary was unable to see her "differences" as assets. In fact, they led her to image confusion and depression, resulting in an identity crisis that stayed with her into adulthood. Mary was no longer the dirt-poor child from the wrong side of the tracks; on the contrary, she was now financially secure, respected by her peers and well liked by her friends. But her disheveled and rumpled appearance reflected her inner confusion and lack of direction—her image wound.

Mary's courage and unrelenting search to dispel her frustration led her to us. She had been traveling the self-help circuit for many years and had spent much of her life working toward "inner" self-improvement. Now she knew it was time to begin matching that improvement on the outside with the development of her personal style.

We asked Mary to take one step toward healing her image wound. We asked her to do something for herself that she would not normally do. The guidelines we gave her were that it must be related to her outward appearance, she must feel it was in her best interest, and it must be purely for her pleasure.

Mary told us that she had always wanted to spend a whole day at a spa being pampered and receiving as many treatments as possible in one day. The idea of a spa day may sound too easy, but it certainly wasn't for Mary. She had never experienced a spa day even once in her life. She had never had a manicure or pedicure; nor had she experienced a massage or a facial. She found it very difficult to comprehend that other people would be taking care of her for a day. She had to make other arrangements for those who usually depended on her, and she had to mentally prepare herself for devoting a whole day to her outer appearance.

Mary shared with us that when she stepped out into the night air after her day at the spa, she felt herself literally glowing—but this time the glow that she sometimes felt on the inside could be seen on the outside. Her skin sparkled; her fingernails and toenails shone with color; and even her hair and scalp had been massaged with special oils.

Mary's image wound was not healed overnight. She did not wake up the next morning and suddenly feel like an aristocratic beauty. When she did wake up, it was to her potential. She gradually dropped the facade of disinterest in her appearance that had been hanging over her like a long dark shroud. She was positive that she was on the right road, one of acceptance of the woman she was becoming.

WILLIAM'S ASSETS

Tall, long-limbed, and trim. Good thick hair. Beautiful teeth. Good posture. Healthy complexion. An attractive combination of fair skin with dark hair and dark blue eyes. If you imagine William as a great-looking guy, you are right. He was a traditionally attractive man. His physical assets were easy for him to identify. His attitude about his looks was healthy and nonegotistic. So have we finally come across someone with a completely healthy and positive body image? Well, no—not exactly.

One evening as we were sitting in his office, William was telling us that he could not remember any image wounds. He picked up a tennis ball from his desk and began tossing it from hand to hand. As we were questioning him, the movements he was making increasingly distracted us. It was as if he were a child, playing with his ball, listening to the adults as best he could. We asked him if he played tennis. "No," he said, "I don't." We asked if this was a "lucky" ball of his. Again, no. But he put the ball down awkwardly and self-consciously, finally realizing it was a distraction—again, quite like a child.

William became still and silent, and it was quite clear to us that he was uncomfortable. We asked him what he was feeling, or if he had remembered something that he'd like to discuss. He became irritated and asked us the relevance of the question. We suggested that the relevance might be directed toward his tennis ball. He told us that the ball belonged to his now-deceased father who had been an accomplished tennis player.

With this admission, William became more edgy—a side of him that he revealed for the first time. His behavior was an indication that we should continue, if he would allow it. As with most clients, William's point of resistance was our point of investigation. Could his memory of his father and the tennis ball have any relevance to the work on body image and image wounds? William let out a long sigh and confided that he really wasn't good at talking about these kinds of things but that he knew they were important.

When he was growing up, William's parents did not allow him to participate in sports or any other extracurricular activities. They were very strict about his academic achievements and insisted that any "fun" should be associated with learning. His television viewing was extremely limited, and he had very few friends. He felt different, which he hated. He was taunted at school for being a "wimp" and a bookworm. As an adult, he believed he had been cheated of his boyhood. He felt that "normal" kids played sports, or had various hobbies and clubs, and that their parents were permissive and even supportive of these activities.

Even though William was a very intelligent man, he was struggling to make the connection between his background and his current body image. Very gently we asked him if there might be any part of his body that he felt uncomfortable with, that felt vulnerable or that he wanted to hide. "Yes," he said. "You know, I've always had this thing about my shoulders. I don't think they're wide enough, and I guess you could say that I try to cover them up." How would he do that? He replied that he always bought jackets with big padded shoulders.

Why, you may be wondering, didn't the adult William just go ahead and take up some sport or go to the gym and fulfill his childhood desires? The reason was his body image. Sometimes it is very challenging for people to shake off a mental image that no longer serves them. He wouldn't go to the gym because he was intimidated—he felt he didn't look good enough without his padded shoulders. He also felt insecure about being a novice. One reason his clothes and image were stuck in the 1980s was that these clothes were perfect for hiding his image wound, and he had found it difficult to move on. He habitually referred to a vision of himself wearing jackets with thick padded shoulders that made him feel strong and comfortable—this was a very powerful anchor for him.

We asked him if there were times when he did take off his jacket. He told us that on the weekends he wore loose, baggy shirts that he felt gave an overall appearance of his upper body's "blending in" and thereby did not bring attention to his shoulders.

There was another reason that William had not yet progressed and further developed his image. Even though he was only forty-three years old, he had always, in the back of his mind, worried about getting older. He couldn't determine where and when this fear emerged. When he intellectualized this thought, he felt "ridiculous" because in the mirror he saw a young-looking man.

Our next conversation with William led to several insights and conclusions that we believe are nearly universal, applicable to many men and women.

William was attached to his "youthful looks" and was fearful of aging. He was confused about the difference between maturity and aging. He saw getting older as a negative experience, and although he intellectually understood the many benefits of maturity, they signaled for him "old, grumpy, and lacking enthusiasm." He felt he had never really experienced growing up in a normal fashion and had never been given the opportunity to learn the invaluable lessons of adolescence. Having leaped from boyhood to manhood without a net, he felt he was ill prepared for the latter.

Whether you are a man or woman, you may well relate to William's story. There are many little boys in men's bodies, and little girls in women's bodies, who are likely to experience a struggle about their image. They are not trying to look younger than their age—that is not the issue here. We are addressing a psychological *stuckness*. From the point of view of your clothes, behavior, and emotions, you may be manifesting a confusing image. In William's case, he tried to build up his shoulders from the outside when in fact he needed to rebuild himself from the inside out.

How might your image be affected by your hesitancy and fear to experience the inevitable pain of growing up? How many old habits have you yet to release?

William made a significant and meaningful move forward while working his way through this session. His desire to get to the bottom of his image wounds was admirable. He also identified certain behaviors that affected his image in negative ways. In the next session, he would be given an opportunity to begin to rebuild his image from the inside out—and learn how to "shoulder" the responsibility of creating a strong self-image.

THE MEDIA AND ITS IMPOSSIBLE MESSAGES

Our concept of what is attractive and what we *should* look like comes from the mass media and marketing. You are supposed to be blessed with beauty and physical perfection, or else you are supposed to buy the products that will help you to attain it. The media play a crucial role in the development of your body image.

We have a great respect for television, film, newspapers, and magazines, and we appreciate the educational and entertainment benefits of all forms of the media. But let us be clear that the media's number-one priority is to hold our attention. It does so by informing, entertaining, thrilling, and exciting us. But if the media are your only standard for your personal and physical self-image, then you are setting yourself up for a huge disappointment—and you will not be self-referred when it comes to developing your personal style.

Suppose we are told that big shoulders are coming back into "style." Who thinks out the implications of that, and what it will or will not mean to him or her? A person who has developed personal style maturely, who is confident of his or her personal style. Such a person will not be bamboozled by the whims and moneymaking schemes of the media and fashion elite. He or she will not be distracted by the "irresistible offers" and dictates of a small but powerful percentage of the population. Such people pick and choose what *they* want to do.

The media have manipulated our consciousness for as long as anyone can remember. Remember the "girdle era," which followed the "corset era"? Women wearing girdles no doubt had a smoother, more svelte look, thanks to the elastic that kept their bodies from being lumpy and bumpy. But at what price? Women lost circulation in their bodies. Soon it was considered improper not to maneuver one's ample frame into a girdle. The message: physical imperfections are not acceptable.

Now we are in the "body shaper era." These undergarments help hold in, smooth out, and reshape women's bodies so that they will look better in the tight and revealing clothing that exists today. Notice the way you react to ads for these undergarments in newspapers and magazines. Maybe you were completely ignorant that they even existed until one morning you opened the paper and there they were. Do they make you feel you really *should* "get used to" being uncomfortable for the sake of your appearance? Some women feel that discomfort is a small price to pay for a smoother silhouette. But others might buy into someone else's values and perception about what looks good, then waste time and money trying to achieve that look, before realizing they are unwilling to pay the price. Reading this book will help you learn to make your own decisions based on your personal choices.

When our clients choose their style icons, most of them, even the ones as young as twenty-three, choose icons from past decades. The reason is obvious. This is an unkind age to be in the public eye, making unrealistic demands for what celebrities "should" look like. Our clients express that there seems to be something real and attainable about the images and personalities of Katharine Hepburn, Gary Cooper, and Greta Garbo. While they were stars of great magnitude, they still seemed fallible and human. They inspired our clients to think, "Yes, maybe I could do that" or "That seems possible for me." But today's celebrities and potential style icons must run for cover from the ever-prying eye of the media. They flee into their own private worlds when not in front of the camera, and as a result they seem less human and less approachable to us.

Another very important difference in today's celebrity atmosphere is the technology of cosmetic surgery. "A nip and a tuck" has graduated to a full-blown body makeover. Now, you may not know anyone who has been the recipient of such a technological miracle, but you can't get away from this phenomenon in the media. Almost every woman on television seems more beautiful, more perfect than just a few short years ago. Every man has an almost nonchalant handsomeness, as if he's really not trying very hard to look so good. And it also appears as if no one ages.

Taking good care of yourself, keeping healthy and strong, looking good—and using technology to do so—are certainly no longer considered vain or exclusive. But the standards for attractiveness that celebrities set are impossible for most people to attain. And with each day that passes in this fast-paced world, the word *normal* is quickly fading.

In our own experiences with celebrities, we have found that they really are beautiful people, yet they complain about their appearance and are never satisfied with it. They have their own image problems, some of which are very serious. Yet they are the very people upon whom others are basing their image desires. They are the prototypes for what is considered beautiful.

The Shrinking Woman

A few months ago we saw an advertisement in the *Los Angeles Times* for a twelve-week body makeover. The woman in the ad said, "I went from a size 8 to a size 4 in just 12 weeks!" We nostalgically remarked that many women used to consider size 8 quite an accomplishment. After all, Marilyn Monroe was a size 8. When did size 4 become so desirable? How unfair it is that women who are having a hard time staying even near size 8 are now told that it's not good enough. Just a few weeks later we came across another ad. This one said, "6 Week Body Makeover—A size 7 to a size 0 in 6 weeks!" What does a size 0 dress look like? Doesn't 0 mean nothing? And what will women have to do during those six weeks to accomplish the feat of achieving it? Does that mean that when they reach their goal, they will no longer be seen at all? Yes, it is funny in a way, but what is not funny is walking into a shop that sells only sizes 0–6. That shop's message is that if you are larger than a 6, then something is wrong with you. In addition, women are supposed to look fit and strong. How is someone who wears a size 0 supposed to look fit and healthy? We really don't know.

For most people, this trendy thinness is impossible to obtain and certainly impossible to sustain.

The Perfect Man

The expectations for men these days are also higher. Contrary to most people's beliefs, it is not only women who hate their bodies. Men suffer too, mostly silently. Many men feel that they are not supposed to be concerned with their looks. But others feel that having a negative body image threatens their masculinity.

Here's the "prescription" for men. Men are supposed to be tall, have broad shoulders, a muscular chest and biceps, a small, tight bottom, a thirty-inch waist, strong facial features, and a head full of hair. This prescription has led some men to jeopardize their health with steroid abuse and excessive exercise. More than ever before, men are seeking cosmetic surgery, hair transplants, face-lifts, liposuction, and chest implants. In the 1920s a bodybuilder named Charles Atlas told boys that his training course would provide them with hope, confidence, and self-esteem by giving them the "perfect" body. Today the Charles Atlas message still exists—"I must be physically attractive in order to succeed in life"—and has been updated by surgery and drugs.

It is very difficult for people not to be affected by the constant barrage of media influences. Many people compare themselves with media images and try desperately to keep up the impossible pace. But others of you rebel. You are the defiant ones. You intentionally distance yourself from as many of the media's messages as you can. You believe there is nothing out there worthy of your attention. You feel that you don't have the time, the money, or the desire to achieve the look you are told is "in." You dress and groom as if you don't care, as if you are marching to the beat of your own drum. But you do care. In fact, you are potentially the most stylish of people.

The price you pay for not listening to your personal style voice is very high, for you are going against your true grain and thus feel conflict and anger. You may suffer from low self-esteem and occupy a space of loneliness that alienates you from being all you can be. You may be fighting to hold on to your identity, without being sure of what it is. But the irony is that it is actually much easier for you to achieve your image goals than it is for most people. For a significant amount of your work has already been done. You have not bought into "fashion," so there is nothing for you to "undo." The media do not cater to or even acknowledge you. You will understand this more clearly and potently in the next session, when you will define your inner style. But consider this point about your rejection of the media's messages as your wake-up call. You are probably very bright. You have a very strong personality and opinions, of which you are more aware now because of the work you've done in the first two sessions. You don't want to be a member of any club that dictates rules and images that are not congruent with who you are.

TAKING ACTION

Media messages, body image, image wounds—the big question is, What *can* you do to begin creating a more healthy and accepting body image? There's good news—modern psychology has given us ample choices. The first step is always awareness, and the next step is action. You have already completed the awareness work. Now it is time for you to think about and perhaps select just one action to take.

What follows are twelve actions that you can take to help yourself change the way you feel about your body image, your image wounds, and media messages.

We believe that people create self-esteem by taking action. To avoid giving people inflated views of themselves, we encourage *warranted* self-esteem. People need concrete reasons to feel good about themselves—and these reasons come from the "doing."

Taking even one of these actions will actively engage you in making contact with your uniqueness. But most of our clients don't stop at only one action—they feel empowered and like the sense of freedom they experience when they begin to change their perspective.

1. Change your avoiding and checking behaviors.
The best way to change any unwanted behavior is to begin with small steps. A new behavior might be uncomfortable at first, but that is all right—isn't the constant repetition of your other behavior uncomfortable too? For example, suppose you avoid dancing, but you happen to really love it. Start dancing at home, either on your own or with someone you trust. Make a pact with the person to go out together, and then don't procrastinate—go!

If you are a mirror avoider, looking in the mirror may be hard for you. We have had extensive experience with people who find it very difficult to look in the mirror. More people than you can imagine share your discomfort! Some of these people bravely go to makeup studios, clothing stores, and hair salons, admirably propelling themselves. But while there they still will not look in the mirror.

We encourage you to practice looking at yourself whenever you feel you can. Another exercise later in this book—our Personal Body Map exercise—will involve spending a period of time in front of the mirror. You will need to be as objective about your body as you can to benefit the most from it. Begin practicing objectivity now, slowly and gradually.

First try looking in the mirror just once a day without turning away. Prepare to do it—talk yourself into it in a loving and caring way. When you get there, stay there, even if you are experiencing uncomfortable feelings. Don't hold your breath—take a long deep breath, and exhale slowly. Breathe deeply and regularly. Keep your thoughts positive by remembering your assets. Do a little bit at a time.

On the other hand, if you can't stay away from your reflection, try avoiding this behavior by delaying it. In other words, when you get the urge to check, tell yourself you are just going to delay that for a little while. Try moving a few mirrors around so that your reflection won't be where you expect to see it.

If you have behaviors that you are not willing to change, try taking a different kind of action. We knew a man who had his shirts professionally pressed—and then felt he absolutely must re-iron them himself. It wouldn't help for him just to press them himself in the first place, because he would still have to do touch-ups on his own ironing. This behavior made him consistently late for work, and he would arrive with a backache from trying not to get his shirt creased in the car.

The remedy we prescribed: he must at least one time put the shirt on immediately after the first pressing (whoever had pressed it!). He must wear it without concern. We told him to think of it as an experiment, or as having a new experience. He tried it. It was very uncomfortable at first, but eventually he managed to put on a shirt after the first pressing. Previously he was in a habit where he would re-press his shirt automatically, without considering his choices. He had been emotionally at the mercy of his habit and the anxiety it brought on. He is now beginning to put the whole experience into perspective by always being aware of what he is doing. Although he may still re-press his shirt on occasion, he will do that only when he feels it is absolutely necessary, not out of an obsessive habit.

2. Talk back to your negative body talk.

By holding negative conversations with yourself, you do yourself a great disservice. Now that you are aware of it, begin to actively change your negative body talk, especially if it relates to image wounds. Be creative. Be honest. Be decisive. Examples:

OLD BODY TALK: My hair looks terrible today. It's a mess.
NEW BODY TALK: No, that is incorrect. I haven't really given my hair any attention today. All I need to do is make a decision about how I am going to wear it so that it feels and looks good.

OLD BODY TALK: Oh, look at the size of my backside in this jacket. I can't do this jacket up. I'm too fat.
NEW BODY TALK: This jacket is not the right fit or style for my body shape.

OLD BODY TALK: Oh no, I look terrible. Look at the condition and pallor of my skin! I look like death.
NEW BODY TALK: The lighting here is unkind; I'll find another mirror with more natural light. I think I'll get a little bit of sun this weekend and think about that holiday I've been promising myself.

OLD BODY TALK: I love this tie, but they would all laugh at me at the office if I wore it. I'd look stupid in it.
NEW BODY TALK: I know this tie is a bit quirky, so I'll only wear it on days when I feel really good.

3. Stop comparing yourself unfairly.

Your negative commentaries on how you compare with the media's messages, real people in your life, or your own idea of what you should look like are a very specific kind of monologue. Once you catch yourself having thoughts like these, change them. Replace any feelings of envy, intimidation, or irritation with realistic thoughts and inner talk that are fair to you. For example, suppose you make this unfair comparison: "Margaret is taller than I am, she always looks good, and she can wear anything she wants because of her great body." Your new thought could be: "It's not Margaret's fault that she is taller than I am. I actually enjoy looking at her. Her looks have nothing to do with mine. I have other physical assets that I enjoy about myself. I have really nice hair."

Have you ever noticed your thoughts after seeing a model, a beautiful actress, or a handsome actor on television or in a film? "Wow, I really should lose some weight. I'm really going to try to exercise this week. I ought to get my hair styled like hers." Stop using words like *should, ought,* and *must* when it comes to your appearance. You now know your physical assets. Use that knowledge whenever you find yourself becoming critical of yourself and making unfair comparisons.

4. Stop magnifying what you consider to be your flaws.

Your inner dialogue may become a broken record about one specific feature, something like this:

"My mouth is really ugly. My lips are so small. In fact, my whole mouth is very undersized. I'm going to have to try to hide my mouth. But how will I do that? I'll think of some really clever way to do that. Look at my mouth compared to the size of my nose. It really is so much smaller. I hate my mouth."

When you look in the mirror, this feature will be all you see. You will be surprised to notice how often you do this. Psychologists call this phenomenon selective attention.

Once again, think of your physical assets when you notice that you are emotionally and intellectually clinging to what you don't like about yourself. Remind yourself of just one of your assets. Think about what you can do to enhance it instead of honing in on the things you can't change.

Also, please try to remember that no one is harder on you than you are on yourself. The only exception would be an extremely critical partner or family member. The "flaws" that you are magnifying are usually not even noticed by others.

5. Stop blaming.

"I didn't get the promotion because I'm overweight." "I can't wear these kinds of clothes because I'm not tall enough." "He got the date with her instead of me because I'm losing my hair." "I didn't get the job because I look too old."

Honestly, many different kinds of discrimination do exist. Your appearance may indeed be a factor in someone's decisions about you. You really won't be a jockey if you are six feet tall, and you won't be a basketball player if you are four foot eleven. The dark-haired, green-eyed, fair-skinned beauty will probably win the Irish Spring commercial. But many, many times, your appearance has nothing to do with an outcome. Don't use your looks as a scapegoat. Often your own discontent with your appearance is what is relevant.

When you find yourself blaming your looks for an event or a disappointment, try taking them out of the equation. Ask yourself, "What are other reasons why I might not have gotten that job?" Could it be that you were overqualified? If you can't take your looks out of the picture, ask yourself if you are confident that you did everything you could to present yourself at your best. Often clients will admit, "Well, to tell you the truth, I did neglect my appearance that day. I had an important meeting and I wanted to appear more together. But I didn't." That is fine—it is an honest assessment of the situation, not self-blame.

6. Stop trying to read other people's minds.

You don't know what other people are thinking. Stop thinking about what they may be thinking and instead change what you are thinking. Instead of thinking, "He must be noticing my large ears" (or big nose, toupee—whatever you're self-conscious about), concentrate on being friendly and communicative.

Stop predicting the future, as in: "If I start going to the gym, people will laugh at me." "If I change the way I dress, I will attract too much attention." "If I change the way I dress, I won't attract any attention." You know you can't predict the future. Figure out what your real objections are. Are you perhaps afraid to change?

7. Stop limiting your activities and your aspirations.

We usually limit our activities and aspirations with *I can't* statements, as in: "I can't wear a certain color." "I can't go to the party with this terrible haircut." "I can't go to an acting class because I don't look like _____." Just choose one thing you think you can't do, and then ask yourself why not. If you are truthful, you will either change your thinking or take action to change your situation.

One of the most common mistakes people make in shopping is to postpone buying clothes because they expect to change their body shape. This usually plays itself out as: "I know I need a new suit, but I can't buy one now. I'll wait until I lose weight." Then you say, "I could spend the money on a new suit, but it will no longer fit when I lose weight."

But you haven't lost the weight yet. If you really need a new suit, then you should buy one without putting pressure on yourself to lose weight first. You can still lose weight in your own time. Meanwhile, you'll have a new suit to wear.

8. Beware of your moods and how they affect your body image.

Have you ever noticed that when you are having a bad day, the negative emotions spill over into your feelings about your appearance? Let's say you are having a very stressful day. You go into the bathroom to wash your hands, and you happen to look into the mirror. Suddenly you become angry at your hair. "Why doesn't my hair ever look right? And my skin just looks awful today too! Plus this stupid jacket looks terrible on me." You're not really having a bad hair day; you're having a bad day.

Or let's say that last night you had a particularly heavy meal—you ate and drank too much. The next morning you feel guilty. You just know that you are fatter than yesterday. Yesterday you didn't feel fat, but today you do. This feeling spills over in your choice of clothing. You want and need to wear something that will make you feel slimmer. But you hate having to do that, so now you're really in a mood. Could this then account for why on some days you feel "fatter" than others? You did not get fatter overnight—it is your guilt you need to address.

When it comes to your appearance, your moods are out to cause trouble. The key here is to realize that your bad mood came first. Ask yourself what was bothering you before you started worrying about your appearance. Then tell yourself, "My appearance isn't really the issue here. I've just had a really bad day, and this isn't a good time to analyze my looks." Shift your focus by attending to something completely unrelated to your appearance. Get back to work, do the gardening, or find a task or hobby that will change your mood. Bad mood times are not good times to make decisions about anything, and they are particularly damaging to how you relate to your body, your clothes, and your general appearance.

9. Relax! Practice breathing and relaxing your body and your mind.

The trouble is, we're addicted to stress. Being stressed out seems easier than just taking five minutes to feel better. As far as breathing goes, we forget to do it. We hold our breath a lot. There are many different types of breathing exercises to choose from—just find one you like. Even if you do nothing more than become aware of when you are *not* breathing, it will help.

How do you practically apply breathing and relaxation techniques? The next time you're standing in front of a dressing-room mirror trying on clothes and for whatever reason you begin to feel bad about yourself, take a long, deep breath, relax your muscles, and let go of the tension. You'll regain control over your mood and mental state. You'll be able to think more objectively and make better decisions about what to do next—whether that is to leave the dressing room or to have a little talk with yourself.

When we are tense, troubled, or angry, we lose emotional control. Body image, image wounds, and appearance pressures are emotional issues. Managing tension is vital for maintaining emotional control. What can you do to reestablish control? Here's a relaxation exercise that workshops, acting classes, books, audiotapes, and videotapes use over and over again. The reason it is used so often is that it works.

Lie on the floor, and tense the muscles in your body, starting at your shoulders. Now let them go. Do this all the way down your body. It only takes a few minutes, and it is a simple way to let go of stress. We use this relaxation exercise with our clients, even when they are in the middle of a high-pressured week. Afterward they feel refreshed, as if they have shrugged off their pressures, at least for the time they spend with us. It is amazing how much more we get accomplished.

10. Think about health and fitness.

Exercising to achieve a certain look does not guarantee that you will have a more positive body image. Physical exercise is most rewarding when you do it to improve fitness and health. In addition to the benefits of weight loss, your moods will improve, and you will be able to better manage stress. Exercising with other people allows you to be sociable and to have fun. As for diets, they don't work—period. Eating healthfully is different from being in denial or negatively controlling your food intake. Take responsibility for exploring what works best for your body and lifestyle.

11. Learn how to deal with provocative people.

You probably have someone in your life who sometimes can be insensitive. It may be your romantic partner, your best friend, a colleague at work, a parent, or another relative. Do not let anyone say negative things about your appearance. People say negative things about others for many reasons: maybe they're jealous, or maybe they're mirroring their own insecurities. It doesn't matter—what does matter is how *you* behave.

When a negative comment is directed at them, most people become passive, aggressive, or passive-aggressive. When it happens to you, try being assertive. Open a conversation with the person who has offended you. Be specific about the problem, and communicate how you feel about it with "I" messages. Don't criticize the person or his or her behavior—that's your opinion. Relate how *you* feel—"I felt hurt," "I felt angry," "I felt embarrassed." No one can argue with your feelings. Express what you need the other person to do: "I'm asking you not to call me pudding face in front of our children." Having the courage to do this and acting in a responsible way will do wonders for your self-esteem.

Other people will be entirely inattentive to your appearance. The presence or absence of compliments is not always an accurate mirror. Everyone likes compliments, but if your need for outside approval is excessive, go back to thinking about your assets. Live with them and acknowledge them on a day-to-day basis. Give yourself the compliments—don't rely on others.

Some people never give compliments to anybody about anything. That is their problem—don't make it yours. Other people are just completely unaware of people's appearance—they don't notice yours and probably not even their own. Even if you look stunning that day, they will make no comment. People whom you are around on a regular basis just get used to the way you look; they take it for granted. Look at your own behavior. When was the last time you acknowledged someone's special effort to look nice? When did you last just appreciate someone's beauty without comparing yourself or having feelings of cynicism or jealousy?

12. For heaven's sake, once a day, once a month, or anytime you can remember to do so, stand in front of the mirror and say something nice about your body.

Say it, mean it, and believe it. This is not the same as standing in front of the mirror telling yourself how great you are or repeating inaccurate statements of "positive thinking." Your statements must come from authenticity and truth laced with compassion. Compassion is a highly underrated commodity. Practicing compassion for yourself and others is incredibly healing and liberating. Again, the dictionary says it better than we ever could: "Compassion—Deep awareness of the suffering of another, coupled with a wish to relieve it." Your own body image is a good place to start practicing.

Your
Inner Style
Inventory

As you read through and contemplate the material in this session, please keep your Personal Style Journal handy. Your answers to the questions in this session will be very important because they will reveal qualities that are unique and specific to who you are.

INNER STYLE: THE INSIDE STORY

It was a cold, gray, and drizzly February afternoon in London. A tall, attractive woman unobtrusively entered the shop. She was wearing gray sweatpants, a dark sweatshirt, and well-worn tennis shoes. Her hair was pulled back with a wide cloth headband. She acknowledged her appearance by saying that she had just been to the Laundromat and was on her way to a movie. With infectious enthusiasm and incredible focus, she said she was interested in buying some clothes for her husband, who was very busy and didn't have the time to shop.

Articulate and clear in her verbal communication, she was specific about the type of things she wanted; yet she was also open to suggestions. She seemed to enjoy being "sold to," but she did not depend on it when making decisions. She was very conscious of her environment and its contents and did not act as if she were the only person in the shop. Even though she had a time constraint, she behaved as if she had no other commitments. She listened in a way that encouraged real communication, not shop chat, and she made wonderful eye contact.

Her exit was as stylish as the rest of her behavior. As she stood by the door, holding several bags full of clothes, she offered her thanks and a sincere smile. Emma Thompson almost floated out the door.

Style, the dictionary says, is "a quality of imagination and individuality expressed in one's actions and taste." We believe that style consists of three very specific elements, which are *attitude, behavior,* and *communication*—the very attributes that Emma Thompson impressed upon us in the most natural and uncalculated way. Her *inner style*—the combination of these three elements—had absolutely nothing to do with the clothes she happened to be wearing that day. And when a person's inner style is allied outwardly with taste, imagination, and individuality, we experience the charismatic, powerful, and magnetic aspects of personal style. Some come by it naturally—others develop it.

Your *attitude* affects your behavior. Your *behavior* affects the way you communicate. And the way you *communicate,* be it verbally, physically, or through clothes, affects your personal style.

Your personal style, your "look," evolves as your sense of self evolves.

So you've passed the fifteen-second first impression test. Your clothes are fabulous, you have a great hairstyle, you made great eye contact and gave a firm handshake, and you're fit as a fiddle. Everyone is practically bowled over by your great first impression. But then what? Can you sustain that first impression? Will you be able to keep it up? How sincere is it? Are you who you say you are?

As we begin this session, we cannot express to you how vital your inner style is to the development of your personal style. This session represents one of *our* passions! Through the years we have seen firsthand, over and over again, that clothing, fashion, good taste, and the money to buy the best of these, is irrelevant when a person's inner style is lacking or nonexistent.

A Beverly Hills hairstylist told us one day of her experience with a beautiful model. When the model entered the salon, all heads and eyes turned—she was breathtakingly beautiful, not your run-of-the-mill, regular beautiful model. Anyone who walked past the model on the street would definitely stop and stare at her. But the longer the model was in the salon, the more demanding she became. By the time she left, our stylist friend said that the model "needed so much attention that she became ugly." The experience so affected the stylist that she now chooses to refrain from working with people whose attitude and behavior are so unattractive.

This story shows clearly that one's personal style cannot be totally dependent on outer image. Beauty, even astounding beauty, is never enough. Personal style has to involve something more lasting than just appearance. Eventually, even if your interaction with someone is brief, you will *experience the person,* if they have developed a personal style. Basically and simply it begins with the handshake, the smile, the eye contact, and the verbal greeting. How you perform these everyday actions defines your inner style.

It is your actions, not your looks, that tell people who you really are.

Makeup, hairstyles, colors, fabrics, cutting-edge styles, who's wearing (or exposing) what—the media always present you with the outside story. The inside story is hardly ever seen as relevant. Relying on a designer garment to create your personal style is like putting the cart before the horse. Your attitudes, your behavior, and the way you communicate transport you to a better, more memorable place.

Corporate clients who employ us to work with their staff eventually do want their employees to improve their personal appearance; however, they are just as, if not *more,* interested in having them develop their inner style. They want their employees to walk into a room and project a unique presence.

These clients readily recognize the importance of both the inner and the outer aspects of personal style. Studies have shown that whenever a business presentation is made, 58 percent of its success depends upon the image of the presenter.

We may not all make business presentations every day, but we do present ourselves daily. And at times we are not entirely happy with some aspect of our outer style. We all need something reliable to fall back on when we feel, for whatever reason, that we're having a bad hair day. Identifying and beginning to develop your inner style will bring you comfort and security in improving your image.

YOUR INNER STYLE INVENTORY

Many times you may see people and think you want what they have. You want their hairstyle or clothing, or you want to copy their "style" or taste. You may say, "If only I could have *that*. *That's* the look I want. How can I look like *that? That's* very me." First, you need to understand what *that* is.

The following scenario, played out often in the London shop, is very representative of what many people experience every day.

Malcolm told it this way: "A man, let's call him John, walks into the shop and heads straight for the suit section. He runs into Steven, who is trying on the most beautiful dark brown wool and silk casual suit. Underneath, Steven is wearing an Italian, Sea Island cotton, pale green mock turtleneck. He does look very striking. Very discreetly John turns toward me and says, 'I want that outfit. I want exactly what he's wearing. Do you have any more of them?' It must be said that John, who had not been in the shop for almost a year, was out of touch with his personal style and obviously in need of a quick fix. I responded by saying, 'No, John, you don't want that.' John said, 'Yes, Malcolm, I do.' Again I said, 'No, you really don't.' But John insisted, so of course it would have been inappropriate for me to dissuade him.

"John put on the clothes in the dressing room and reappeared looking uncomfortable. He stood before the mirror, disappointed and perplexed. 'Why doesn't this outfit suit me?' he asked. 'I look terrible in it.' John did not look terrible, but he did not look like Steven either. In fact, he had lost the smile and happy appearance he was wearing when he arrived that day."

It was not that John was less handsome than Steven; in fact they were of the same proportions and height and even had similar skin tones. What had happened?

When John saw Steven, it was not the brown suit or the beautiful mock turtleneck that he wanted. He wanted to project his own inner style in a way that honestly represented him, and to choose the clothes that would enhance it. This is exactly what Steven had done, and John had seen this without understanding exactly what he was seeing.

Steven is a low-key kind of guy. He is reliable, kind, and well mannered. He has a bright, youthful demeanor that reflects his light-hearted view of the world. With a personality that is warm and inviting and an infectious smile, he encourages people around him to feel better. Steven is also very confident and comfortable in his own skin and with his masculinity.

Steven's clothing choices that day were right on—for him. They spoke to him about who he was on the inside. The warm brown color, the soft, friendly-to-the-hand fabric, and the casual and relaxed structure of the suit were in sync with his inner style. It said everything about him that he wanted it to say. Steven could "get away" with the pale, almost feminine green color of the sweater because of his subtle male assuredness. This color is also very inviting and kind to the eye; it was soothing to his skin tone, which is slightly tanned year-round, and his unusual whitish-blond hair color.

When John saw Steven standing before the mirror that day, Steven had not yet bought the suit and sweater, but they looked as if they already belonged to him, as if they had come from his wardrobe. He had connected to them. He wore the clothes—they did not wear him.

John, on the other hand, has a completely different inner style. He has a good sense of humor and communicates in a clear, charming, and engaging way. He is a quick, sharp thinker and responds to challenges in a heartbeat. Where Steven is slow-moving and casual, John is quick and sprightly. His view of the world is one of wonderment and surprise. He is an eternal optimist who sees only positive outcomes. He is not shy of admitting his faults and mistakes and uses them as a learning tool—which is exactly what he did in this instance.

After his brief moment of disappointment, John immediately turned himself around and wanted to know what *would* work for him that day. It had been a while since we had last seen him, so we asked him a few questions—some of the same questions we ask you in this session.

We suggested that he look around and observe what fabrics and colors he was drawn to, keeping in mind the qualities that speak of his inner style. John immediately became completely engaged and selected a midnight blue, wool crepe, single-breasted suit with a deep maroon silk lining. It was a moment of importance: he had found his way and done so on his own.

John was drawn to the element of surprise in the jacket's lining, whose maroon color and luxurious silk made him smile. The midnight blue color of the suit communicated clarity and richness, and the wool crepe fabric was tactile. Wool crepe is more alive than some fabrics, which complemented John's sprightliness. The style of the suit was crisp and sharp, and the cut well-defined. John's suit was more "out there" than Steven's. When John tried Steven's suit, the soft, informal cut had submerged his personality—the softly constructed shoulders of the jacket had even made his body appear a bit stooped and round-shouldered. But in the more structured, tailored, and trimmer blue suit, he stood more erect and his personality brightened.

John told us he needed to take a moment to "get over" the turtle-neck and walked around again to become inspired. He was drawn to a shirt in a very beautiful, vivid shade of mauve. When worn against the midnight blue, the dark, rich color made a powerful statement. The shirt looked and felt luxurious. It was a blend of silk and cotton, and it reflected a flat look with a soft luster. John wore it well. The colors and fabrics he had chosen enhanced the handsome combination of his warm reddish-brown wavy hair and his skin tone, which was just a bit ruddier than Steven's.

We have known both Steven and John for years. Other factors were involved in their clothing decisions that spoke of their passions and the way they feel about their bodies. But on that day it was their inner style qualities that were seeking attention. Steven's warm, friendly, and easygoing manner contrasted greatly with John's smart and funny quickness. Neither man is better or more appealing than the other—they are just different.

In earlier sessions, you've spent some time identifying aspects of yourself that make you special and unique, including your passions, the things you dislike, and the kind of people you are drawn to. You have gained insight into details of your past experiences that relate solely to your body, and you have acquired a new, intimate perspective of your body image.

We would now like you to meet your inner style. You may very well be uncomfortable either complimenting yourself or admitting that things about your inner style need improvement. Please don't worry about how good or bad a person you are! Take the perspective of the keen observer, or the great detective.

Authenticity is the goal here. If you put on a good show when first meeting someone but it isn't really who you are, then you are taking a big risk. Of course we all behave differently at home than in business or with friends; but the less disparity between the two, the more of "you" will be experienced.

Our Inner Style Inventory will clearly show you how your inner style is inseparable from the way you are viewed. It consists of three parts: attitude, behavior, and communication. With the knowledge and awareness you derive from this inventory, you will begin to raise your self-esteem and increase your self-confidence.

ATTITUDE

Your attitudes are a subtle backdrop for your behavior.

Your attitude is your mental outlook, your state of mind. You "wear" your attitude like a garment, and you can do so either with style or without. There are several things that can ruin even a beautifully put-together outfit, and a bad attitude is one of them. When you are in the presence of a person with a bad attitude, you don't care or even notice what he or she is wearing. All you care about is how quickly you can get away!

You can choose to leave your problems, negative emotions, and stress at home, or not. If you are unable to convey a positive attitude when you need to, then you need to be aware of the consequences. At times we all have to do things that we just don't want to do. A person who makes his or her best effort to do those things with a good attitude is a person of style.

HOW YOU LOOK IS HOW YOU FEEL IS HOW YOU LOOK

Your feelings are inextricably linked to the way you look. When people look at you, what they really see is how you feel about yourself—your level of confidence and your sense of well-being. These qualities are apparent in your attitude.

Let's talk about charisma, defined as "personal magnetism or charm." People who have charisma arouse our curiosity. They are compelling—we want to be around them and know more about them. They draw our attention by an almost magical force, even though they may be entirely silent. They aren't necessarily beautiful, nor are they always fashionable. They do not wake up every morning in sunny moods. They are not perfect by any means. But they do possess a few qualities and perform certain actions, whether naturally or by design, that set them apart.

But charisma also means an optimal attitude, a self-sufficient attitude. Charismatic people are not needy of compliments or applause for their successes. With each success, they move on; they do not linger in the past.

People who exude charisma live by the Three D's:

- Desire
- Discipline
- Determination

People whose attitudes you admire, whose charisma attracts you to them, do not have it all—no one has it all. What they do is apply the Three D's to their life on a daily basis.

Their *desire* is an engine that drives them to do their best and be the best they can be. Yet to be the best is not what drives them. It is their passions that drive them. As we are drawn to them by their magnetism, they are drawn to their passions and maintain a constant relationship with them.

Their *discipline* keeps their desires on track and in touch with what is attainable. When charismatic people have bad days, they pull themselves up by their bootstraps and perform the task at hand without complaint, and with finesse. Their discipline enables them to pull this off. They have learned to compartmentalize their problems. They are aware that if they are having a problem in one area, it shouldn't affect them in other areas. Even though their relationship has just failed, or they are in debt, or their beloved pet has just died, they can still walk into a meeting and perform well.

Their *determination* keeps them going, as you will recognize should you make eye contact with them. They never, ever give up. When the old ways fail to achieve their desired outcomes, they try new ways. They are open to any method that will bring them closer to achieving their heartfelt desires.

They keep their agreements with themselves. They have a heightened awareness of themselves and all things around them. Their personal style is usually very specific—even if it appears that their clothes are not important to them, there will be some sign of self-respect: their clothes will be neat, pressed, clean, and well groomed.

Christopher Reeve, Martin Luther King, Jr., Mahatma Gandhi,

Helen Keller, and Mother Teresa—all of these people, against almost impossible odds, managed to get things done. Not only were their actions extraordinary, they were performed—and in the case of Christopher Reeve are still performed—with grace and dignity. These are people with great attitudes! They tackled their goals with their *successful* attitudes.

The visual appearance of these people holds no surprises. In photos Martin Luther King, Jr., looks dignified in his 1960s suits, Gandhi appears before us in his handwoven loincloth, Helen Keller is impeccably dressed and groomed even though she could not see, Mother Teresa wears her blue-and-white starched-cotton uniform, and Christopher Reeve is clean-cut and *GQ* handsome, even though he is more challenged physically than we can possibly imagine.

These icons of inner style went a long way toward being the best that they could be.

It is not necessary for you to be charismatic or accomplish deeds of heroic proportions. What is important is for you to acknowledge that you could.

YOUR ATTITUDE INVENTORY

Please use your Personal Style Journal to answer the following questions.

- **What is your overall outlook on life? Do you consider yourself to be a positive person?**
- **How do you think other people view you?**

Learn to play detective. Listen carefully to what other people say about you. Do not directly ask them for their comments, because that puts them on the spot and often they will think up something to say that might not be accurate. Just quietly observe. People are surprisingly free with their opinions even without being asked! Some comments will be obvious, like "You have a great sense of humor" or "You are very efficient." Some comments will be more subtle. For example, suppose someone tells you that you are not a pushover. Gently ask them what they mean: do they mean you are confident and determined, or pushy and a bully? All comments are valuable to you—even if someone says something about you that is not true, it is important for you to know that you are somehow giving them the impression that it is.

- **Are you comfortable with your attitudes?**
- **When you feel yourself heading toward a negative attitude, can you catch yourself before it affects your behavior?**
- **How flexible are you with yourself?**

You need to learn how to change a negative attitude, and to make attitude adjustments on a regular basis. You already have the tools to change your attitude, such as humor, concern for others, and the demands of the task at hand.

If your thoughts promote negative attitudes, then your thoughts can also change them, especially your attitudes about people. You cannot always control whom you spend time with, but if you can find it within you to give something of yourself to a person toward whom you have negative feelings, and to do so with compassion, you will feel better in that very moment.

- **In what specific ways might you be "wearing" your attitude?**

It is not humanly possible to always sustain a positive attitude. Your attitude directly affects your image. Your body language may reveal that you are bored, impatient, preoccupied, or angry. If you are aware that your body is giving off these signals, then you can change the message simply by changing your body language. For example, if you are in a seminar practically lying in your chair from lack of interest, try sitting up. After putting your body in a more alert position, you will actually learn something or hear something of interest to you. Then you will change not only how you are perceived but also how you feel. Scientific research has shown that when a person just pretends to change his or her attitude or mood, a chemical in the brain adjusts, so that that person actually does feel differently. Similarly, researchers say that if you act self-confident, whether you feel it or not, eventually you will gain confidence. And it happens quickly—try it!

- **Are you aware of your attitude as you begin your day?**

On days when you wake up feeling good or looking forward to the day, it is much easier to get yourself dressed. The morning seems to flow in a natural way, and you automatically know what to wear. You may pick a flattering color, or maybe a brighter one than you normally would, or you might be inclined to express yourself more creatively with a witty pair of socks. Your vintage sweater feels and looks absolutely right with a skirt that you never paired it with before.

But no one wakes up feeling good every day. Sometimes you begin your day thinking that you would rather be doing something else, or wishing it were Saturday, or suffering from a fight with your significant other. These are not days when you open your closet door delighted to clothe yourself—anything but.

Think about the personal scenarios that most often start your day. What attitudes do you most often bring to your closet? Is it your "This is the last thing I want to think about this morning" attitude? Maybe it is your "I really don't care, I don't have the time for this" attitude. Delve into why you hate getting dressed in the morning. Do you grumble and moan? Does your attitude get progressively worse as you choose your clothes for the day? Or do you calm down once you've gotten dressed?

THREE WAYS TO OVERCOME YOUR DILEMMAS ABOUT GETTING DRESSED

1. **Change your attitude.** Use the tools we have offered you in this session. Use humor, think about something positive, or focus on the importance of your image for that day. Use your body to change your attitude—go for an early morning walk, stretch, beat a pillow—do something.

2. **Some days you cannot change your attitude or don't want to. Having the right clothes in your closet will relieve the indecision that usually accompanies a negative attitude.** You are still in the process of learning what the right clothes for you will be. In a later session, you will discover and learn to rely upon your secure-making clothes. These are the clothes you will not have to think about on days when you don't have the patience or inclination to bring your full attention to your image.

3. **When your clothes are housed in your wardrobe in a way that represents your *emotional* categories as well as your lifestyle categories, you will dilute the potency of your bad days.** We will discuss this in more detail later as well.

• **Are you aware when certain attitudes prevent you from conveying the image you would like?**

Sometimes the mental process of projecting an outcome helps exacerbate a negative attitude. You imagine the worst-case scenario happening at an upcoming meeting that day, and you walk into the room with a cloud of pessimism hanging over you. Others often feel your presence as being "heavy." You meticulously planned your wardrobe that day, but telltale signs indicate that something is not quite right: a missing button, a label sticking out, odd socks, or a forgotten belt. The meeting turns out fine—the opposite of what you imagined—but look what you did to yourself: you took a risk with your image and left yourself open to doubt.

Is this a familiar scene in your life? How can you make those days better? What would you change if you could do it differently?

- **Choose and write about people whose attitude you admire.**

These people, like your icons, can be real or fictional characters and need not be limited to people you actually know. Perhaps you've met someone whom you've remembered solely for his or her attitude, or who has faced considerable challenges yet still manages to have a great attitude. Do you know such a person?

- **Is there anything about the attitude of these people that you aspire to? What is it?**
- **Now that you are more aware of how your attitude is connected to your inner style, what can you do to better serve your personal style?**

BEHAVIOR

There is one component of your personal style that can really bring a sparkle to your image, enhancing it and making you feel and appear special. It costs nothing in monetary terms, yet its rewards are too numerous to mention. It is not exactly magic, for it often calls upon your inner strength and patience, but its benefits are palpable. This ingredient is *behavior*. Your behavior is so much a part of your personal style that to separate the two would be impossible.

Behavior is attitude in action. How you are feeling on the inside and the attitude you adopt will eventually evolve into your behavior in one way or another. The important thing is to become aware of how your behavior affects you and those around you. For the sake of your personal style, we would like to share with you the elements of "good behavior" and also "stylish behavior."

We have had many outstanding and diverse teachers on the subject of behavior. People have been generous to us, and we are very grateful to them. Various cultures in the world have taught us valuable lessons in the fundamentals of good behavior. And we have had the pleasure of experiencing good behavior taken to the plateau of truly stylish behavior.

Everywhere in the world we have been, no matter what the culture or economic background or education of the people, the basics of good behavior have been the same. Several members of a communal farming community in the Middle East sacrificed their food allowance for weeks to feed us as if we were royalty. In Milan an Italian clothing manufacturer, away on a business trip in America, called us to ensure that everything was satisfactory in the restaurant where we were his guests, even though he was not present. Japanese friends have taught us appropriate communal bathing etiquette—as if we would need it anywhere else! The consistent and generous hospitality of family members in the American South still amazes us. In each of these scenes, our hosts were generous, made sacrifices for our comfort, and gave of themselves without wanting anything in return. They were willing and patient teachers without even knowing it.

It is easy to behave well when you have something to gain from it—a raise, a job, a chance at something. But very good behavior is dynamic when you don't want anything in return. It is engaging and encourages people to feel good in your presence.

If your intention is to leave a positive lasting impression, then good behavior is a must.

SELF-ESTEEM

Researchers have found that the self-esteem of even highly successful people varies not only daily but hourly. Due to the inevitable ebb and flow of our experiences, our self-esteem comes and goes.

In general, healthy self-esteem does not come from being happy about the way you look or what you wear. It comes from being personally and socially responsible.

Good behavior and self-esteem are intertwined. You build self-esteem bit by bit by behaving well. As you behave well, you begin to feel good about yourself. And when you feel good about yourself, you become more attractive to others.

When you behave responsibly, you take care of yourself, your family, and those for whom you are responsible at work. When you do that to the best of your ability, you automatically create self-respect.

Life throws at us the seeds for change. When the challenges of life become overwhelming and difficult, our sense of self is threatened. When people are faced with such challenges, you can immediately see their self-esteem drop: their head hangs low, their body slumps, they may gain weight, their personal appearance begins to show that less care has been taken.

Even though our self-esteem seems to disappear when we least want or expect it to, we can still retrieve it and bring it back to life. When you call upon your inner strength to make the needed changes, you then create an even greater level of inner strength. That is why you sometimes see people who are humble or gracious, and you cannot quite put your finger on why they are so compelling. They draw on enormous inner strength and self-discipline to support their behavior.

Good behavior produces an immediate result. Anyone at any-time can raise his or her level of self-esteem by behaving well.

You have the power to own your space, create a positive atmosphere, and even steer the outcome of a meeting simply by being on your best behavior. What a confidence booster! But it takes practice, and it must be real and genuine.

Many of our clients have experienced an increase in self-esteem. No two clients' quests for a higher self-esteem have been the same. Some seem to plod along, slowly accumulating self-respect, while others seem to be doing very little but then suddenly burst forth, as if their stagnant energy had propelled them to take action.

In each case something always shifted: from an intellectual understanding of what they needed to do, they took an action, however small, that would warrant higher self-esteem. Interestingly, the more clients raised their self-respect, the more they wanted to go shopping right away! They wanted to experience how it felt to buy and wear clothes while feeling better about themselves and being more self-accepting.

Martha: Raising Self-Esteem

Two ladies in particular were remarkably different in the way they progressed. You have met them both before: they are Julia, the red-haired "superwoman," and Martha, the woman who was too stressed to even consider losing weight.

Martha was soft-spoken, warm, and very bright. Her way of moving through the world was slow, diligent, and sometimes hesitant, which was also how she approached the work in this session. Her key to achieving healthier self-esteem was to increase her preparedness. She lacked preparation in every aspect of her life, from her clothing and grooming to her readiness for meetings. As a result, she projected the image of someone who was messy looking and unreliable. She would walk into a meeting wearing clothes that she felt uncomfortable in—either they were too tight, which restricted her freedom of movement, or they were too baggy to be crisp and fresh looking. Because she was not mentally prepared, she could not focus herself and was unable to make direct eye contact with people in the room. When the meeting was over, she lost self-respect because she knew she could have done better. This cycle continued until her employer suggested she meet with us.

We addressed grooming issues straightaway, because small outward improvements would probably bolster Martha's self-esteem immediately. They did for a moment, but she was inconsistent in maintaining the improvements. We didn't badger her but instead decided to move on.

We suggested that Martha would benefit from behavioral changes related to her work, and she agreed. We began to practice simple and small role-playing scenarios with her. This struck a chord, for during the role-playing she discovered that she had an overabundance of empathy. At meetings she was so concerned with how she could accommodate everyone else's needs that she never really aired her own views. Yet it was her views and ideas that her employer respected and wanted to promote.

We began slowly with Martha: we first practiced telephone skills and making eye contact, then eventually graduated to mock meetings and presentations. She even enacted a confrontation with a colleague with whom she was in conflict. She had no problem acting out these scenarios with us, but when it came time to put her new behavior into action at work, she was hesitant. She was experiencing something similar to stage fright.

At this point we pulled back, to give Martha the space and time she needed to find her way. She resisted being led and wanted to stay in charge of how she progressed. This, we discovered, was not stubbornness or a refusal to conform but her strength. The trick with Martha was to let her take the initiative, while we remained in the background, ready to support her. She still needed encouragement and reinforcement, but from a distance. It was almost as if she were incubating.

Then one day at work she took a risk and used the skills she had learned in an important meeting. In true Martha form, she did small but noticeable things. She went to the hairdresser the day before. She bought a new blouse to wear with her favorite suit. The night before the meeting, she made a list of three points that she was determined to put forth the next day. And she decided that if she was able to make one of those points successfully, she would have accomplished something. She arrived at the meeting early to locate where she would sit and stand to make herself more comfortable. These actions may seem small and irrelevant, but to Martha they were not small. They were the result of the time and effort she spent on improving herself and her image. After the meeting, Martha's self-esteem was raised a few notches, an invaluable gain in self-respect.

These accumulated changes produced another result: they gave Martha the impetus to attend to her weight. Since her self-esteem was higher, she felt capable and worthy of taking care of her body as well. This happened with absolutely no prompting from us—we even heard about it from someone else in the company. This behavior was also true to Martha: she was modest and would not have been comfortable drawing even that amount of attention to herself.

As Martha learned how to incorporate preparedness into her life, she acquired an image of greater reliability. Her employer was impressed with both her behavioral changes and her improved self-presentation. Now he could tell just by the way her hair looked or her choice of clothing whether she would be giving her best that day. Her appearance had become a clear signal of her confidence level, her professional ability, and her emotional state.

When Martha learned how to be prepared, her behavior in personal care and in taking care of business became consistent, and with this consistency she earned self-esteem. This is what impressed her employer. Her consistent *behavior* proved to him that he could trust her and depend on her. For the first time, her progress report at work reflected a significant improvement.

Martha deserves credit for having made so many wonderful improvements. She had great potential within her that was just waiting for her to cultivate it. Fortunately her employer was keen enough to recognize her potential. In the end, he was very satisfied to be able to offer her what she had now earned—a promotion to the job of her dreams.

Julia: Treating Others with Respect

Where Martha was unhurried and tenuous, Julia was quick and eager. Everyone around her was under the impression that she could have it all, but she herself felt insecure about her abilities, and she confessed to us that she felt like a fake. She did indeed want it all, but she was having trouble admitting it to herself. So her behavior was defensive, guarded, and even unfriendly at times—a mask. Her uniformlike clothes were a part of the mask that concealed her fear that someone would find out that she was a fake. (We call this *armoring*.) The blandness of her clothes, their overly mature style, and their coarse fabrics acted as an invisible shield and helped keep people at bay. Her severe image made her seem inaccessible. In fact, she was standoffish and demanding and appeared to be uncaring. She was not an unkind person, but she did not have the tools to better her relationships. She behaved toward people the way she had been treated by her parents, her former employers, and even some of her friends. She had been conditioned and didn't know better.

Julia found one of the keys to her personal style in her work in this session. Her behavior, she discovered, was holding her back and was stifling her true image.

Julia was ripe and ready for change. She especially wanted to change the way she treated other people and in particular her staff. But finding her inner strength and creating healthier self-esteem took a great deal of hard work and a lot of tears. When she finally experienced how good it felt to drop her guard and that it was safe to do so, her behavior changed, and she relinquished her mask.

We gave Julia very specific tools that enabled her to have better experiences immediately.

SELF-RESPECT

We use *self-respect* and *self-esteem* interchangeably—and our trusty dictionary agrees. But here we differentiate the two for a single purpose. While self-esteem is "all about you," self-respect is less about you and more about others. A person with self-respect talks and listens to a fifth grader with a paper route the same way he talks and listens to his bank manager. Although he may have a much more intellectual or physical prowess than others, he would never blatantly display it. Self-respect is gained by giving it.

We asked Julia to become aware of what it felt like to give people respect for no reason at all. They did not have to particularly earn it—she had to offer it without conditions or results. Julia's version of this was to open the door for her colleagues if she happened to arrive at the door first. When she saw the pleasure it brought to people, when they made eye contact and smiled in thanks, she did a mental double take. By doing so little, she got so much in return.

EMPATHY AND COMPASSION

Empathy and compassion are closely linked to self-respect. Taking time out for others, putting yourself in their shoes, and having an awareness of their feelings—these are qualities that promote self-respect and command respect from others.

Julia did not have a natural facility for giving unconditionally. This is a perfectly normal way of being, and there are many valid reasons why people do not naturally have this quality. Julia's experiences with "being taken" had left her with a need to protect herself, which produced her guarded and slightly jaded attitude. Yet Julia made a decision to try to express empathy, compassion, and respect for others and herself.

To begin to connect with people, Julia used two more tools to teach her how to experience empathy. The first one was learning how to listen.

LISTENING

The ability to listen well is a very important inner style ingredient. Listening, not talking, is the great and gifted role. The true listener is much more magnetic than the talker, much more imaginative in his or her silence. Listening has always been considered the passive role, but it is extremely active, because to be a good listener, you must at the same time be tranquil and present—using all your senses and powers of observation. This kind of listening creates empathy. You walk in another person's shoes; you try to know him or her without arguing, changing the subject, or forcing your opinion.

Some people who think they are listening are actually being self-assertive. Their body may lean forward a little too attentively, which is not a pose of receptivity. They may be making eye contact, yet their thoughts may be pressing invisibly into the talker's space.

A good listener will have a healthy curiosity. He or she will be genuinely interested in others, wanting to know who they are and what their thoughts and feelings, their fears, hopes, and dreams, may be.

Good listening requires patience. Sometimes you must listen a long time before you receive the speaker's purer thoughts. Always underneath dull or dry thoughts are bright thoughts that are creative, true, and alive. When people are listened to in the right way, they reveal those bright thoughts. Think of how good you feel when the person you are talking to is really listening.

PATIENCE

"Our patience will achieve more than our force," said Edmund Burke, an eighteenth-century, Irish-born British politician and writer.

With everything at our fingertips, our society has become more convenience-oriented and faster-paced than ever. Yet, even though we as a culture seem already to be traveling at the speed of light, that is not fast enough. Our society's insatiable hunger for immediacy can be best characterized as impatience run riot. This anxious impatience affects our manners, civility, body language, communication, attitude—just about all the ingredients of inner style. If you look carefully at what it means to have patience, you will understand why practicing it might be a challenge in this age of immediate results.

> **Patient—bearing or enduring pain, difficulty, provocation or annoyance with calmness. Tolerant; understanding. Capable of calmly awaiting an outcome or result: not hasty or impulsive. Patience emphasizes calmness, self-control, and the willingness or ability to tolerate delay.**

We're not asking you to accomplish a major overhaul of your personality and become a monklike shining example of the virtues of patience. But huge benefits are to be gained from cultivating patience as part of your personal style.

Julia instinctively knew that she needed to practice patience in order to further develop her inner style. She was well aware that her impatience at work attributed to her image of being uncaring and unapproachable. When she took the time out to really look at what that meant to her reputation, her attitude immediately changed.

When we discussed with Julia the concepts of empathy, listening, and patience, she was able to evaluate her behavior in these terms. She took the initiative and began to monitor her behavior. In so doing, she focused on key elements that were not working for her and chose to discontinue them. She practiced being more considerate, she sacrificed her time, and she really listened to her family and co-workers. People began to perceive her and treat her differently; she gained respect and graciously accepted compliments on her appearance. The transformation in her image was remarkable.

If Julia had made improvements only in her outer style, the results would indeed have been short-lived. No new clothes, hairstyle, or makeup alone could have created Julia's true personal style. It was the development of her inner style, which was beautifully emerging, that truly enhanced her image. Fortunately she already had within her the desire and the facility to project a better image.

HUMOR

Would you rather be criticized for wearing a certain tie or scarf, or for not having a sense of humor?

Everyone has a sense of humor. Granted, people have many different ways of expressing and experiencing humor, and a person's sense of humor may be well hidden, surfacing only on rare occasions. But humor is vital for developing one's personal style.

First of all, humor takes the edge off of many situations, especially extremely personal ones. It almost allows you to be intimate in a way that is safe. Through imparting these healthy feelings, it encourages better relationships. How many times have you laughingly told a story about a traumatic or embarrassing event?

Humor is also a very specific and personal form of expression in behavior and manner, personal taste and style. When your humor is authentic, it allows people to experience your uniqueness. We encourage all of our clients to investigate their humor, both in what delights and amuses them and how they might delight and amuse others.

We are not talking about adding joke telling to your personal style or becoming a comedian. And we are certainly not referring to offensive, tasteless, or sarcastic humor that hurts and offends others. You can use your humor in small but effective ways to season a conversation, presentation, or even a negotiation. Humor is often used to ease painful situations and disagreements.

One of our clients arrived late for a meeting with us, breathless, flustered, and disheveled. She apologized and slumped into a chair, dropping her briefcase onto the floor. We had recently introduced her to the idea of discovering her own specific humor, since her very dry wit often cropped up on its own. We suggested that she reenter the room and somehow create a better atmosphere by using humor.

She entered the room calmly and made good eye contact with us. She then gently placed her briefcase on a chair and said in her best deadpan manner, "Good morning. I'm sorry I'm late, but I have just arm-wrestled one of our company's competitors and held a prayer meeting for my boss's ailing cat. Well, not really. There was a crisis in the office that needed my immediate attention. Thank you for waiting."

This worked for her and us because her brand of humor was very much a part of who she was. We will help you to discover aspects of your own sense of humor in the Behavior Inventory on pages 120–23. Become aware of when you make someone chuckle or smile. How did you do it? Please note that you must never "try" to be funny. There is nothing worse than thinking you are funny when you are not. But when you do get it right, humor is very engaging and can bring a human touch to relationships in both personal and business circumstances.

MANAGING YOUR EMOTIONS

In addition to improving her image, our "running late" client was also using humor to manage her emotions: to get through a moment of frustration. Entering with her own brand of personal humor—a specific element of her personal style—worked for her. What did not work for her was entering the room showing us how upset, angry, and frustrated she was.

When people talk about things they feel passionately about, they are usually very focused and can articulate specifically why they feel the way they do. As a listener, you can easily get caught up in their passion for their subject, because you are experiencing their heart. But passion and emotion are not the same thing. Being emotional can involve expressing a passion, but it can also mean ranting and raving, being overwhelmed, or being unable to control one's behavior or speech. As witnesses to such emotional behavior, we tend to back off both physically and mentally. The absence of heart and the presence of ego, intellect, or the need to be right often accompany emotionality.

A successful personal style, in part, is derived from emotional stability, something very few people have been taught to strive for. Your parents may have allowed you, as a child, to freely express your emotions inappropriately anywhere at any time, or they may have demanded that you suppress your emotions in unbearably stifling ways. In either case, what often emerges in the adult is emotional immaturity.

This is not to say that you should be void of feeling and sensibility—just the opposite. But it is your sensitivity and awareness of yourself and others that develops emotional maturity and restraint—two very important elements to include in your personal style. If you use emotional maturity and restraint, you will make better decisions and avoid making mistakes.

The subject of emotions enters our world because we help people to present themselves successfully. Many of our clients have issues about their image that have been lying dormant for most of their lives. And when given a platform to express their long-term pain and dissatisfaction about their image for the first time, they understandably behave with deep emotion. When you can release your emotions in the right place with the right person, safely, securely, and without judgment, then you are on the path toward healing. But if you choose to vent your emotions to inappropriate people, or at inappropriate times and places, then you are setting yourself up for criticism and judgment and injuring your image.

We are not experts in the field of recognizing and managing emotions; these are lifelong skills that we ourselves continue to learn. But when you learn to manage your emotions, you improve your image and stay true to the development of your personal style.

MANNERS, ETIQUETTE, AND CIVILITY

Today good manners, etiquette, and civility are quite clearly on the decline. They are even considered artificial and unnatural. We disagree. Nothing is more transparent than insincere civility or pushy do-goodism; and nothing is more becoming than the simplicity of a sincere "thank you" and a polite and genuine "please."

A person who has no manners, etiquette, or civility has no style. Unlike a clothing item, these qualities will never go out of style. Including them in your personal style elevates your image to a level that no designer outfit could ever achieve.

The push toward constant casual attire in our society begs to be addressed as well. We can't tell you how many clients, especially men, have come to us completely stressed about "casual Fridays." Both men and women complain that their "casual look" is private and they would like to keep it that way. They feel that casual Friday is actually intruding on their weekend. In some cases, they lament, their colleagues' casual attire is matched by casual behavior that is inappropriate for the office. Women have complained that the men sometimes become a little too free with their weekend chatter and begin to cross the boundaries of professional behavior.

We once attended a series of meetings with entertainment companies in Los Angeles. Although Los Angeles has a reputation for being the King of Casual, for the most part we found the executives at the first meeting to be pretty straight-laced dressers. Our second meeting, with a company in Beverly Hills, happened to be on a Friday. We walked into the office—and the man who had been wearing a beautiful suit when we met before now appeared before us in jeans, a T-shirt, and moccasins. We were both astonished. We suddenly felt as if we had been transported to Malibu and should have brought our beach towels. When we sat down, the man proceeded to place his well-worn moccasins on the table, propping his legs right at eye level with us. As far as we were concerned, he had lost all credibility. It didn't matter what day of the week it was, his self-presentation was too personal, too revealing for a business meeting. His casual dress and manner, and his bad manners in placing his feet on the table, were memorable—in the wrong way. (In Session 9 we will address the many consequences of this new dressing-down phenomenon. For some companies, Casual Friday is becoming Casual Monday through Friday.)

YOUR BEHAVIOR INVENTORY

Please use your journal to answer the following questions.

SELF-ESTEEM

1. **When do you feel your self-esteem is at its highest?**
2. **Why do you feel good about yourself on those days?** Is it because you are more relaxed? Did you take better care of yourself that day? Is there a certain clothing item that you feel good in? Did you do a good deed? Did you spend time with your family or partner? Did you feel satisfied from a certain achievement? Were you at peace?
3. **When do you feel your self-esteem is low?** Can you identify the reasons why your self-esteem is lowered? (For Martha, it was her lack of preparation and her discomfort with her weight.)
4. **When you hit a low point in your life, how does this affect your behavior?** How do you behave toward others during these times?
5. **How would you define healthy self-esteem?** Describe how you think healthy self-esteem "looks." What are its signals, in your estimation? How close do you fit that description?
6. **How has your self-esteem affected your personal style?**

SELF-RESPECT

1. **How important is self-respect in relation to your image?**
2. **Why?**
3. **When do you feel self-respect?** From an action that was well completed? From standing up for yourself? From keeping your word when you were tempted not to?
4. **How do you show respect to others?** Do you show respect selectively? Is gain ever involved? Do you show respect because you feel it is deserved?
5. **Does your wardrobe say anything about self-respect?**
6. **Does your personal style reflect self-respect?**

EMPATHY AND COMPASSION

1. **Are you aware of other people's feelings?**
2. **How thoughtful are you?**
3. **Do you have compassion for yourself?**
4. **Are you able to lend emotional support when needed?**

5. **Do you have the capacity for genuinely caring about others?**

6. **Do you ever step into someone else's shoes and think what it is like to be him or her?**

7. **How are compassion and empathy manifested in your behavior?**

LISTENING

1. **Do you enjoy listening to other people?**
2. **Why or why not?**
3. **Do you consider yourself to be a good listener?**
4. **What makes you a good or not-so-good listener?** To help you out with this one, several things are signals. What kind of body language do you adopt when listening? What does it reveal about you? Are you antsy, uninterested, impatient, or bored? Do you think about other things? Are you more anxious to be heard than to listen? Do you mentally jump ahead of the speaker, either guessing his or her next words or preparing your comments? Do you interrupt a lot?
5. **Do you use listening as a learning tool?** You learn more about people through good listening, and you build better, stronger relationships. You also gain credibility for having listened and truly comprehended what the speaker was saying.

PATIENCE

1. **Are you a patient or impatient person?**
2. **If you are patient, please list the qualities and behavior that make you so.**
3. **If you are impatient, please write about what makes you lose patience.** When you ask a question, do you require an immediate response? Does waiting in line change your mood? What kind of driver are you? How do you treat others when you become impatient with them? Are you drawn to people who you think are patient?
4. **Are you less or more patient than you were in your youth?**
5. **What one thing can you do to develop more patience?**
6. **How would patience manifest itself in your personal style?**

HUMOR

Before you can begin to use your sense of humor effectively, take time to identify it. The following questions will help you to pinpoint what amuses you and how you would characterize the "amusing you."

1. **Do you have the ability to laugh at yourself?**
2. **Does your humor emerge in a spontaneous way?**
3. **Is your humor physical?**
4. **Do you have a dry wit?**
5. **Is your sense of humor intellectual?**
6. **Responsive humor—the quick comeback—does that describe yours?**
7. **Is your humor improbable, imaginative, or surreal?**
8. **Are you eccentric or quirky? How so?**
9. **Do you have a conservative sense of humor? How so?**
10. **Have you ever used your humor, however subtly, to improve a situation or relieve tension?** Did it work? If not, do you know why? Was your timing off, the situation wrong, or the humor unappreciated?
11. **Are you comfortable with your sense of humor?** Have you ever felt that people just do not appreciate you outlook on life? Has your sense of humor become a secret affair between you and you? Would you be willing to let the cat out of the bag every once and a while, when you feel safe and are with people who you think might get it?
12. **What people, places, or things tend to bring out your sense of humor?** For example: When I am with _____, I always make him laugh.

MANAGING YOUR EMOTIONS

1. **Do you consider yourself to be an emotional person?** If you do, please describe how this is manifested in your behavior. Do you readily express what you are feeling to people? Do people usually know what kind of mood you are in by the way you behave?
2. **If you don't consider yourself to be an emotional person, are you managing your emotions?**
3. **How do you manage your emotions?** Do you make a point of taking care of your emotional needs?
4. **Have you become less emotional as you age?** How as that affected your behavior? Do you seem to accomplish more when your emotions are balanced? Do you have more energy? Do you make better decisions?
5. **What effect do your emotions have on your personal style?** Do you think people view you as an emotional person or a passionate person? Have you ever been told that you are "too emotional" or "too sensitive"? How did you feel about that? Are you an "emo-

tional shopper"—do you fall in love with items? Or do you shop dispassionately?

MANNERS, ETIQUETTE, CIVILITY

1. **What were your feelings as you read the previous section on manners?** What are your personal views and thoughts about manners, etiquette, and civility? Are they important in how you behave and how others behave toward you?

2. **From whom did you learn your manners?** Was it a parent, a relative, or a mentor who taught you basic lessons in how to behave? Did you learn by observation? Did you copy icons who behaved a certain way? Were you ever told why you should behave in a certain way? That it was the right thing to do? That you would get along better in life? That people would like you if you "minded your manners"?

3. **If you think back to all of the things we have brought to your attention in this session—humor, patience, managing emotions, listening—are any of these things related to why you do or do not make manners, etiquette, and civility a part of your personal style?** For example, do you use humor to keep your manners in check? Is it your impatience that keeps you from acting civilly? Do your emotions sometimes prevent you from behaving as well as you would like?

COMMUNICATION

"Everybody is talented, original, and has something important to say," says Brenda Ueland, a writer, editor, and teacher. And one of the most empowering elements you can bring to your personal style is the way you communicate. Throughout this session you have been exploring your attitude and behavior, both of which affect your communication.

Part of personal style is knowing what you have to say. Your clothes, your hair, and your grooming all communicate many things about you, sometimes accurately and sometimes not. But you also communicate verbally and physically, in ways as unique as your DNA.

Some experts will tell you that there is one right and accepted way to communicate. For example, they will tell you to stand or sit with "open body language" or to use a clear, even-pitched tone of voice, devoid of any regional or national accent. As if people could not communicate effectively with a Boston or a Cockney accent! As if crossing your arms always means you are being defensive! Human beings are more complex than a list of stock gestures and cookie-cutter symbols.

Learning how to communicate well has advantages and positive outcomes. You might be interested in improving the way you communicate, and you might want to stop doing things that negatively affect your ability to communicate. But before you do any of that, you need to be aware of what kind of communicator you are. Our approach is focused on how the way you communicate makes you different, sets you apart.

YOUR VERBAL COMMUNICATION

Have your journal on hand for the rest of this session, and please answer the following questions.

WHO ARE YOU VERBALLY?
- Are you a good storyteller?
- Do you get to the point?
- Are you a humorist?
- Are you a smooth talker?
- Are you a highly energized, fast speaker?
- Are you a thoughtful, considered speaker?
- Are you the town crier, the circus barker?
- Are you a melodic speaker?
- Are you a sound bite speaker?
- Are you a verbal introvert or an extrovert?
- Do you often speak with emotion?
- Do you speak with intention?
- Describe yourself verbally in other ways that are not listed here.

Look over this list of questions. These are not categories to try to fit yourself into—the only thing you need to do is be aware of your verbal style. Your verbal style may change depending on the situation or people you are around. Many of the categories may be ways of describing yourself verbally, or one specific category may describe you perfectly by itself. If you don't know the answers to these questions, it will be interesting for you to figure them out. You may do that in two different ways.

First, try observing yourself verbally for a few days. While this might seem a bit unusual, it can become quite fun. As you tell a story, notice whether you are holding someone's attention. (Is he or she a particularly good listener, or are you a particularly good storyteller?) If you are speaking very loudly in a quiet place, or whispering for no reason, notice that. If you are a shy person, notice what you do and how you feel when you are called upon to speak. Do you speak to family members differently from store clerks, co-workers, or strangers? How?

If you are an extrovert and have no trouble speaking in public and meeting new people, ask yourself whether you are sensitive to others when they wish to speak. Be specific about what kind of extrovert you are. Do you shelter a shy introvert deep inside you? Many actors do. Or is it possible that you just can't get enough of the limelight?

A second way to answer these questions is to ask someone to help you or give you their observations. The person you choose must be someone close to you whom you trust and respect.

Your Voice

Many clients have told us that they hate their voice. A few have even sought the help of voice and speech experts. But there is no such thing as a perfect voice. Some of the most interesting and magnetic voices are unusual and quirky. The "perfect," accentless, crisp, and clear voice can drone on and on until your nerves are on edge.

We are not suggesting that you consider speech training or voice lessons. Instead, we are asking you to go inside to allow your voice to speak in a way that truly represents you. Kristin Linklater, one of the greatest teachers of freeing the natural voice, would have new students do nothing but relax and become aware of their breathing for weeks before she would allow them to even *practice* the one-syllable sound of *ahh*!

It is not your voice but your perception and awareness of your voice that needs attention. When you spend time getting to know your voice, you will find out things about it and come to appreciate how different it is from everyone else's. You may begin to realize that what you thought was a _____ (fill in the blank) voice is actually a charmingly eccentric, melodious, resonant, sophisticated, soft, delicate, strong voice!

The following questions will help you to begin thinking about what makes your voice unique.

ASSESSING YOUR VOICE

- **Are you aware of the tone of your voice?** Is it rich and full, highly pitched, soft, deep, nasal, soothing, sweet, raspy, resonant, or clear?

- **When you hear your voice on tape, what is your first reaction?**

- **If you don't like hearing your voice (and most people we know don't), what is it that you don't like?** Please be specific. Is it your speech, your voice itself, or is it your accent? Is it the pitch of your voice—would you want it to be lower or higher?

- **Are you aware of when you are speaking too loudly or too softly? Are you aware of the volume that you use most often?** Is your voice loud, booming, soft, whispery, or midrange? Do people often ask you to speak up or lower your voice? Do you try to comply with their requests?

- **What pace do you most often use when speaking?** Do you speak quickly or slowly, or do you keep a fairly moderate pace?

- **Does your voice have any unique qualities? Use several words to describe your voice.** We've listed a few possibilities to get you started:

Bubbly	Whiny
Deep	Soft
Rich	Monotone
Breathy	Languid
Raspy	Spirited
Shaky	Breezy
Clear as a bell	Resonant
Gruff and rough	Vibrant
Screechy	High
Muffled	

A woman once told us that people had always made unkind comments about her voice, calling it "squeaky," "monotone," and "irritating." She couldn't care less, because she has turned what she calls her most unique and identifying asset into a moneymaker. She is now a busy, well-paid voice-over artist!

YOUR PHYSICAL COMMUNICATION

What you communicate with your body often says more than words. Your eyes, your touch, the way you walk, even the way you stand in the movie line speaks volumes. Your physical being communicates your attitudes, your manners, your feelings, your emotions, and even your sense of humor.

Your physical communication is connected with your body image, which we discussed in the last session. For instance, your body image might affect the way you walk or move. If you are having an "I feel fat day," you might feel self-conscious maneuvering yourself in between people in a social or business setting. If walking into a roomful of people makes you uncomfortable, you may physically communicate that you are shy, embarrassed, or uncomfortable. On the other hand, you may experience a great deal of "body pride" one day and find yourself almost strutting. People will probably get the message that you feel pretty good about yourself. People make automatic and instantaneous judgments about you based on your physical communication.

Your physical communication also relates to your moment-to-moment emotional state. When your boss refuses your request for a raise or time off, he or she will probably watch for physical communication from you. A person you are on a first date with is sensitive to your physical responses. Your children will watch your facial and physical reactions as they push your patience. You respond with physical communication that is uniquely your own. Let's find out how.

HOW DO YOU PHYSICALLY COMMUNICATE?

- **Have you ever considered that your physicality sends messages to others about you?**
- **Are you comfortable shaking hands with people?**
- **Are you a "toucher"?** Do you make physical contact with people fairly easily? Do you casually touch people often, with a pat on the back or a slight touch on the arm? Do you hug people easily?
- **Do you avoid touching people?**
- **Do you consider yourself aloof?**
- **Do you have a relaxed body language?**
- **Do you have active or nervous energy?** Do you tap your feet, legs, or hands? Do you look around a lot?

- **Do you consider your physical communication to be relaxed?**
  - **Do you consider it to be alert?**
  - **Do you sit neatly or sloppily?**
  - **Do you try to control your body language?** Do you manipulate your physicality because you are aware that people are observing you? If so, how?
    - **Do you talk with your hands? What do you say with them?**
    - **How would you describe the way you make eye contact?**
  - **When you are standing in line, at a party, in a business environment, or anywhere in a group of people, are you aware of your physical space? Are you aware of theirs?**
    - **Do you think you are a physically dominating person?**
    - **In what other ways would you describe your physicality?**

YOUR ESSENCE

Essence—the intrinsic or indispensable properties that characterize or identify something. The most important ingredient; the crucial element. The inherent unchanging nature of something.

The most subtle ingredient in you as a person and in your personal style is something called your *essence*. It is the concentrated and pure part of you that makes you who you are and that reveals your uniqueness. It is communicated whether or not you are aware of it. The qualities that represent your essence actually exist in spite of you! It is not easy to identify your essence, because it is almost intangible. Your essence is often felt by others, but it is not something you think about very often, if at all.

Our favorite recipe for deep-dish apple pie includes one unusual ingredient. Instead of cinnamon, it calls for rose water. Substituting this one ingredient changes the whole identity of the pie, making it special and unique. Guests always say it is the best apple pie they have ever tasted. It may not be *the best,* but it is certainly different.

In this session you have explored, discovered, and identified many of the ingredients that make up your inner style. Within all of these ingredients exists your essence, however small, however subtle. The more self-aware you become and the more you strive to reveal about yourself, the more in touch with your essence you will be. It is then that your essence will become stronger, purer, and more felt by others.

To help define your essence, we would now like for you to identify your inner style assets.

YOUR INNER STYLE ASSETS

It is very important for you to recognize your inner assets—the qualities of your inner style that shine, the positive aspects of yourself, whether you have cultivated them or were born with them. They are the purest part of you. They include the highlights of your Inner Style Inventory, but you may also discover an asset that is not in your inventory.

List anything that you feel comes naturally to you or that you do without effort. For example, if it is easy for you to be empathetic, then include this on your list of inner assets; but if you are still working on making good eye contact or being more straightforward, then don't include those yet. To make it easier for you, we have listed several possible inner style assets, but please go back through your work in this session to find all of yours. You can always add more to your list later. When you know that you own these assets, then even on "bad days" you can rely on them to see you through.

Reliable
Kind
Well-mannered
Honest
Warm
Friendly
Inviting
Empathetic
Good sense of humour
Clear communicator
Straightforward
Charming
Positive attitude
Good listener
Calm
Good etiquette
Gracious

Surprising
Sharp-witted
Charismatic
Disciplined
Flexible
Prepared
Good eye contact
Comfortable physically
Interesting, strong, or nice voice
Well-spoken
Compassionate
Emotionally balanced
Sensitive
Patient
Vibrant
Civil
Physically elegant

We're sure that you have other highlights from this session that you may list as assets. Yours may be more specific and personal than the ones we have listed.

REVIEWING YOUR PERSONAL STYLE STATEMENT

This is the final exercise in this session, but an extremely important one.

Go back and review your Personal Style Statement. Is what you want to project in your personal style congruent with the results of your Inner Style Inventory?

KEVIN'S REVIEW

In our client Kevin's Inner Style Inventory, he discovered the following things:

- He had a great sense of humor.
- He had okay but not great manners.
- His voice carried well, and he was sometimes told that it was loud.
- He loved helping people.
- He was better at talking than listening.
- Patience was not a strong point.
- He was civil equally to children, friends, and strangers.
- The thought of his essence flew right over his head.
- His inner style assets were that he was charming, reliable, witty, philanthropic, honest, and trustworthy.

Kevin's Personal Style Statement was: **"I project a sophisticated, charismatic, and reliable image."**

The words *charismatic* and *reliable* do actually follow from Kevin's Inner Style Inventory and his assets; they make sense. But what in his Inner Style Inventory suggests *sophisticated*? Well, nothing. Having completed his inventory, Kevin needed to decide whether he would still like *sophisticated* to be a part of his personal style. He didn't necessarily need to change his statement, but he did need to look at the facts. More important, he needed to decide how strong was his desire to include sophistication in his personal style.

If Kevin decided he still wanted sophistication, then he needed to improve on a few things. He said his manners were "okay." Improving them would definitely help him be more sophisticated. He had been told that he sometimes spoke too loudly. Learning when and where to lower his voice would not only help him to become more sensitive and aware, it would also help him to improve his listening skills—all qualities of a truly sophisticated person. Practicing all these things would automatically help him develop patience. These simple acts of awareness cost nothing and do not take up a great deal of time, and Kevin probably already knew how to do them. All would add a little sophistication to his personal style.

Your Inner Style Inventory contains a plethora of easy-to-recognize aspects of yourself that you might wish to improve, as Kevin's inventory did. You can use your inner assets—the wonderful ideas, thoughts, and truths about who you are—in many different ways. Sometimes people take the trouble to identify their assets yet never use them. Don't do that! Improvements do not need to be time-swallowing, grand gestures. Small, subtle, yet meaningful improvements can be made easily.

You can enhance your assets just by bringing your awareness to them. For example, if you are in the middle of an intense, heated conversation with someone, ask yourself if this is a good time to use humor, or to be compassionate or silent and just listen. How you choose to use your inner style assets says a great deal about you and your personal style.

ANNA'S INNER STYLE

Remember Anna, the woman who started life as an individualist but lost a part of herself because it felt easier and less painful to conform? As Anna established her assets in this session, she made several important discoveries.

It had been fairly easy for Anna to establish her physical assets in Session 3. Now it was important for her to identify her hidden inner assets, so that she could start rebuilding her confidence. Anna's inner assets included a good sense of humor, excellent listening skills, and an ability to call upon her inner strength. She was everybody's favorite friend; a good problem solver; quick, empathetic, and thoughtful; and able to express her creativity in different ways. Through the writing exercises in earlier sessions, she was beginning to remember things about herself that she used to enjoy. She was reacquainting herself with her individuality. With the benefit of hindsight and maturity, she was able to reignite her flame of creativity. This process was becoming exciting for her.

Anna's Personal Style Statement was: **"My personal style exudes quality and individuality."**

Quality was certainly represented in Anna's inner assets by the kind of person she was and by the way she behaved in the world. She was beginning to rediscover her individuality as well. This Personal Style Statement truly fit its owner. She would now begin to work on how to manifest these qualities in her tastes and her wardrobe.

To give you a little preview, Anna gradually began to incorporate into her wardrobe items that resonated with her specific tastes. She did this with subtlety, using the good taste she already had. As we have seen, she found a pair of fabulous 1930s sunglasses that looked as if they had been made for her. She revamped one of her very-good-quality but conservative black suits by adding accessories that totally changed its look and made it unique. An excellent-quality ivory-colored, pure silk mock turtleneck looked sleek under the jacket and enhanced her exotic skin tone. An antique lace handkerchief and a pair of very-good-quality, Italian-made, man-style shoes spoke of her individuality and pleased her specific taste, as did a wider-than-average black leather belt fitted with an unusual buckle that she found tucked away, forgotten, in her drawer. Not only did Anna regain her individuality, she once again became self-reliant, which boosted her confidence and self-esteem.

WILLIAM'S INNER STYLE

William's Personal Style Statement, if you recall, was **"I make an elegant and sophisticated impression."** When it came time for William to delve into his inner style, he participated with sincerity and honesty, but he was very hard on himself. He admitted to very few assets, and his list of things he wanted to work on consisted of more items than anyone could be expected to take on. This behavior was reminiscent of the work ethic demanded of him as a child by his parents.

We encouraged William to reduce his "to do" list. That way he could transcend his expectations of himself rather than constantly chase after perfection.

WILLIAM'S INNER STYLE INVENTORY

- William's overall outlook is optimistic.
- He can see how his attitudes are sometimes "stubborn."
- He admires Tiger Woods's ability to achieve excellence. He thinks Tiger Woods is a go-getter with a great attitude.
- His self-esteem varies greatly; he labels it "shaky."
- His wife and children receive empathy and compassion from a real and warm place within him, but he admits that he struggles to achieve it in business. And it is practically nonexistent with people he does not know personally.
- What he lacks in other areas, he makes up for in patience. He is very patient with most people and situations, such as standing in line or driving in traffic.
- He has a good sense of humor but uses it sparingly.
- He is well educated and articulate. He is a good and entertaining storyteller. He is soft-spoken, and his voice is relaxed and informal, with a nice, melodic rhythm.
- He thinks it is unmanly to show emotions.
- He admits to laziness when it comes to manners and etiquette.
- He spends a significant amount of time behind his desk and says that he is comfortable there. The desk represents a boundary line; it keeps things impersonal. His hellos and good-byes are good; he is not comfortable with the "in between."

We asked William to list his inner assets.

WILLIAM'S INNER STYLE ASSETS

- Optimistic outlook
- Charming communicator
- Good sense of humor
- Mentally adroit
- Generous
- Forgiving
- Patient
- Honest
- Humble

After compiling these lists, we asked William to look again at his Personal Style Statement: **"I make an elegant and sophisticated impression."**

Did he still feel connected to it? Was he still comfortable with it? Did anything stand out as being relevant for him to work on right away?

William asked us how he could develop an elegant inner style. We answered him in the same way we would answer anyone. If you look at your Inner Style Inventory and if you have been as honest and as detailed as you can be, the answers will be there.

When William looked at his inventory, he decided on several things he could do to develop a more elegant and sophisticated inner style:

- Work on his stubbornness and his attitudes
- Work on becoming a more compassionate person
- Work on his manners and etiquette
- Make an effort to engage and to be more forthcoming with people

William knew that any improvements he made in these areas would act as a strong foundation for his outer image desires.

MARY'S INNER STYLE

Did you find it difficult to reveal (even to yourself) the ingredients of your inner style? Is it possible that you censored a few pats on the back? Did you dig deep enough to discover your assets? Were you as honest as you could be about your human frailties?

Like many people, Mary found it difficult to see herself both as how she thinks she is and as others see her. But the attempt to do so resulted in healthy and revelatory questioning: *Am I really an honest person? Is being on time considered an inner asset? How patient is patient?*

Be kind to yourself. If we were with you in person, we would monitor your openness and help you widen your vision of yourself. We encouraged Mary to do this, and it made a big difference as she excavated her inner style.

We found Mary to be abundantly blessed with inner style assets. But what would she see in her own inventory of her inner style?

What would she list as her assets? The difference between our inventory of Mary and her own is striking.

OUR INVENTORY OF MARY

- Mary has an endearing smile.
- She is warm and genuine.
- She is gracious in both her manner and her behavior.
- Verbally she is clear and has a way of speaking that is open and friendly.
- Her voice is smooth, rich, and strong.
- She has a quiet enthusiasm.
- She is sincere.
- Her most prevailing attitude is determination.
- She has a sunny, delightful disposition.
- She is good company.
- She is inquisitive and has an ability and strong desire to learn.
- She is courageous.
- Her body language doesn't communicate how spirited she is. She desires freedom of movement.
- Her physical communication portrays someone who sometimes "disappears."
- She is philanthropic.
- Her icons—Grace Kelly, Mother Teresa, and Audrey Hepburn—also represent her attitude and behavior goals. She is very connected to the qualities in these women. The words she used to describe them are relevant to her—*grace, dignity, elegance, meaning,* and *sophistication.*

OUR LIST OF MARY'S ASSETS

Mary had many assets. The following represent the core of her inner style:

- Gracious
- Warm and genuine
- Quiet enthusiasm
- Sincere
- Determined
- Good company, nice to be around
- Courageous
- Inquisitive

MARY'S INNER STYLE INVENTORY

- My attitudes toward my children and my husband are good and positive; my attitudes toward myself are on the negative side.
- I often struggle at the beginning of my day, especially when I get dressed.
- I find it easy to give to others, but I am not a good receiver.
- I wish I could own more of the qualities that I admire in my icons, particularly dignity and sophistication.
- I know how to empathize.
- I am generous, loving, and reliable with my family but less so with myself.
- I am an honest person.
- I think my voice is barely passable and would love to speak more slowly.
- I don't have a vocal style.
- I have to work hard at making eye contact and shaking hands.
- I consider myself a spiritual person.
- I am nervous about getting attention but enjoy it when I do get it.
- I know how to put on an air of confidence but feel intense fear.
- Even on a good day I am aware of my insecurities and work toward attaining higher self-esteem.

MARY'S LIST OF HER INNER ASSETS

- Empathetic
- Generous
- Honest
- Hardworking

Mary was being honest, but she had only touched the surface of who she is. She hadn't experienced any surge of emotion or any strong feelings when she wrote about herself. We urged her to take more time and keep digging until she came to something that evoked a feeling.

She realized and acknowledged that people like her. Her friends and acquaintances often said nice things about her, which gave her a warm feeling. She interpreted this to mean:

- I am friendly, easy to get along with, and loyal.
- I am a good listener.
- I am compassionate.

She looked again at her commitment to her spiritual growth and at her unrelenting desire for self-development and doing good. She didn't recognize her spiritual quest as being an inner asset or part of her inner style. Nor did she think of her desire to be of service as anything special. She found that she had underestimated these values and what they said about her.

Mary realized that she had come a long way from the poor little misfit to the woman she is now. She still had not acknowledged the substantial improvements she had made, but she was beginning to understand that her attitudes would have had to be incredibly positive to get her where she is today.

Her manners, her etiquette, and her communication had improved enormously over the years. She had earned the respect of her family, friends, and business acquaintances simply by being who she was. She was finally aware that she must be doing something right!

MARY'S ADDITIONAL INNER ASSETS

• I have a conscious awareness of my actions.
• I am a "people person": a good listener, compassionate, empathetic, and able to be selfless.
• I am always looking for positive outcomes to challenges and problems.
• I have a good smile.
• I am a philanthropist.

Mary felt very connected to her new assets and satisfied to know what made her special. Her inner style "workout" had given her confidence a boost. Now she was even more committed to discovering her personal style.

When Mary reviewed her Personal Style Statement—**"I project a substantial and meaningful presence"**—she told us she was considering adding the word *refined*. She still felt that *substantial* and *meaningful* were important and were connected to her inner style, but she also believed that refinement would smooth out the rough edges of her outward physical appearance. We agreed and were impressed that she desired to incorporate a new element that was intuitively right for her.

What is the lesson in Mary's inventory?

- Say more about yourself rather than less.
- Don't hold back; nothing is insignificant.
- Any thought is worth mentioning.
- Don't talk yourself out of your first thought, intuition, or feeling.
- There is no need to be rational.

Each and every person with whom we have worked has been fascinating, special, and extraordinary. Know that you are one of a kind, and that you are special. When you believe that, you will surmount all kinds of obstacles.

SESSION 5

The Aesthetic Field Trip

It's time to play! You have accomplished much in defining the most personal and intimate aspects of yourself. You have created a solid background for your own tapestry. Soon you will fill it in with the colors and patterns and textures of your liberated and authentic image.

Knowing your tastes and your aesthetic opinions is very important for discovering your personal style. Sometimes people think they love or are attracted to something but find themselves magnetically pulled toward the exact opposite. Many times the reason is that they are out of touch, or they are stuck in a comfortable habit or rut. The habit may actually no longer please them, but they may be unaware of their displeasure.

Such people need a change in scenery! And this is what our Aesthetic Field Trip will bring you. When you are in a new environment, something happens to you. All of your senses become heightened—even the air becomes somehow different. It really is very simple. When you travel to a new destination during a field trip, whether it is in another town or country, or just on a street around the corner, you will discover new things about yourself that you can use in your personal style.

One of our clients took a different route home from work, in an effort to break a visual pattern. Her eye was taken with a restaurant facade just a few city blocks from her home. She sat down alone at her table with new eyes and fell in love with the colors in the murals on the walls. The murals inspired her to find one of the loveliest scarves she had ever owned.

Another client, in London, developed a passion for all things French on her field trip to Paris. In this new environment, she observed the understated way that many of the women dressed. London has many sophisticated and understated women, but this client's eyes had grown accustomed to what was for her a workaday world.

In this session, you will choose an environment for your Aesthetic Field Trip. If you select it with thought and care, the experience will be refreshing, creative, and enlightening. While all of your senses will be alerted during this outing, your visual sense will be most affected. When you allow yourself to have visual treats, you will feast your eyes on your surroundings.

PLANNING THE FIELD TRIP

Think of the field trip as an investment in your creativity. You have a creative spirit within you that is waiting to express itself in your tastes and that is aligned with your Personal Style Statement. Taking this field trip will help you to understand and define your tastes. Its results will help you to become more clear about what is aesthetically pleasing to you and emotionally comfortable for you.

Because of the work you have done in the preceding sessions, you are now receptive and alert enough to make the most of this exercise. You are about to use your imagination and your creativity in a way that you may have not used it before.

By recognizing your tastes, you can add your own special touches to your personal style. Using your creativity takes your experience out of the realm of the intellectual and makes it more personally meaningful. Inspiration is fundamental to creating your personal style— and it comes from experiencing new and sometimes surprising things.

As you plan the field trip, keep in mind that this a fun, rejuvenating, and easy thing to do. It is not a chore! It is not hard work! Consider the field trip as a reward for having gotten half way through the work.

Make an appointment with yourself.
Ideally, giving yourself a whole day to do the trip would be fantastic. But less than half a day will just not work. Choose a time when you

have no other commitments, so that you will not be clock watching. You don't want to have any time pressure.

Go alone or with the right person.
It can be fun to take this trip with another person. But it is for your benefit; the other person must understand this. You will be deciding where to go and how long to stay; if you walk into a place and then want to leave immediately, you must have the freedom to do so. Again, you should be under no pressure to adjust to or think about anyone else's needs or desires this day. If your friend is working through this book too, you should take two separate field trips.

Choose a destination that you have not visited before.
Plan to travel to an area that you have never visited before, or not for a long time. If you live in a large city, it could be a different neighborhood. If you live in a small town, it could be another town, village, city, or even country! If you travel frequently for business, you may want to schedule a little extra time in a place you normally whiz through.

Choose a specific area, street, or place.
The types of places best suited for the trip are those that can focus and train your eye.

Here are some suggestions for places that have inspired and motivated our clients to develop and understand their tastes.

• **An art museum.** Any kind of art museum, be it modern, traditional, or specialized, is fine. If you have never been to an art museum and don't know where to find one, you can look in your local newspaper, call the Chamber of Commerce, or use the Internet to find one near you. By choosing a museum to visit, you have already begun your Aesthetic Field Trip.

• **An ethnic neighborhood.** These are wonderful places to experience the colors, food, fabrics, clothes, designs, furniture, art, and people of different cultures. Particular colors and fabrics of a certain culture may stand out and attract you: saffron cottons from India, red silks from Tibet, simple designs of Japanese clothing. Smells from the bakeries, restaurants, and homes of different cultures will wake up your senses, as will displays of food.

• **An "old" part of town.** In America, old is not really that old, but refurbished Main Streets and well-maintained "downtowns" from bygone eras are still interesting and different. In Europe and Asia cities contain well-known "old cities" that are unique as a culture within a culture.

• **A hip and happening area.** When you visit a neighborhood that is hip and happening, you are not going to try to be part of the "in" crowd. In fact, quite the reverse: you are just going to observe as if you were a tourist. What kinds of stores are there? What music is playing in the stores? The people, their attitudes, the way they communicate, and the way they look—what are they like? Even if you don't appreciate it, what makes this place hip and happening? How do you feel here? These places are precursors for what will eventually become mainstream and available at your local mall. Often you are seeing fashion in the making and what many designers consider "street." In the past these areas have included Carnaby Street and King's Road Chelsea in London; Saint Germaine and Le Quartier Marais in Paris; Via Brera in Milan; Soho in both London and New York; South Beach in Miami; and the meat district, Tribeca, and Harlem in Manhattan. These are a few of the better-known areas, but other places that are just as interesting and original are not far from you. They always have been, they always will be.

• **An up-market, high-end shopping area.** High-end shopping areas (which are not malls) are usually found in cities. Here you might go to an up-market gourmet food shop, a kitchen store, a lighting shop, a furniture store, or a beautiful stationery store. Look for the equivalent of these best-known "shopping streets": Via Montenapoleone in Milan, Rodeo Drive in Los Angeles, Bond Street in London, Fifth Avenue in New York, and the Champs Elysées in Paris. You'll have no trouble finding these areas—their close equivalents exist internationally and are vigorously promoted and advertised.

• **An antique shop.** Here you will find a variety of furniture, rugs, carpets, jewelry, clothing, fine art, sculpture, and home furnishing fabrics.

• **An art and photographic gallery.** This will be a different experience from a museum. Art galleries are often grouped in the same part of town, and you will be able to visit several in one after-noon. They are excellent places to discover your taste. The types of artwork and photography you see will be rich in variety.

• **A furniture shop.** Modern, antique, and even secondhand furniture stores are fine. You will see furniture from many different eras, designers, and countries—the possibilities are endless.

• **A home furnishings or fabric store.** These are wonderful places to explore your connection to colors, fabrics, and textures. What is new and interesting to you? Do you like simple, elegant designs? Or do you like ornate, highly colored, or very plain items? Do you prefer lightweight or heavy fabrics?

You may be wondering why there are no contemporary clothing stores on this list. It is too early for you to go to a clothing store. We really do understand how tempting this may be now. But you are still in the process of building your personal style. Visiting a clothing store before this process is finished will dilute your experience and act as a distraction. You need to stay on track. Trust us on this—a clothing store would disrupt the purpose of the field trip.

If you are unsure of where to go, review your Personal Style State-ment and your journal entries. Here you will find clues that are exclusive to you. For example, Mary, whose statement includes the words *substantial, meaningful,* and *refined,* will probably not go to a hip and happening area. A trendy area's transient nature is the reverse of what Mary desires for her image, which is more conserva-tive, classic, and reserved. Choose your destination carefully. Select an area or environment that you actually like. If you hate antiques, then do not choose an antique store. If a museum feels wrong, then choose another destination. But if you really want to do something extremely and outrageously different for you, don't let intimidation hold you back.

GUIDELINES FOR THE BEST TRIP

Adopt a positive attitude about the trip.

We've heard every possible excuse for not going on the field trip. The number-one excuse is not enough time. Sorry, but you *are* worth it—

please find the time. The real reason you might not want to go is that you might feel uncomfortable, insecure, or intimidated about going to an unfamiliar place. It is not uncommon to feel reticent about doing new things and venturing into unknown territory. But if you are interested in expanding your vision of yourself, it is essential to do so. In fact, feeling resistance is a sure sign that you need to go on this trip. By going, you will gain new insights that might surprise you.

Dress comfortably and appropriately.

Put some thought into what you will wear. You will want to be comfortable, but you are not going to a ball game or a movie. You're going to a public place, and you will probably be surrounded by beautiful things. If you make an effort with your appearance, you will feel more confident, and your confidence will encourage your creativity. Wear an item of clothing or use your favorite grooming method to encourage confidence and a feel-good factor. For some it will be a better-quality clothing item; for others, a good pair of shoes or a special trip to the hair salon.

Take your journal or a small notebook.

Write in your journal when you are inspired to do so, and when you are comfortable. There will be questions for you to answer when you arrive home, but you might want to record things that you could forget. You will benefit from noting anything that immediately jumps out at you. Record thoughts or feelings that seem important as well as those that keep coming up. Make notes about things you dislike, as well as those you love.

Once you arrive at your destination, roam.

Do nothing but walk around and let your eyes and your instincts lead the way. Do not shop—this is not a shopping excursion. Simply observe yourself and the way you respond to things visually. Touch things (unless you are in a museum), ask questions if appropriate, and spend as much time as you wish in areas or shops where you feel particularly comfortable.

If something is not working for you—an atmosphere, a person, music, anything—then leave immediately.

There is no reason for you to be uncomfortable. This is your treat. If you are not enjoying yourself, then leave. In a retail store, graciously telling a staff member that you are just looking should suffice. But glances from a snooty sales assistant or a feeling of pressure to do more than "just look" are signals that you should leave. If you walk into an art gallery or a fabric store and something about it doesn't feel right—perhaps the music is too loud, or there is chrome everywhere and you dislike chrome, or the lighting distracts you—don't stick it out; leave. Use the experience as a discriminatory learning tool. There is much to be learned from things you dislike—they are just as important as things you like. Be sure to write about those things.

If you are trying something that is really new for you, make sure you are prepared.

If you have never been to a museum before, you will observe that most people who visit are soft-spoken and well behaved. Museums generally have a special atmosphere that requires more respect and reverence than other places you might visit. Before setting out for your destination, find out what days and hours it is open—a whole shopping area may be closed on Sundays or Mondays. Find out about restaurants, coffee shops, and cafés before you go. You may need to get directions to make your journey easier.

Be open-minded, flexible, and willing to learn.

WHAT TO LOOK FOR

When you arrive at your destination, notice what you are drawn to.

Stay in the present, and notice if you become absorbed in what you are doing. If you feel comfortable and if it is appropriate, write about what pleases your eye. (You might not be able to do this until you take a break.) Be specific. Depending on where you are, describe what you like in detail.

Keep in mind that you may be drawn to a "part of a whole."

For example, if you are in an antique rug shop and you like only the border of a certain carpet, that's fine. Why do you like it? Do you love it? If you are in a furniture store and you just love the shape of a chair but nothing else about it, take note because you have made an emotional connection to something. The shape itself may be inspiring to you.

Keep in mind that your tastes may have changed.

Please take special note of this. If for ten years you only liked French country furniture and now you find yourself drawn to 1960s Scandinavian lightwood and metal-framed furniture, you may be a little surprised. It means you have moved on—and that is exactly what you are looking for: a conscious awareness that your taste has changed or broadened. It means you are receptive to something new and open to change.

Observe the people.

How do they look? How do they behave? What are their attitudes? Are they enjoying themselves?

Have plenty of patience with yourself.

There is no goal here. You do not have to accomplish anything except just be there and observe.

Resist buying anything!

If you are tempted to buy something, make a note of it. See if you still love it a week later.

Take a rest when you need to.

Eat lunch or dinner in this new area. Explore the cafés and coffee shops. Sit down for a while and write about what you have experienced. Please don't overdo it—when you feel tired, stop.

Enjoy yourself, and please wait until you get back home to finish reading this session.

HOW WAS YOUR TRIP?

After you have arrived home and have had a chance to assimilate the experience, please answer the following questions in your Personal Style Journal. They will help you to formulate your opinions and identify your tastes. Please transfer any other writings from your field trip into your journal at this time.

1. Were you engaged in the experience, or were you purely an observer? Did you feel the need to be entertained, or were you able to generate your own excitement?

2. Did you enjoy being in places where many objects were clustered in one area—for example, one wall with ten paintings, a furniture store crowded with furniture—or were you happier in an environment with one piece of sculpture occupying a vast space? In short, did you like crowded spaces or minimalist spaces?

3. Did you like quiet environments, or did you prefer the hustle and bustle of busy environments?

4. If you were in a retail space, did you notice the music? Did you like it? Did you prefer high-energy or calm and melodic sounds?

5. What about smells?

6. What objects, things, colors, or textures do you remember the most? What specifically has stayed with you?

7. Were you inspired by anything? If so, what and why?

8. Was there anything that you saw that you would like to learn more about? What is it? Why?

9. What did you dislike? Why?

10. What confirmed something you already knew about your taste?

11. What surprised you?

12. Did you learn anything about your preference for a particular era?

13. If you visited a neighborhood, were you able to soak up the atmosphere? What did you experience? Did anything in particular stay with you?

14. What were the people like in the places you visited? How did you feel about them? Was there anything memorable about them? How did they make you feel about yourself?

15. What is the most important thing you learned from your trip?

By now, you are used to reading about our clients' experiences, and you might be wondering how William's or Mary's tastes emerged in this session. We will share that with you later—for now, it is more important for you to immerse yourself in your own experiences. We do not wish to influence or distract you. You must choose your own destination and have your own observations. As we mentioned, one of our clients went to Paris, and another went a few blocks from where she lived. The intention is to find a different environment—no matter where it may be!

SESSION 6

The Spirit
of Clothes

The great and golden rule of art, as well as of life, is this: That the more distinct, sharp and wiry the bounding line, the more perfect the work of art; and the less keen and sharp, the greater the evidence of weak imitation, plagiarism and bungling.

—WILLIAM BLAKE

Your creative juices are flowing, your passions have been tapped, you are becoming acquainted with your inner style, and your Personal Style Statement has been made. You have learned about your body image and how you perceive yourself. You are discovering your tastes, both old and new.

We would like to take you in a new direction now. By this session our clients are ready and prepared for the natural progression into the practical world of clothing. And we are sure that you too are now ready to step into the "outer" world of your personal style. In this session, you will receive a unique education into the often closeted world of clothes.

We love clothes. We love all kinds of fabrics, from hand-loomed Indian silk to Scottish cashmere, from hand-dyed Irish linens to fine British tweeds. In our quest to learn more and to inspire our creative juices, we have visited some very unlikely venues. But the process has inspired us to create many new designs, color palettes, and even whole collections. Our visits to some of these unlikely venues became our own aesthetic field trips.

After a lot of traveling in Europe, North America, Asia, and the

Middle East, we felt a desire to explore more of our own backyard, which at the time was the British Isles. We decided that Scotland would be a new, different, and visually interesting part of the world to visit, not least because of its fascinating history, landscapes, and ancient ruins. We opted for the rugged coastline of the northern-most part of Scotland, the Isle of Lewis. We were aware that it would be very cold, but nothing could have prepared us for what we encountered.

When we arrived at what could barely be described as an airport, the wind was so forceful that we had to hold on to something firm for support. Our hosts, who met us with beaming smiles, looked uncommonly jovial and not in the least fazed by the inclement weather. They drove us to their hotel, a glorious seventeenth-century manse that they had been restoring. It was dark by then, and we were tired from the journey. When we awoke the following morning, we looked out the bedroom window and found that our room was perched on a cliff, almost hanging over the Atlantic Ocean.

Our host offered to drive us around that day, and as the conversation loosened up, he asked us what profession we were in. We explained that we were in the clothing business. To our amazement, he responded, "Really? What kind of clothes do you design? What kind of fabrics do you use?"

When we explained that our collections were exclusive both in design and fabric, he told us about a local weaver of tweeds whom he knew. Would we be interested in meeting with him? We didn't hesitate. As we drove along the perilous-looking roads, we glanced down at the huge waves crashing against the rocks.

Literally out in the middle of nowhere, we came to a crofter's cottage. It stood by itself on a cliff, with only storm clouds and the sea behind it. Upon entering, we were greeted by a towering Scotsman who was wearing a gray and black hairy tweed jacket, a colorful tweed scarf, and dark brown, soft corduroy trousers.

He escorted us through his kitchen into a one-room studio that contained only one item: his loom. It took up the entire room. We noticed a small window by his stool that looked out over the ocean. As he led us out, we imagined him sitting at it, solitary, weaving.

He then showed us into a storage room, where he picked up a rough-looking, undyed cone of yarn. By *rough*, we mean scraggly looking, hardly identifiable as yarn. He had purchased the yarn from the local wool traders. He explained that he would dye and treat the rough yarn. He opened a cabinet door, and we saw shelves and shelves full of multicolored yarn. Though still rough, it was now dyed every color imaginable, ranging from rich, muddy earthy tones to vibrant and dense hues. These yarns were later woven into sample swatches, which he would review. He sat us down with tea and biscuits and leisurely laid a multitude of fabric swatches before us. The swatches were small and loosely woven, so that we could clearly make out each thread that formed a swatch's final pattern. They were some of the most beautiful tweeds we'd ever come across.

Remarkably, our host, the weaver of these tweeds, was surprisingly familiar with landscapes other than his own; Bond Street in London, rue Saint-Honoré in Paris, and Fifth Avenue in New York. His fabrics had graced many international designers' collections. He was even familiar with our London shop and complimented us on the Malcolm Levene–designed wool chenille coat he had seen in a recent edition of British *Vogue*. As you can imagine, we were both very surprised. It was a serendipitous treat.

So there we were, between the roarings of the Atlantic Ocean and the rolling pastures around the craggy hills. We had stumbled upon a fortuitous combination of atmosphere and history. The weaver's exceptional commitment to quality and his uncompromising attention to detail and authenticity were unique. This was a perfect environment in which to create fabrics that evoked dramatic contrasts. It was a field trip that neither of us will ever forget.

This is the true culture and spirit of clothes—it just doesn't get any better. Here is where creativity meets culture and melds them to create a form of art that has commercial applications. We've seen scores of men and women, in the heat of the hottest August day, sweating to try on a tweed jacket from the new autumn collection—not because they are fashion victims or "have to get there first" people, but because they truly appreciate the spirit in which the tweed jacket was born. They will glance at it in their wardrobe, enjoying it for its own sake and looking forward to wearing it. They know that come the first cold autumn day, they will reach into their closet, delighted and excited to wear their fine new tweed jacket.

THE REAL WORLD

Sadly, the form of creativity that existed in the Scotsman's cottage is almost extinct. Very few artists and craftsmen are replacing the older generation. The weaver had no computer, no fax, not even call-waiting on his telephone. He was self-sufficient and content to create his fabrics without the buzz of activity around him. Although we met him over ten years ago, even then he lived and worked in a bygone era.

It is very expensive to produce fabrics that way, and it is not commercially viable for the huge corporations that manufacture jeans and other generic clothing items. As we lose the one-of-a-kind specialty shop, the already diminishing demand for the artisan decreases even more.

Fortunately, pockets of clothing-related craftspeople still exist throughout the world. Today, a tweed jacket produced with similar spirit, care, and quality might be found in the United States in a very up-market, high-profile department store or an exclusive boutique. Clothing made with a great deal of spirit is available in the capital cities of Europe. We relate this information to you not because we expect you to search for these special clothing items, but because they begin to give you a standard—a reference for quality.

Today designers, stores' buyers, and retailers buy versions of handcrafted clothing, albeit watered-down versions. The passion of the buyer or designer will determine how much of the original spirit of the garment is left.

The Savile Row suit, for example, has been undergoing a revival among both men and women for quite a while now. If the original Savile Row suit were to be made today to the exacting standards of highly trained and experienced craftsmen, it would cost between $4,000 and $6,000, affordable only by Sultans and other royals and by the very rich and famous. It would be made completely by hand. The fabrics would be of the finest quality and would include pure wool, pure cashmere, and pure silk. Any physical "imperfection" in its future owner would be taken into account and accommodated for. Several fittings would be required to achieve the perfect fit and level of comfort. In effect, you would be having a suit built specifically for you. You would be pampered and treated as if you were the only customer in the world—and in the period of time that you were there, you would be!

The $800-to-$1,500 version of the suit has a label that says Savile Row. It is made entirely by machine, not by hand. But it has elements of the spirit of the original—the fabrics, buttons, lining, and shape are very similar. The fit is usually good and comfortable but, of course, less personal. The more "average" your body shape, the more likely that it will feel comfortable on you. At this price range, if the suit does not feel comfortable and fit well, then you are paying for a label, not a suit. The fabrics are usually good quality, but not the best, and the design is current looking. When you touch this suit's jacket lapel, it should feel malleable but not soft. If it feels hard and unkind, then you are paying too much.

For $500 to $800 you can get a Savile Row–"looking" suit. Its only similarity will be its marketing. It will be marketed to get your attention. The suit itself might carry an impressive designer label. The fabric range will be very restricted—classic business fabrics such as wool worsteds and flannels in navy, gray, and black, maybe a pinstripe or a plaid. The linings and buttons will be more generic. You could very well be moving further and further away from the spirit of the original garment; but if you choose a retailer or designer who has the spirit of clothes at heart, you can still purchase a really wonderful suit.

For $500 or less, it is still possible to find a small element of the spirit of the original suit in certain shops on certain occasions. Mass-produced and treated with less care, the suit will be stiffer and feel less comfortable. It will not drape on your body or have the fluidity of a better-quality suit. The fabric will probably contain a synthetic mixed with wool. Less material will be available in the inseams, making alterations more difficult. The biggest sacrifice will be comfort. Where the better-quality suit literally slips over your shoulders and sits comfortably, needing no tugging and pulling to "put it in place," the lesser-quality suit will feel flimsy and stiff, and you will find yourself trying to make it conform to your body. For example, should the wind blow your jacket open, it will not return to your body immediately, and you may have to constantly adjust it. It will not slip comfortably over your shoulders; it will need some persuading to do so.

But a trained eye, a bit of research, and some savvy shopping will achieve a fine-looking suit even at this price range. The selection may be limited by comparison, but the rewards will make up for the effort.

This quality chain exists in every type of garment for both men and women, from T-shirts to overcoats. This is the multifaceted, complex world of clothes!

When your body has a positive physical relationship with your clothes it is because those clothes have a spirit with which you have connected.

This feeling, this relationship with your clothes will manifest as inner confidence, higher self-esteem, and a more positive self-image.

By habit, most people try on clothes while they are looking into the mirror of a dressing room. What happens is that before you have given yourself a chance to experience the feeling of the garment on your body, you are already making visual judgments. These visual judgments are often based on your emotions, how you are feeling that day, how you are feeling about your body that day, and so on. In that moment you are concerned with how you *look,* not with how you *feel*.

Suppose you were in a dressing room without mirrors, and someone brought you several jackets to try on. You would know immediately which were of better quality—not by sight, but by the way you feel and the way the jacket feels on you. This "feeling" is ease, comfort, and a sense of confidence that begins to percolate within you. It is not your vision of yourself in a mirror that creates this feeling, but the feel of the article of clothing itself. You are experiencing the spirit of clothes. You feel good, and you feel alive.

Once you have experienced a jacket that makes you feel alive and vibrant, you will have a frame of reference when you then try on the jackets of lesser quality. You will know the difference—not because someone tells you about it but because you can feel it. And the next time someone tries to sell you an article of clothing that doesn't feel good to you, even though it has a prestigious label and an expensive price tag, take it off and try something else.

Certainly clothes that are void of spirit can be livened up. This is exactly what happens when a lesser-quality clothing item is paired with a better-quality item. The spirit of the better-quality item enlivens the lesser-quality item, especially when the personal style of the wearer is defined and confident.

So unless you are able to spend very large amounts of money regularly, you always have to compromise quality. Some of your clothes will have more spirit than others.

INVESTMENT CLOTHING

Clothes that have spirit and that are of good quality are an investment. They are clothes you should be investing your money in, because they are the most important part of your wardrobe. These are your secure-making clothes, your safety valves. They increase your self-confidence, make you feel better about your body, and enable you to send out an image message that is positive. These secure-making clothing items are the backbone and building blocks of your wardrobe. You do not need many of them, as it is quality, not quantity, that is going to provide you with a strong foundation for your wardrobe. In addition, these clothing items have a personality that transcends fashion, and therefore they will never go out of style. They are designed and made to stand the test of time.

Let's start with some basics. At some time or other, you will have a need for certain clothing items that you can "fall back on." These items will be different for each of you, and later in this book you will begin to define exactly what they are. But right now we can tell you what some of the most common investment clothing items are. Some people refer to these items as "clothing essentials." Well, they are essential only if they are essential to you and your personal style. Nevertheless, the following is a short list of some of our clients' investment clothing items. Each item listed will be of very good to better quality.

- A pair of midweight wool pants
- Two or three pure cotton, current-looking shirts or blouses
- Two pairs of very-good-quality shoes
- Two leather belts
- A business/dressy suit
- A skirt and a dress
- Two sweaters or knitwear pieces
- Outerwear: a coat and a raincoat
- A casual jacket
- Ties (quantity as appropriate to your needs or wishes)

- Casual/weekend clothing items: perhaps a cashmere sweater, a leather jacket, or casual trousers

Pretty vague, yes? Of course it is—this is not a generic one-fits-all list. Your essentials can come only from you. It might just be that you need a great pair of jeans and that you should find the best quality available. Or perhaps you often attend charity events that call for dressy clothing items. Only you will know exactly which items should be worth the investment in a better quality than you are used to.

As you get closer to defining your personal style and making decisions about your investment items, there are specific things for you to be aware of. Any and all of these investment items will have several important commonalities:

All secure-making clothes have the same elements of quality, fit, and design.

Whether it is a jean jacket or a business suit, the elements that represent both spirit and quality are exactly the same. These are the principles that are universal to any clothing item that you deem to be part of the "backbone" of your wardrobe.

RECOGNIZING QUALITY

Your education about quality is simply about learning the differences between all the levels of quality that are on offer. Once you have this awareness, you automatically become a more discriminating shopper.

Probably you are not very interested in how many stitches to the inch a good quality shirt collar has, or the intricacies of how a clothing alteration is achieved. What you most likely do want is to be introduced to what quality *feels* like.

Trying on a great pair of pants for the first time in your life may well completely change your frame of reference and your appreciation of good quality. The trousers will flatter you, feel good, and fit well—and you will *know* they look good.

If you raise your level of quality even a half of a step in certain items, that alone will be enough to make a difference in your wardrobe.

We are suggesting that you eventually allocate a reasonable proportion of your clothing budget to a few good-quality clothing items. This will mean buying less quantity and more quality. Even if you start with one item—perhaps a shirt or a pair of pants—you will begin to experience a different relationship with your clothing. You will respond better to your clothing both physically and emotionally. You will introduce yourself to a new habit, a habit that unequivocally states that you are worth a little more investment.

If investing your money in good-quality, better-designed clothing is inappropriate for you right now, you can still make better decisions about the clothes you do buy next. By paying attention to quality and design, you will be better able to detect the best that is on offer in your price range.

For example, no matter what store you are in, it will always offer clothing items of different quality. Even if they are at the same or similar price level, the quality will vary. Always enter a clothing store with the intention of buying the best quality available at a price you can afford. Don't just buy "something"—take off the blinkers by learning to recognize quality. Don't blindly reach for any old white T-shirt— look for the best in your price range. Try them all on if need be. Remember, you are worth it!

TEN EASY TIPS FOR RECOGNIZING GOOD QUALITY

1. When you first see a quality garment on the hanger, it looks "beautifully finished." It will have no creases or folds from lying in the box it was shipped in or from being cramped on a rack.

2. A quality garment will drape, or flow down from the hanger. It should not look stiff or unfriendly. Even a conservative suit should drape.

3. Good-quality knitwear will spring back to life when it is scrunched. It will look beautifully finished and will have no loose threads. Its body, sleeves, and neckline will not be misshaped.

4. A shirt collar should be malleable yet crisp. It should look fresh and defined without being stiff. The points should sit on your collarbone (if you are trying on the correct collar size); the further they move from your collarbone, the less quality you are wearing.

5. The more stitches per inch on the outside of a collar, the better the quality.

6. The body of a good-quality shirt should rest over your shoulders, not stand away from your shoulders.

7. Buttons should be made of a good-quality material, such as pearl, wood, or horn. Flat and weighty metals are preferable to shiny and flimsy ones.

8. The cuffs should not be too stiff. They should not have the cardboard feeling of generic French-cuff dress shirts.

9. When you try on a good-quality garment, its feeling should be friendly and kind, yet you should also be able to feel the "guts" of the garment. It should feel substantial.

10. Even if the garment is not your size, style, or color, it will still feel and look surprisingly good on you.

GOOD-QUALITY FABRICS

Good clothing design begins and ends with fabric. Almost every country in the world produces some kind of fabric, from the far reaches of Peru to the mountain ranges of Switzerland. Some countries are renowned for producing the very best fabrics, and others are known for their specialty fabrics.

Generally speaking some of the best fabrics come from Italy, Britain, and Scotland. Equally good, sturdy fabrics come from Germany, while Swiss cotton shirting is much sought after by the best shirt manufacturers. Delicate Irish linens and colorful tweeds still boast the best in quality and design. Spain produces very good-quality classic wools and cottons. In North America, the Carolinas produce beautiful specialty cotton, and the gorgeous silks from Asia are well-known. Novelty fabrics from Japan, such as creased cottons, techno fabrics, and shirting cotton, are also desirable.

If the garment bears the label of the fabric manufacturer—in addition to the designer's label—it is often a sign of a superior-quality fabric.

RECOGNIZING GOOD-QUALITY FABRIC

What does a good-quality fabric look like? What does it feel like, and how does it behave?

Comfort and Feel-Ability

A good-quality fabric is sensual to the touch. Donegal tweed is crunchy. Pure cashmere is for stroking and petting. Pure silk is a fabric that you love to have right next to your skin. These fabrics are all made of natural, breathable fibers. They have the "spirit" and "aliveness" that we speak about. They are comfortable, either because of their solid, secure sturdiness or their soothing, cushioning coziness. The best way to explore fabric is to touch it with your fingers. How does it feel next to your skin? You are looking for comfort. (Unless you have decided to forgo comfort for other reasons. Women know about this only too well! Those beautiful woolly sweaters look luxurious but begin to itch after an hour's wear!)

Ease of Movement and Fluidity

A good fabric moves with your body. It makes your physical expression easier for you and easier on the eyes of others. It has less rigidity, like a "second skin." You feel more flexible, both physically and mentally. When you take your jacket off and hang it on the back of a chair, the jacket drapes, just as it did on the hanger. Even in the pants or skirt of the suit, you still appear substantial because the fluidity of movement continues with the drape of the material on your body.

Recovery

How well and how quickly a fabric recovers from a day at work, play, or just sitting around depends on its quality. A good-quality fabric will recover overnight from a long journey, from being tightly packed, or from being worn for several hours. Any creases will appear soft and acceptable, as if they were caused by normal wear. Acceptable creases from your normal daily-life activities, such as in the back of the knee from sitting or at the elbow from writing, are familiar and hardly noticeable.

Staying Power and Durability

Good-quality fabric enhances the longevity of a garment. Almost as if the fabric has a memory, it withstands cleaning and pressing, inclement weather, and a certain degree of carelessness. The garment holds its shape better and longer. When you are too tired to hang up your clothes properly in the evening, good-quality fabrics keep the garment fresh.

Good-quality fabrics have staying power from one fashion trend to the next. The better-quality the fabric, the more likely the garment will remain in style. In fact, good-quality fabric will allow you to get away with a less current-looking item of clothing. The reason is that the eye is drawn to the fabric, be it leather, wool, cotton, or any other good-quality fabric.

The Third Dimension

A good-quality fabric has a depth and a spring to it. It almost jumps out at you. It can be soft and smooth and at the same time richly textured. When you rub it between your forefinger and thumb, it almost ripples. Making an emotional connection to these kinds of fabrics is very easy, no matter what your personal style is! Good-quality fabrics are expensive, but where lesser-quality garments are in the garbage after two years, those of best-quality fabric, if well taken care of, will be beautifully wearable for at least four years.

EXAMPLES OF GOOD-QUALITY FABRICS

New fabrics come and go. There will always be passing fads for fashionable fabrics. In the 1990s, designers used state-of-the-art techniques for weaving and new and unusual synthetics to create a highly contemporary look. One of the biggest fabric revolution of the 1990s was stretch. Everyone was "stretching," from the chic boutiques to the most basic clothing retailers. Stretch fabrics are fun, interesting, and original, and sometimes they are cheap and cheerful, but ultimately they will have a shorter life.

Here, then, are the fabrics that have been around longer than any of us and will continue to be around long after we are gone.

Wool crepe	Silk
Wool hopsack	Silk and cashmere mix
Wool twill	Silk and wool mix
Wool gabardine	Silk and wool tweed mix
Superfine wool worsted	Cotton gabardine
Wool flannel	Cotton and linen mix
Vicuña	Cotton and silk mix
Cashmere	Cotton poplin
Cashmere and wool mix	Two-fold cotton poplins

Sea Island cotton   Pure merino wool
Pure Irish linen   Angora
Italian linen   Mohair

GOOD FIT

A tailor and a client are standing in front of a mirror. The tailor is working on the customer's jacket. He asks his client, "How does it feel, sir?" This question raises the single most important aspect about a garment's fit: the way it feels.

For its wearer, the fit of any garment can make the difference between feeling comfortable and confident and feeling uncomfortable and unconfident. A good fit can sometimes compensate for less-than-good design, while a bad fit can detract even from beautiful design. Let's take the dress that Gwyneth Paltrow wore at the 1999 Academy Awards ceremony. The design was very good, the fabric was superb, and the quality of manufacture was second to none. But the fit was far from good—the bustline of the dress was too full, and therefore it was unflattering to Paltrow. It was distracting. If you actually saw the broadcast, did you notice that your eyes were glued to the bodice of the dress? It was hard not to be fixated on the less-than-perfect fit. This is the nature of fit: it can make or break any article of clothing.

Retailers, custom tailors, and alteration tailors often say that a good fit "sits well." If they say, "This jacket sits very well," for example, they mean that the garment is almost "hugging" the person in the most important places—the neck, the shoulders, the chest, and the upper back. This kind of description is usually reserved for formally tailored garments, but we firmly believe that a good fit on almost any clothing item that isn't strictly beach-related or sports-oriented or reserved for gardening should "sit well."

RECOGNIZING A GOOD FIT

• A good fit is one in which your body makes contact with a garment in a way that does not feel intrusive or flimsy. The garment should touch you in such a way that it feels as though it is a part of you.

• One of the most effective ways to ascertain whether a garment fits you well is to be aware, from the moment you try it on, of how your body responds to it—or doesn't. Don't become emotionally attached to a garment that does not fit well. Don't talk yourself into buying something because you like the color or the price tag!

• A good fit can change the way you hold your body. For instance, if your jacket fits high and snug under your arm, as it should, you will achieve a look that appears more defined, and you will probably stand with your chest slightly more pronounced.

• If a shirt or blouse stands away from your neck, it doesn't fit. If the lapel of your jacket is either caving in or billowing out, it doesn't fit.

• Trust yourself. When you find yourself in a dressing room, become aware of when you feel good. Move around in the garment. Raise your arms, sit down, walk, and return to the question "How do I feel?"

WEIGHT LOSS OR GAIN

If you are having difficulty finding garments that fit you well, the reason may be that you have lost or gained weight recently. Or perhaps your body shape changed for other reasons, such as exercise, which can give you a new toned, muscular body. If so, you may be trying to make yourself fit into a smaller or larger size than you now need.

When people have lost weight, their image of themselves sometimes lags behind their new body shape. Instead of wearing new, flattering clothes, they still cover up their bodies with oversized clothes; they are still in hiding. They might wear too much fabric around the hips, or clothes with a less defined waistline and long sleeves; the shoulders of their garments might be too big, or the skirt may be overly long and full. If this sounds like you, try to get a sense of proper-fitting clothes by experimenting with one or two items. We are not encouraging you to parade your body or to be more extroverted in any way; we simply suggest that you begin to reeducate yourself about what is a good fit for your body shape. But don't overcompensate, either, by buying clothes that fit too tightly. Everything you have achieved in regard to your weight loss will be spoiled by a bad fit.

If you are heavier than you'd like to be, do not buy clothes that fit tightly. *We are not suggesting that you camouflage yourself with loose-fitting, baggy clothes.* We are saying, rather, that you need freedom of movement. Your clothes should have contact with your body, but in no way should they be snug. We cannot tell you exactly what styles and cuts to look for. Many books that do that disappoint their readers because the recommendations do not work for them. You must learn what cuts and shapes flatter you. No one is physically identical to anyone else. Some heavier body shapes can easily wear a style that other heavier body shapes cannot. But please remember this: the better the quality of the clothes you buy, the more flattering they will be and the better they will fit. You must experiment and develop more intimate knowledge of your body. This will help you tremendously with fit.

The one-size-fits-all era is over. Now that our society is more body conscious, the whole "fit culture" has changed dramatically. Clothes have become more defined in the way they fit; the emphasis is on showing the body, not on trying to cover it. Yet a good fit is never challenged by fashion or trends—it is perennial and always in style. Expensive designer clothes are not a prerequisite for great style, but well-made clothes in quality fabrics do produce a better fit. Your body shape may change, or the style of a garment may become out of date, but if the basic fit is good and the style and fabric are of good quality, it can be altered to accommodate your new needs.

GOOD DESIGN

Good quality design does not necessarily mean "designer clothes."

An expensive designer item is not necessarily well designed and does not always represent the best quality.

Many of the most beautiful clothes in the world are made by very high-profile designers, and the world of clothing design is all the better because of them. But when you learn to select well-designed, good-quality garments, then you will be investing in clothes—not in a label or a logo.

Good design changes only subtly. A suit is a suit is a suit. Good design can be fashionable, but it does not necessarily have to be so.

Good design has its very own spirit. It emanates from the designer's vision and from attention to every detail, no matter how small. When a costume designer creates a character's clothes for a movie, the design significantly contributes to the actor's portrayal of that character. The actor becomes better connected to the role if the clothes are designed well and if all of the details are in place. Many times the smallest detail is a key facet of the character's personality. For example, the unique television character Inspector Morse is by day a top-notch detective and in the evening a very aesthetic, cultured human being with a fine appreciation of the arts. When he arrives home, he changes into a pure silk, handmade dressing gown, in design chosen specifically for his personality. The dressing gown is in keeping with his refined sensibilities, as he settles down to listen to his favorite opera and sips an aperitif.

Good design is part of the essential mix that will encourage *your* character to come to life. If you look in your wardrobe today and are able to find any clothing items that you bought three years ago that still look good on you, you were fortunate to have purchased good design. One of the hallmarks of good design is practicality. If a zipper or a button doesn't have a practical application, the garment is not well designed. If the garment has any superfluous embellishments that exist only for show, then design has been compromised. The only attention that good design brings is to the wearer, not to the clothes themselves.

The essence of good design is a passion for understatement. (Certainly good designers do sometimes create garments that are far from understated, even "over the top." But these kinds of clothes are reserved for very special occasions and are not the kind of clothes we are talking about here.) Understated clothes are the epitome of sophistication; they can travel anywhere in the world and always appear appropriate. They can be enigmatic, appealing, and even intelligently witty. They possess much more than meets the eye. Their inherent purity of design and their attention to practical details make them special.

Well-designed clothes are designed with you the customer first and foremost in mind. Your lifestyle, tastes, sensibilities, and personality will all come into play and somehow be integrated into good design.

The old cliché image of a "fashion designer" usually conjures up a prima donna artiste who is precocious, temperamental, and somewhat hysterical. But many, many good designers have nothing to do with this stereotype.

A good designer knows about people, especially his or her customers. He is perpetually curious and is willing and eager to learn. He knows how his customers live, what their passions are, and where they are vulnerable. He respects them and their opinions. If a customer remarks in passing that she dislikes shiny velvet, the designer will hear it, understand it, and relate it to his own taste, talent, and judgment. For the next collection, he may use flat velvet instead of shiny velvet. The designer's customers are his partners—and his unknowing collaborators.

WHAT IS GOOD DESIGN?

Good design has *clarity, purity, and simplicity of form.*

Before you read another word—how do you feel about those three words?

Did you automatically jump to conclusions about them? Many of our clients do. They exclaim that they don't want to be simple, and that clarity and purity have nothing to do with their passions, their Personal Style Statement, or their personality. *But good design has everything to do with your personality.* It means using your clothes as a backdrop for your personality to come through. A few simple guidelines about good design will give you a framework for projecting your personality.

Lyle Lovett is a perfect example of someone who uses good design to project his interesting and unusual personality. Lyle has taught himself to recognize well-designed clothes and uses his knowledge to choose clothes that enhance his personality and his uniqueness. Although he has a vast wardrobe, every item is selected primarily because of its design. He chooses only clothes that flatter, never distract, and have longevity. Whether he is wearing a leather motorcycle jacket or a suit for a concert, it is Lyle's personality that you experience, not his clothes.

Whether you are aware of it or not, you already know what good design is.

When customers came into our shop, we did not expect them to know anything at all about good design. Yet 90 percent of them could differentiate between a garment that was designed with clarity, purity, and simplicity and one that was not. They were even able to distinguish an imbalance in the smallest detail. At first, they did not know exactly which detail; they only knew that something didn't feel right because it didn't please their eye. But when we gave them the tools to make them consciously aware of what they already knew, they quickly tapped into their own innate sense of aesthetics.

The tools they learned to use were the following simple questions. One of our clients, Tony, showed us a jacket that he loved but never wore. He wasn't sure what he didn't like about it, but he didn't want to make the same mistake again.

TONY: There's something about this jacket that I don't like.

K&M: What is it that you don't like about it?

TONY: I don't know.

K&M: Is it the way it fits?

TONY: No, I like the way it fits.

K&M: Is it the fabric?

TONY: No.

K&M: Is it the color?

TONY: No, I love the color.

K&M: Is it the position of the pockets?

TONY: The pockets are fine.

K&M: Is it the lining or the buttons?

TONY: No.

K&M: Is it the lapel?

TONY: Yes, I think it might be that.

K&M: Do you like the shape of the lapel?

TONY: I'm not sure.

K&M: Is it too wide?

TONY: No.

K&M: Is the space between the collar and the lapel too wide?

TONY: *Yes!* That's what it is!

K&M: Well, you have a good eye. There is an imbalance between the shape of the jacket collar and the lapel.

TONY: When I put the jacket on and looked in the mirror, I sensed a visual discomfort in that area. I couldn't put my finger on it. I'd take it off and put it back on again, or I'd change the shirt or tie, but I couldn't make it work. I would almost get in a bad mood about it. But now that I really look at that area I can see what I don't like. Would that small detail really make me so uncomfortable?

K&M: Yes, absolutely.

Tony didn't recognize immediately what he didn't like about the jacket. But once he was given a method of discovery—an elimination process—he was able to identify and articulate what his eye knew: the jacket had an imbalance. The purity of line was broken at the lapel. The lapel line is often what makes or breaks a jacket. Tony didn't know how crucial his discovery was—and he didn't need to know. But lo and behold, there he was reaffirming his ability to discriminate good design. It took all of two minutes.

PURITY AND CLARITY

A well-designed garment is one that has been made with the fundamental element of purity of line. Pure lines are those free of anything extraneous or inappropriate. Achieving purity and simplicity is actually the most labor-intensive effort that any designer undertakes. It entails strong discipline, extreme focus, patience, determination, and passion. It requires a forceful, no-holds-barred vision coupled with a flexibility and openness to anything that will provide improvement.

At the former Malcolm Levene shop, no matter what the current trend or the era might have been, we always offered a clutch of clothing items that represented pure lines. These might have included a plain black cotton shirt with no visible stitching on the collar. Or a cashmere sweater without a clinging waistband and with a "clean" unstitched neckline. Or maybe a suit whose jacket pockets were "invisibly" inserted into the side seams.

A clothing item that is designed with pure lines will outshine and outlast any "trendy" garment because it will allow you, the wearer, to convey the most important aspect of your image. No matter your size, shape, lifestyle, or current wardrobe, you will always feel and be seen as being well turned out, a person of style, if your clothes embody purity of design.

A garment that hides imperfections with embellishments or whose minute details have not been finished properly is not of good design. A garment of pure and clear design never hides anything; nor does it hide behind anything. A well-designed garment must embody purity and simplicity so that it reveals an image of clarity. The object of this purity is to expose and express your personality, uniqueness, confidence, self-assuredness, and reliability. You can truly achieve this only when you allow not only your outer sense of style to come through but your inner style as well.

Purity and simplicity of design become a testament not just to the designer but to you the wearer. Well-designed clothes have a chameleonlike quality and are infinitely flexible. Even though they may be seasonal, they do not project a specific "fashion season." They are adaptable and fit into your wardrobe easily, comfortably, and appropriately. The great advantage of good design is that you can dress it up or down. You can add special items to create an overall look of your own: by adding an unusual pair of shoes to a suit, a beautiful silk shawl to a summer dress, or an antique bag to a sweater and pants.

Everything we are talking about here is a part of a whole. Good design will allow you to experience a wonderful garment and enjoy clothes. Clothes are much more than just things that go on your back: they are the closest objects to our body. It is very important that we understand them and give them the respect that they deserve. They in turn will earn you the respect that you deserve.

THE LOWDOWN ON LOGO

When Louis Vuitton designed his now–incredibly famous luggage in the late nineteenth century, he made it first and foremost of excellent quality, as well as practical and attractive. Then he added the initials of his name, so people would be able to distinguish his luggage. It was a clever marketing tool, combined with his purity of design. Vuitton was the only person using this marketing tool in that period.

What Vuitton conceived and executed as a wonderfully practical and pure addition to his product has since been manipulated into a logo-driven sales tool. Logos now overshadow products. People now buy Louis Vuitton items for their prestige value rather than for their quality. An item with a prestigious logo, whatever it is, whether you like it or not, sends the message "I can afford this; I am a member of this logo club."

One of the reasons our retail customers were so loyal, consistent, and frequent in their patronage was that the Malcolm Levene logo was never found on the outside of a garment. Customers were relieved and delighted, especially in the 1980s, at the height of the insatiable appetite for logos, that all of the emphasis was on the quality and design of the clothes.

The success of Malcolm Levene clothing was founded on the fact that every garment had its own unique characteristic, whether it was an unusual lining that came from an almost-extinct fabric manufactured in the north of England or hand-carved buttons from Santa Fe. The responsibility of the Malcolm Levene label was to always express uniqueness coupled with simplicity.

The added bonus about well-designed clothes is that they can be tailored with greater ease than most other clothes. For instance, if you lose or gain weight, or if the style is less current looking than you would like, any good alteration person would be able to reinvent the item for you.

That is not to say that there were no "fun" or "quirky" things in the collection—there were, like a paisley velvet smoking jacket that was a great conversation piece and straw boaters dyed in different colors, made by Maurice Chevalier's original milliner. Those kinds of items were intended to get the customers' attention. In fact, they often were what brought customers into the shop, if only out of curiosity.

The loyalty of our customers was instigated by their "relationship" with our brand. Having the right clothes, the right prices, the right environment, and excellent professional service was what created that relationship.

The following is a list of what we consider to be extraneous, distracting, and inappropriate additions to clothing *as they relate to good design*. This list is not a judgment, an opinion, or a criticism—it is forty years of experience in creating and developing the kinds of clothes that help people's personalities come to life.

THE LIST: EXTRANEOUS ADDITIONS

1. Stitch details that have no practical reason for being. Generally they are used to cover inferior-quality manufacturing.
2. Epaulettes (except on uniforms)
3. Printed or embroidered logos
4. Suede and leather elbow patches
5. Nonworking buttons
6. Hoods attached to sweaters that are not sports clothing items
7. Fake fastenings that do not work, such as buckles on shoes
8. Pockets or pocket flaps that have no function and are for show only

9. Elastic or belted side adjusters on waistbands in addition to belt loops

10. Mock wooden or fake metal buttons

11. Oversized anything—pockets on pants, shoulder pads, buttons, or zippers

12. Inappropriately and overly adorned clothing items (like mock jewelry on sweaters, sequins on T-shirts, fringe)

13. Any pleat that does not provide freedom of movement

14. Additional shoulder pads

Everybody has items in their wardrobe that have at least one of the items on this list. This is very, very normal. You, the consumer, are cajoled, enticed, tempted, and bombarded with marketing for items that are overly adorned and that scream at you to buy them. You become emotionally seduced by an item of clothing that looks pretty or unusual or "busy." We are not asking you to do anything right now other than to be aware of what you feel and think about this idea.

The items on the list are not the best way to reveal your personal style. Epaulettes don't reveal anything about your personality. Oversized pockets don't project your creativity. A logo does not raise your self-esteem.

You will be less likely to make expensive mistakes in buying clothes if you put quality first and foremost. Make sure that the label is not taking advantage of you.

Don't be seduced by glamorous, expensive marketing or glossy advertising. You may still purchase a high-profile designer item, but insure that it is of good quality and good design before you do so.

THE BEST QUALITY AT YOUR PRICE LEVEL

It is perfectly understandable that some of you may never choose to buy even one item of high-quality designed clothing. Maybe you live in an area that doesn't offer this kind of selection, or maybe that is not where your priorities lie. But you still must someday buy new clothes. And when you do, you will gain an immeasurable amount of value by searching for the better-conceived, better-designed items that are on offer. Even in well-priced, fashionable yet generic, clothing stores, you will find different levels of quality amongst their standard-issue T-shirts. Some garments in these stores are made of better-quality fabric than others. Some items fit better and are better constructed. They will be better finished and have a "cleaner" look. Even the dye will have more depth and richness. Some possess more spirit than others. But you have to look for these items, feel the fabrics, and try them on. They might even be hanging right next to each other.

TRENDY, FASHIONABLE, AND CURRENT: KNOWING THE DIFFERENCE

TRENDY

It's easy to be trendy. Trendy clothes can be found anywhere, at any price level and at any quality level. They may come to your town long after they have left the larger fashion centers, but you can be sure that they will arrive. Trendy clothes are disposable, entertaining, and even visually arresting. They celebrate the young. They use the low-price items to begin to form and experiment with their developing identities. Trendy clothes are what parents don't understand but teenagers must have. Teens want to be different and don't want their parents to understand them—they are beginning to cut the ties, and they use clothes to do it. They also use clothes as a way of communicating to each other. Cliques, coded messages, clubs, and friendships are formed, and they are signaled by trendy clothing statements.

Initially, trendy clothes make heads turn, but then the market becomes saturated with them and the young and restless become bored and must move on to something else—the next trend.

Trendy is only about the clothes, while being current enhances and projects personality.

Most people have an insatiable appetite to look younger than they are, and we all want to look our best. But when adults wear trendy clothing, they must do so carefully. How you wear it, and how much of it you wear, makes all the difference. For instance, if you just love the newest 1970s revival halter-top or Clarks desert boots, you must first decide whether you have the body, lifestyle, and personality to carry them off. If you buy trendy clothes without considering how they relate to your taste and your true self-image, you will probably end up looking and feeling disconnected from your clothes.

FASHION

Fashion is directed toward men and women enjoy the outward influence that fashion brings. It announces and identifies you as a person of "fashion." There are numerous categories of people who are associated with high fashion; here are a few of them. We are not condoning or promoting any of them; we are merely offering you the information, in the hope that it will enlighten you.

He's sitting on the Paris Metro on his way to the boulevard Saint-Germain, one of the fashion centers of Paris. He wears black, hip-hugging, very-high-fashion, designer-labeled, stretch techno fabric trousers. His black military-style belt carries the initials of its maker on the brushed-steel buckle. His perfectly-worked-out upper body (not too big, not too small!) is clad in a black, very-high-quality, cotton-stretch, 1970s-styled, short-sleeve, tight-fitting shirt. His shiny black, flat fronted, wide-toed, high-fashion shoes-of-the-moment are a perfect complement to the very narrow trouser bottoms that just graze his shoes.

In Tokyo his doppelgänger sits on the bullet train heading toward the Ginza; another heads toward Covent Garden in London, and yet another is in a Manhattan taxi whose destination is SoHo. They are part of an elite tribe, a self-created subculture in and of themselves. They have their own visual language that is spoken internationally— to those who recognize it. They pass one another on the street, shooting split-second glances of acknowledgment that they are of the same world.

Their passion for fashion is unrelenting, and their dedication knows no bounds. That's a good thing, because being fashionable is very demanding, financially and emotionally.

Followers of fashion sacrifice a great deal of time and money to obtain and maintain their image. The young man in Paris takes the train (instead of a taxi) so that he can have a drink (instead of dinner) at the newest fashionable restaurant. He carefully allocates his money for clothing so that he stays in vogue. Fashion is his serious hobby, and he devotes much of his free time to staying in the groove and keeping on top of it all. In order to be a dedicated follower of fashion, you must integrate it into your life in a very serious way. You must always know what is in, what is out, what's about to come in, and what's about to go out. Some would say that these people are addicted to fashion, while others call them fashion victims.

The aspiring fashion person has a different relationship with fashion. She builds her wardrobe slowly but surely. She studies all the fashion magazines, shops, movies, and fashion television. She places her attention on the details of fashion. She alters a dress to a new fashionable length. Inspired by a wide polka-dot belt that is all the rage in Milan that season, she searches the vintage shops until she finds a satisfying original. She is dedicated, but she is not spending every waking hour and every cent to keep up with the fashion trendsetters. For her, fashion is fun, a hobby, and not to be taken too seriously.

Members of the fashion/celebrity/high society culture are a closely knit group who enjoy their like-mindedness and respect one another's tastes and talents. A common thread links them to everything fashionable. Their aesthetic relationships with clothing are sensitive. They care a great deal about the newest designs, fabrics, and shapes. Their relationship with fashion is as important as their relationship with fine art, good food, and luxurious vacations. Their lifestyle almost demands that they be seen to be wearing the height of fashion—always.

It is as if a subliminal fashion mantra is transmitted to clothing designers, textile designers, fashion mavens, and trendsetters. These messages may echo the culture or the economy, the past or the future. At any given moment the receptors of the fashion elite are almost eerily wired to the fashion message. They descend upon the tiny little London mews store selling one-of-a-kind Japanese bowls that no one else yet knows about. It's called fashion radar. The thrill is in the hunt. It exists in every aspect of fashion, be it in clothing or napkins.

High-Fashion Clothing

High-fashion clothing is expensive; it is made in limited editions and is sometimes exaggerated in design. It often sets the standard for what eventually appears in the malls.

High-fashion companies often look to the street for inspiration and to feel the pulse of a culture—an all-important method, particularly when designing for a younger audience. They enlist advice from a stream of experts, ranging from "culture watchers" (people who pick up on trends and analyze their impact on society) to established fashion industry leaders. Like any business, the fashion industry seeks to make a profit, and high fashion is a tried and tested arena for doing so.

High fashion is striking to look at. It is expressively designed and uses interesting and innovative fabrics. The high-fashion houses of Europe and North America direct their looks toward a well-heeled group of men and women who enjoy a fashionable international lifestyle.

One of the assets of high-fashion clothes is that they are created as "collections," which makes them easy to coordinate with each other— their colors, fabrics, design, and fit all complement each other perfectly. Just as you might pair a beautiful 1940s silk scarf with a traditional classic suit, you might also pair items from the high fashion of one designer with those of another. They all seem to be working in harmony, albeit with their own individual stamp.

High-fashion clothes are tactile, sensual, surprising, innovative, contemporary, and international. They are wonderful things—if you can afford them and are able to put them together with *your* own personal stamp.

BEING CURRENT

Being current is a state of mind, an awareness that can further develop your personal style.

Interestingly, it's the very small things that keep you feeling and looking current. Let's say that one of the new season's colors is petrol blue. It is a color that you love, and it flatters you. But you must be able to integrate it into your wardrobe—otherwise you will be stuck with yet another "loner." You come across a petrol blue jacket and a pair of trousers. But you don't need the jacket, and the trousers are too expensive. Looking further, you find the color available in everything from handkerchiefs to raincoats. You choose a silk long-sleeve T-shirt in petrol blue that you can wear under your own black suit. You have now integrated a "current item" into your wardrobe.

Suppose that in one season jackets are cut in a trimmer, more tailored silhouette. You review your own jackets and discover that one of them might take well to this new trimmer look. A good tailor will tell you if this alteration can be done successfully. You make the final decision on whether to invest in creating a look that is more current. But you can only do this when you are informed.

Being current is far easier, less demanding, and a great deal less expensive than being fashionable. The secret to being current is researching and reviewing.

Suppose you are really out of touch. (Due to today's demands on some of your time, you probably are.) Before you do anything else, you must establish where you are in relation to what is current. The best way to do so is to go to the shops you love at the beginning of a new season. Look at the designs, cuts, and shapes; note the new colors and fabrics; and look at the people. In better-quality stores, many of the sales staff will be wearing combinations of the new season's clothing. (Use these people as references only—do not copy!) Once you have become aware of what is current, remain alert to the direction the season's clothing is taking. And keep an open mind to elements of the clothing that you would like to include in your personal style.

A QUESTION OF TASTE

The elements of this session—good quality, good design, good fabric and fit—all have an important common denominator that affects the very essence of everyone's personal style: taste.

Personal preference is sometimes confused with taste. There are so many different styles and designs in the clothing world that sometimes it is hard to distinguish whether someone's personal preferences constitute "good taste" or "bad taste."

> **There is no such thing as *bad taste*. There is no such thing as *good taste*. There is only *taste* and *no taste*.**

Bad taste is an oxymoron: you either have taste, are developing it, or are not interested in it. People who are accused of having bad taste are actually those who have not yet developed a sense of who they are aesthetically. Their lack of self-knowledge and their restricted vision of the world make it difficult for them to make appropriate decisions about their own visual world, whether it is in their taste in clothing, art, or furniture. These limitations prevent them from developing any aesthetically based taste at all. But dismissing someone as having "bad taste" is a flippant judgment call, and it is wrong. Underdeveloped, inappropriate, or nonexistent taste are truer descriptions.

Please consider the meaning of the word *taste*:

Taste—appreciation or enjoyment of a personal preference. The faculty of discerning what is aesthetically excellent and appropriate. The sense of what is proper, seemly, or least likely to give offense in a given social situation.

We consider this definition to be highly accurate, especially as it relates to clothing and accessories. Notice that it does not include the following words:

Pretty
Cute
Colorful
Fun
Sexy

Rhinestone studs placed on a T-shirt may be *pretty* in some people's opinion, but they do not relate to taste. *Cute* and *fun* are better reserved for young children and teenagers. More often than not, adults run into trouble when they try to emulate the young and hip. They violate the taste guidelines of *appropriate, proper,* and *least likely to give offense.* They give priority to looking young or fun or sexy, not to taste, which cannot play second fiddle to any of these desires. Rather, taste evokes comments such as *sophisticated, urban chic, elegant, enigmatic,* and *unique.*

Tasteful living involves a healthy, mature attitude and relationship with your body, age, lifestyle, and image. Social maturity accompanies self-respect and is vital to acquiring taste. Taste never sends "ouch" signals—inappropriate behavior or exaggerations to seek attention for attention's sake. Nor does it alert people to question your credibility. Thus taste is always acceptable—anywhere.

Unless you had the good fortune to be born into an ambience of taste or have acquired it on your own, you must then work at developing and cultivating it. Some people do not have the passion to do this, but you must do so if you want to be a person of taste. This is where discipline comes into play. When *you* become your hobby and *you* become one of your passions, you cannot help but develop taste. This is not about developing an egotistical, self-absorbed, "all about me" attitude. It is about creating a history.

Acquiring taste is akin to tasting life in its various forms, from new food to new cultures. Even in your town, no matter where that may be, different cultures exist. Exploring them adds character and new dimensions to your life. It helps you to cultivate your tastes and widen your aesthetic view. Tasting life is about becoming acquainted with it in a nonintellectual fashion. For new experiences to have any meaning or educational value, they must make a connection with you in a sensual and tactile way.

Taste comes from all of the experiences in which you allow yourself to participate. Some of them you will find exhilarating, and some you will not want to have again. All are necessary for creating a history—your history. Trying to create a personal style without history is empty and therefore without taste.

Once you begin to accumulate various experiences, your system automatically begins to filter them. You begin to eliminate what is superfluous, unwanted, or inappropriate. For instance, suppose you experimented with "trendy" and discovered that it represents only a very small part of who you really are, a part so peripheral to your personal style that you do not want to invest any real time or money into it.

Whatever is left over from the filtering process is the beginning of the creation of your taste, which will then take a form unique to you. Others might not necessarily appreciate it, but you must never allow yourself to be influenced by the media or sometimes even well-intentioned friends.

People with taste expect more from themselves and aspire to better. They are selective; they ask if what they are doing serves them, feeds them, or educates them. In short, they *edit*.

People with taste develop a discipline for knowing, as they edit, what to include and what to exclude. People with very refined taste are the most ruthless; they will pare down every detail of their wardrobes to the bare minimum, to allow the quality to speak. A person with eccentric taste is the least likely to conform; sophisticated taste is more worldly and urbane. These people make editing choices that are specific and unique to them.

All people with taste have an appreciation for other tastes, tastes different from their own, even though they may not like them.

Taste, at the very least, must be appreciated. A heightened self-awareness, sensitivity to textures and colors, originality, form and function, harmony and balance are all interpreted in different ways by others; whether it is the design of a clothing item, the dinner you eat, or the chair you sit in, taste too has a spirit. We often hear from clients and customers, "I don't know what it is, but I really love the way that _____ looks." They are tuning in to their taste and to that which gives them visual and emotional pleasure. For them, the key is to find out exactly what it is that they loved about the item. Taste makes an emotional connection; when you see taste, you feel it. It moves you.

WHY HAVING TASTE IS NOT BORING

"Wait a minute. If I can't have a fun, colorful, pretty, sexy, and cute wardrobe, then won't my personal style be boring?" you may ask. Actually, taste allows you to bring creativity to your image without being superficial—in a way that works *for* you, not *against* you. It brings life to a part of you that has been dormant but is longing to be acknowledged. Taste adds another dimension to your personal style. It brings character to your life and life to your character. You win respect from others because you look as if you've "got it all together," even on those days when you feel as if you have not.

Lauren Hutton continues to be an American icon, even though she no longer graces the covers of the world's glossiest fashion magazines. It is her own grace that continues to charm us. Part of that seemingly effortless charm emanates from her taste and how it is revealed through her clothing choices. If she chooses a red sweater, it is a "fantastic red." If she wears simple white linen pants and a shirt, she adds a pair of orange tennis shoes. If she wears a business suit, she will top it off with a pair of glasses in an unusual shape or color. Her taste is developed, not boring. Her taste allows her to choose clothes that bring aliveness and dynamism to her look. Her look would be hard to copy because it so enveloped in her specific taste.

When you develop taste, your choices become more adventurous and unpredictable. You now have permission to play. You can afford to experiment, to wear the well-chosen "surprising "item, because now you can carry and support it—you have something to back it up: your self.

WHAT YOUR CLOTHES SAY ABOUT YOU

Each time you leave your doorstep, you send messages about yourself via your clothing: "Today I feel sporty or casual," or "I feel like dressing up tonight and being glamorous." Your clothes may indicate "seductress," or "fashion victim," or "power suit." These messages, which you send either consciously or, more often, unconsciously— add to the overall message you send through your Personal Style Statement. Clothing messages are more specific to the environment or situation you encounter. Ideally, each message you send on any given day will connect to your Personal Style Statement. If your statement is that you are elegant and sophisticated, you will project those qualities whether you are attending a wedding or going to a spa, a baseball game, or the ballet. Your personal style is conveyed through multiple avenues—your behavior, the way you communicate, your body language. But for the moment we would like to focus solely on the specific messages of clothes.

The following stories describe people whose clothes send very diverse messages to others. Some of the messages are not consciously sent; they come from conditioning, lack of information, and fear of change. Others are painstakingly conscious; they make too much effort to say something.

All these people wanted to change their image. They knew they needed help and had a strong desire to go deeper into the discovery of themselves rather than participate in a solitary, superficial shopping spree. They come from very different walks of life and represent a wide range of income brackets.

GRETCHEN

What you saw:
Gretchen was wearing a long, baggy, green chenille cardigan with oversized fake mother-of-pearl buttons. Underneath the cardigan she

wore a contemporary but retro-looking 1920s light green silk blouse, with red-printed strawberries with darker green leaves. The collar was wrinkled and sat far away from her neck. Her skirt, made of a rust-colored cotton sweatshirt material, hung almost to the floor, stretched out from wash and wear. She walked toward us in black All-Star sneakers, carrying a beige canvas shoulder bag, from which an umbrella, newspapers, and an orange, black, and beige silk scarf stuck out of the top.

Why she wore what she wore:

Gretchen was covering up. She was overweight and very self-conscious and uncomfortable with it.

She felt she could not express her true personal style until she lost weight. She equated weight loss with being able to buy better clothes, cute clothes, clothes that would make her look younger. Until then she had to find ways to cover her body and hide her weight. She was very creative, cared a great deal about her image, and loved clothes, but she thought she could express her creativity only with colors and prints and patterns. She even tried a quirk—the All-Stars—but they didn't work. They made her look as if she were grasping at anything to take your eyes off of her body.

She chose colors that she loved, but they were not appropriate for her hair color or skin tone. She couldn't really see what she looked like because her relationship with the mirror was only about, as she told us, "how fat" she was. She couldn't see her beautiful blue eyes, her healthy fair skin, or the luscious gold tones of her hair. She forgot that she was intelligent, witty, and a great conversationalist.

Her message:

Gretchen's clothes communicated "I just don't know what to do. I'm lost. I hope this is okay." She was a careless mess, trying desperately to express herself and hide herself at the same time. She dressed herself in individual items, without paying attention to the whole picture: "This is a nice blouse, I'll wear this. Oh, and I like this sweater, so I'll wear it too. And this green color will make me feel better—I'm not sure it's right with the other things, but that's okay."

She intended to lose weight tomorrow. Tomorrow was two years ago and counting. And she didn't believe that she could make significant improvements without losing the weight first. But she did.

By having the courage to face herself and her clothes in the mirror, Gretchen began to really see what a distracting image she was projecting. She recognized that she was actually uncomfortable in her clothes. When she learned that she did not have to be uncomfortable, she was relieved and even a little excited about buying a few items for her current weight.

Gretchen's new clothes:

Gretchen bought a slate blue wool gabardine pantsuit that had several twists. The jacket buttoned all the way down, but the buttons and buttonholes were hidden under what is called a *fly front* or *concealed front*. The gabardine was a midweight fabric that hung well. It gave the garment the effect of being sleek and long. At the jacket's neck, a very tailored mandarin collar sat just a bit higher than lesser-quality designs, which set it apart from the generic look of cheaper copies. The jacket was neither tight nor baggy; it was tailored to fit, and its length was measured by where Gretchen's fingertips ended when she placed them by her sides. The jacket was a longer look than she was used to, and it is worn closed to keep the slimmer, cleaner line.

The skirt, of the same fabric, fell close to her ankles. The back inverted center pleat provided even more freedom of movement and added a dash of depth to the simplicity of the lines. The skirt was tailored at the waist and it fell straight down comfortably over the hips. This gave her a longer and narrower line.

The suit was of very good quality; the fabric, design, and superb fit made it work for her. Anything of a lesser quality would not have allowed the smooth, elegant lines.

The shoes were mahogany brown, of the finest Italian calf leather. While they nodded to fashion, they were not trendy but were very solid and substantial. She would wear them out before they went out of style. They had a square toe and were slightly chunky, with a particularly interesting heel. They gave her a little height but are easy to walk in. She carried a shoulder bag in a similar shade as the shoes. It had an interesting shape, like an elegant bucket with beautiful brushed-stainless-steel fittings.

The clothes were beautiful, but it was Gretchen who stood out. She moved more gracefully, and she felt protected and safe—not by hiding but by offering to our eyes the whole of her. Her confidence was heightened by her comfortableness. She used only two colors, but they were calming and striking, which gave her a strong identity. Visually we were drawn to her face and the very top part of her upper body, closing in on her gold hair, blue eyes, and the slate blue-gray of the mandarin collar.

Her new message:

"I'm interesting. I have self-respect. I'm attractive. I know what I'm doing."

JACKIE

What you saw:

A stiff, bright white cotton jean jacket covered a tight, acid-yellow T-shirt, which was fairly low cut. Both the jean jacket and the T-shirt were made of inexpensive fabrics, which looked uncomfortable. Her black pants—very tight hip-huggers—were of a slightly better-quality stretchy synthetic fabric. Her black leather boots were a classic, chunky-high-heeled, short boot in a midrange quality.

Why she wore what she wore:

Our first impression of Jackie's clothing: Not bad. But taking another look, it seemed cheap. She was trying too hard to make a bold statement but instead made a cheap statement. She felt she had the ability to spend next to nothing yet still "create a fashion statement." Her message was "I'm tough. I'm sexy, but don't mess with me. I know exactly what I'm doing. I can compete in a man's world and still be all woman." But this message was mixed. Part of it was seductive, but the more hidden part was "Don't try to penetrate my veneer." So she invited you in but emotionally, would only let you go so far, and then she put up a wall. Hence the stiff white armorlike jacket paired with the low-cut tight T-shirt and tight pants and sturdy boots.

Here's the surprise for you: Jackie was over fifty years old. By showing off her body, she was obviously trying to make a young statement, an "I can pull this off" statement. But underneath it all lay a fear of vulnerability. Jackie had real feelings of "I'm afraid of getting older. I'm not traditionally beautiful. Sometimes I feel all alone in a man's world. I care deeply about my image. I don't want to be pigeonholed as conventional, but I don't really want to stand out too much."

But she tried very hard to push down those feelings and have no emotional connection with her image, her clothes, or her identity. In her "trying to look younger" clothing choices, she actually limited herself and her willingness to seek out new things. She also lacked sensuality, as indicated by her choice of unkind colors. Young people usually wear these colors—acid yellow and bright white—for the fun of it or because they can actually get away with it! Jackie was looking to the wrong age group for inspiration.

Jackie was very, very clever, and she *had* made it in a man's world. But she had also paid a price for it, which created confusion in her identity. She actually loved clothes but was afraid to literally step into the ones that would reveal her true personal style. She had an incredible amount of power and a sense of humor that tempered it, as well as a great deal of compassion. She actually did possess the kind of body that could wear a wide variety of styles. She didn't need to try to project anything, for it was all there. In projecting more of who she was, it was very important for her to adhere to two things: quality and softness.

Jackie's new clothes:

She began with a long sheath dress. It was made of two fabrics, one on top of the other. The layer closest to her body was pure silk satin in a lusciously deep chocolate brown. The second layer, which lay perfectly on top, was a lighter version of the same color and was made of a translucent, fine silk chiffon. Its separateness from the bottom layer was almost indistinguishable. It was very subtly etched with a small design placed strategically in a uniform pattern. In other words, you would barely notice the design at all. The dress itself was very simple in design; it was sleeveless, was cut well, and hung perfectly. The rich color made it interesting, and its simplicity made it versatile—Jackie was comfortable wearing it to work as well as for informal social occasions. There was one more very important aspect of this beautiful dress: it was ageless. A woman of any age would be equally flattered by it.

She chose plain but interesting dark brown sandals. The fine, soft leather straps ran vertically across the top of her feet, making them look sleek. They had no buckles or fasteners—they slipped on and stayed secure.

When Jackie first tried on the dress and the shoes, she was truly amazed. While she was used to looking in the mirror to see if her clothes enhanced her already-good body, she wasn't used to feeling good in them. In the past she would check to make sure her outfit put some part of her body on display, such as her legs or her bust, and she would disregard her discomfort with the itchy fabric or the bad fit. But when she slipped into this dress, she became aware of what it felt like to feel good in her clothes. She was shocked that she actually looked more feminine in a garment that showed nothing but her arms and ankles!

Relieved to be able to appear softer yet feel confident, she explored other possibilities for her wardrobe. Her new favorite and reliable outfit consists simply of a jacket, a blouse, and a pair of pants. But she upgraded the quality of these new items, and they completely changed the way she felt as a woman, both socially and in business.

The blouse, made of a polished cotton of the best quality, in a cool ivory color, gave off a rich luster and was strikingly feminine. The collar shape was fairly big and full, without being oversized or cheap or trendy looking. The collar was designed to be worn either up, à la Katharine Hepburn, or down. The deep cuffs of the blouse were turned up gauntlet style, a tiny bit dramatic.

A contemporary version of the classic pleated designer pant replaced Jackie's trendy, poor-quality hip-huggers and enhanced her slender shape. The small details gave these black trousers an edge. They were made of a midweight wool crepe, which recovers beautifully from a day's work. They had no side pockets, which produced a sleeker, smoother line on Jackie's slim hips. They had a "ticket" pocket (a small working pocket with an equally small flap that was literally intended to carry bus and train tickets) on the front left-hand side attached to the waistband and a matching larger ticket pocket at the back on the right-hand side. The buttons of the pockets were hidden under the flaps, which allowed a smooth line. The pants had no belt loops, and the waistband was an inch deeper than a normal waistband. The bottoms were plain, with just a hint of a flare. The whole effect was sleek, sophisticated, and current looking.

The jacket aided Jackie's business image: its color and fabric spoke volumes. The fabric was the softest cashmere and wool mix, a "feel-able" fabric that made for a very tactile garment; it was inviting and luxurious to look at. The shoulders were relaxed yet not insubstantial. The jacket was single-breasted with one button, and it had a peak lapel (a narrow double-breasted lapel on a single-breasted jacket). The bottom of the jacket was square rather than rounded at the front edges.

The color was a dark sapphire blue, not loud or glaring but very dense and sumptuous. This deepest of blues is an unusual color for this kind of jacket and totally unpredictable. Yet it is surprisingly easy to wear with almost anything—black, gray, and certain shades of brown and beige.

Jackie's new message:

Instead of "I'm tough and intimidating," Jackie's message is "I have strength." Instead of "I'm trying to look younger than my age," it's "I look very good for my age." And instead of cheap and trendy, her message is "I am successful."

OSCAR

What you saw:

A shiny black leather sports jacket covered a rose-pink shiny silk shirt with a wide, open collar. The jacket looked a little shabby; it was wrinkled, the buttons were loose, and a bit of the lining hung from the back. The shirt was worn outside the trousers, and its bottom was square. The shirt's large buttons were cream-colored bone. The trousers were gray silk and wool and had a slight luster. The shirt's fit was a little tight, the jacket was a little too baggy, and the trousers were a little too long. The shoes were black suede Chelsea boots that had seen better days.

Why he wore what he wore:

The message Oscar wanted to convey was: "I'm hip, I'm cool, and I'm a little bit rock and roll. I do not conform. I'm different. I'm not interested in formalities. I'm easygoing and friendly." There was nothing wrong with this message, as long as it accurately describes the person.

But Oscar was trying too hard to appear hip and cool. He thought he knew what he wanted to say about himself, but his choice of clothes were not really who he was. He hadn't established his own identity and was borrowing from images of people who impressed him, making clothing choices based on other people's lifestyles and values.

Oscar's painstaking effort to project an easygoing nature was an act. He was not a bad guy, but no "Mr. Nice Guy" either. He was very intelligent and very witty and had a great deal of business savvy. He had great taste in furniture design and art and was highly aware of the finer things in life. He was very well read and was considered to be up on all things current. These are great qualities to have; Oscar didn't know that he didn't have to act at being a "nice guy" too. The leather jacket and pink shirt did not project all his good qualities or reflect his taste. They were not of bad quality, but they made him look unkempt and slovenly, because the way he wore them produced a too-relaxed, laid-back look.

Oscars' new clothes:

Oscar's new custom-made suit was of very good quality, although not the most expensive. The fabric was closely woven vertical twill wool in a dark charcoal gray. The jacket was single-breasted, with two buttons placed a little higher than on the traditional version of this suit. It had one center back vent, and the side pockets were jetted, with no flaps. The lapel and collar were traditionally American classic. The shoulders were lightly padded and fit accurately to Oscar's own shoulders. The shape of the jacket was the traditional "sack" shape, with two small changes; it was just a bit more tailored at the waist and slightly narrower through the hip. This made the traditionally handsome suit look more current. The jacket was lined in a pearl-gray silk satin lining. The trousers were high in the rise, with single pleats. They were quite a bit narrower at the bottom than traditional classic trousers, and they were cuffed.

The shirt, made of Sea Island cotton, was a dark cherry red. Because of the superior cotton fabric, the dark red had a soft sheen to it. The collar, shaped as a traditional English cutaway, sat perfectly on Oscar's collarbones. The vintage American 1950s tie, with a dark navy background and small ivory-colored polka dots placed closely together, was chosen for its originality and its absolutely mint condition. The combination of colors was a tiny bit theatrical in a way that was right for Oscar and replaced his rock-and-roll fever.

Instead of a belt, he chose plain navy canvas suspenders. Their black leather fastenings complemented his black leather shoes, which were a quirky version of the traditional classic men's business shoe.

Oscar's new message:

"I have a strong sense of self and a strong identity. I am my own person. I am unique, distinctive, and memorable."

TATE

What you saw:

Tate's baggy beige cargo pants fell just below her knees. She wore a grayish-white spaghetti-strap T-shirt and a light navy blue cotton/synthetic cardigan with a couple of buttons missing.

Why she wore what she wore:

If Tate had been a twenty-year-old college student, this outfit would have been fine. But Tate was thirty years old, owned her own small business, and was in her own way ambitious. Something was not right: there was a disconnect between her intelligence and her image. Her message was "I am unfocused, careless, immature, and not in the least professional." Her clothes were rebellious and antisocial, even though she was in the people business. But the most damaging aspect of her image was that she had taken "casual" to the point of projecting a lack of self-respect. Even her reliability and trustworthiness seemed questionable.

Yet none of these messages were accurate. In her business Tate was reliable, trustworthy, professional, focused, and good-humored, and she communicated effectively. Her first impression portrayed none of her positive qualities. She was unable to see herself as attractive.

Whether or not she was actually depressed, Tate was projecting what psychologists call the clothing language of depression. Carelessness, dishevelment, buttons missing, inattention to details, inappropriateness—these are signs of a person who has low self-esteem and may be depressed. Tate was not a slovenly person, and she was very conscious of things being "just so"—except when it came to her own image.

She actually didn't like clothes: to her they were a boring necessity, and it showed. Going to a store to buy clothes was like going to the grocery store—a burdensome necessity. She believed her work spoke for who she was, and she didn't feel the need to dress up for anyone, let alone herself. She wore drab, dead colors in fabrics that had never seen an iron, which made her clothes look older than they actually were. She was a sparkling role model for uniformity: one color, one fabric, one style, and one size fits all.

Tate's clothes reflected her image wound. Literally from the time she was born until she reached the age of sixteen, she wore hand-me-downs. She was tossed from foster home to foster home. Clothing was a frivolous consideration compared to figuring out where she was going to sleep, eat, and fit in.

Tate's coping and survival skills became sharp, and she concentrated on using them to begin her own business. When she began buying her own new clothes, they literally felt uncomfortable to her until she had "broken them in." "Dressing up" seemed like an out-of-body experience; she just didn't know who she was. She put on a long clingy skirt and a knitted twinset and felt out of place. So even when she tried to add different items to the cargo and T-shirt basics, the new clothes would end up in the back of her closet. The "homeless waif" clothing was what pushed her emotional buttons.

Finally Tate's accountant put his foot down. The time was right, he strongly suggested, for her to expand her business. She absolutely had to buy clothes that were appropriate for meetings with the bank manager. That was how she normally shopped for clothes—she called it "emergency shopping."

Tate's new clothes:

The main item in Tate's new outfit was a short jacket in vanilla-colored "gloving" leather. It was softer than velvet to the touch, but strong and durable. It had a front center zipper, which was concealed behind the leather. The collar, which resembled a man's shirt collar, sat softly around her neck. The only other adornments were two side pockets with concealed zippers. The square bottom sat precisely at her waist but in no way gripped or hugged—it almost floated.

Beneath the jacket, an athletic-looking and sleeveless mock turtleneck in a deep, dark mauve fit her like a glove. The strong stretchy silk fabric was young, fresh, and fashionable but not trendy. The skirt was very, very simple: no pockets, no extraneous seams or vents, just a center back zipper. It was calf length, which was both flattering to her long legs and perennially stylish for her age group. The skirt, of a solid navy, cotton drill fabric (generally used for work clothes), was controlled, neither tight nor flowy.

Tate bought a bonus item to wear with the leather jacket and turtleneck on more casual occasions: a fantastic-fitting pair of jeans. The denim was very dark midnight blue, and all the stitching was the same color. The fabric was weighty and dense. The jeans were slender looking but not tight and were cut like a man's jeans but made for a woman. They had a well-proportioned flare at the bottom, and Tate wore them just a tiny bit too short.

Tate couldn't bear to think of wearing either heels or boots. Through a process of elimination, she decided on a pair of Bordeaux leather platform slides—which could not have been better suited for her.

Each item was very carefully chosen to accommodate Tate's emotional and physical needs. She was tall and thin with a boyish frame, extremely athletic, resembling a long lean foal spiriting across a field. The jacket, although completely modern, had an "old leather" feel to it, which Tate emotionally connected with. And the skirt's cotton drill fabric reminded her of a past era and made her feel "at home."

The sleeveless mock turtleneck in the tight stretchy fabric kept her both mentally and physically in the present. The Bordeaux shoes were quirky and rich, a part of her personality that had been hidden. All the colors were chosen to brighten up and enhance her long red hair, green eyes, and unusually tannish-colored skin. They brought her to life. Experiencing these feelings, these emotional and physical connections with her new clothing, allowed her to entertain the idea of developing a new image.

The four new items were obviously very different for Tate, and they were also of a much better quality than she had ever worn before. But they were not out of her league. Passing from hand-me-downs, cargo pants, and T-shirts, to a fabulous leather jacket, a sophisticated skirt, and a sassy top, Tate was in a transition. To help her feel as if her new clothes were a second skin, she had to practice wearing them before going anywhere where she would be judged. She did so, and by the time she met the bank manager, she was prepared, both in her business acumen and in her self-presentation.

Tate's new message:

"I'm a feminine tomboy. I'm focused. I've got my act together. I'm enigmatic. I'm accessible."

·   ·   ·

We do hope you can appreciate the magnitude of Tate's courage and that of the other clients. Their stories may have given you insights into the deeper messages you may be sending via the clothes you choose to wear. Perhaps they will help you to develop an awareness of the messages you would like to convey.

We have covered a lot of ground in this session. Before we return to your specific style profile, we have one more topic to explore about clothing.

You no doubt noticed the importance of color in the description of the clothes and of the clients themselves—the red hair, the pale skin, the sapphire jacket, the dark cherry-red shirt. Color is very, very important, and we devote the entire next session to exploring its uses.

Color

Why did fuchsia and orange become the rage last summer? Why was mid-gray to charcoal the hot color two winters ago? How does it happen that certain colors are seen in all the stores, from the Gap to Gucci, at any one time?

Many of the fashion colors that appear in the stores today have their origin in the remote hillside villages of northern Italy. Foremost among them is Biella, which is located approximately thirty minutes from Milan, one of the world's fashion capitals. Here, twice a year, the principals of the region's premier mills that weave yarn into fabric come together to discuss new fibers, new techniques, new technology, new trends—and new colors. Decisions are made about colors as much as eighteen months in advance. One factory positioned its offices for hillside views, so its fabric designers could look onto the changing colors of the seasons for inspiration.

Together this elite group works through a series of questions to determine what will be the "color of the season." Will the color be relatively easy to manufacture? Is it new and distinctly original enough? Will it suit all the different cultures and constituencies they supply? Is it marketable? How many styles will it translate into? Can both men and women wear it? The final decision is based less on aesthetics than on whether the particular color will be profitable for the mills.

Although Biella is one of the main sources of this process, this scenario is simultaneously being played out in other parts of the world as well. Hong Kong, South Africa, Germany, and Canada, among others, have their own versions of this process.

Once the decision is made, international color researchers, color experts, and color forecasters descend upon these international centers to retrieve the important news and information, which they take back to their people. Merchandising directors then instruct their buyers to be on the lookout for the "color of the season."

In this way, the colors available to customers in stores are dictated to you. It may be hard to find a beautiful shade of red next winter, if Biella has decided that everyone is to wear warm brown. What will you do? Will you give in to fashion and buy the warm brown because it is easy—or will you work a bit harder to find an independent-minded retailer who has his or her own point of view about colors?

COLOR MYTHS

Color is a phenomenal workhorse. It can get all kinds of jobs done if you know how to use it and respect it. But it can be as stubborn as a mule and refuse to budge, draining you of energy and visual life. It can be used cleverly to stretch a small budget, or it can break the bank with bad choices.

Choosing the right colors for a wardrobe is one of the hardest things to do. Whenever we meet with resistance from clients, students, and customers, it is usually about color. Many people choose colors for their wardrobe in order to "add some fun" or "brighten it up." Most people call upon color to feel secure, bold, strong, or happy, and they have deeply ingrained emotional habits relating to it. They've often been conditioned into believing that they can never, ever wear a certain color. These myths are misrepresentations of the true role that color plays in clothing.

MYTH 1: COLOR IS FUN

Color is not fun. Color decisions are as serious as the rest of the decisions you make about self-presentation. The wrong color can wash you out, but the right one can make you stand out—you, not the color. If you throw on a red scarf or a bright tie to add some color to your outfit, we suggest that you think again. Do you know exactly what you are doing? Are you trying to gain attention or divert it? Are you trying to bring attention to the scarf or to yourself? Are you trying to divert attention from yourself or some part of your body? Any of these objectives can be acceptable—the point is, are you aware of them?

If you are combining colors in order to appear "colorful" and "fun," look again at your Personal Style Statement. Do the words *colorful* or *fun* appear in it?

Color decisions can actually be quite scientific, even manipulative. A male executive once told us that he wore white shirts to certain meetings because he didn't want to stand out—he wanted to make himself part of the background so that others could freely get their ideas across. He didn't realize that his very healthy, ruddy complexion actually stood out against his bright white shirt, or that his charm, his good looks, and his strong physical presence magnified his prominence. His white shirts certainly didn't hide any of those qualities. A soft blue shirt would have calmed him down, gently blending him in to his surroundings.

MYTH 2: THE COLORS I LOVE ARE THE ONES I SHOULD WEAR

It sounds reasonable to wear the colors you love, doesn't it? We all have emotional and psychological connections and reactions to colors—if we have a passion for kelly green, then why not wear it? But just because you love a certain color doesn't mean that you should wear it. Your skin tone might not love it. Your hair color and your eye color might not love it.

Our client Bonnie had a favorite color, and she found it difficult to let go of it. The exercise helped enormously to shift her awareness.

MYTH 3: RED IS A POWER COLOR

Red is not a power color. Neither is blue or black or green. Color has no power at all if it does not look good on you. Red is a *strong* color—in certain shades and if it is of good quality. (Yes, color has quality too, as we will discuss later.) But then, many colors are strong when they are worn on the right person. If we are confusing you a little bit, that's good.

Bonnie's Love for Orange

Bonnie loves the color orange. It makes her feel warm, and it cheers her up. Psychologically, it is her antidepressant. The problem is that orange looks terrible on her. She has auburn hair with reddish-gold highlights, and her complexion is florid and warm looking. Her body is slightly fleshy, and she is always a bit breathless. All of these characteristics already make Bonnie look hot (not as in "happening" but as in heat). When Bonnie wears her favorite color, she looks as if she is about to explode. But Bonnie often chose clothes that were brightly colored and busily designed.

When we visited an art museum with her, she liked the Van Goghs and Matisses in their gilded frames and also the ornate European furniture. But she truly "found herself" someplace entirely different: in a room of modern art. The paintings she saw there had simple lines and only two or three colors. She was surprised by how much she loved looking at them and how comfortable they made her feel. Her favorite was a painting with what she called "clean lines" in different shades of blue and gray. There wasn't a hint of orange to be seen!

Bonnie decided to explore clothing items whose colors were cooler and calmer: the blue-grays, creams, and charcoals she had admired in the paintings. Soon afterward, we went shopping with her. As always, she gravitated toward the brightly colored, overdesigned clothing. When she spotted these clothes, she was drawn to them at once. We watched her cheeks flush as she hurried through a rack of multicolored print blouses, stopping at an orange one. Suddenly she looked up and met our eyes—and we all burst into laughter. She had returned to her old pattern.

The blouses she was looking at bore no resemblance to her Personal Style Statement, which was "I project clarity and strength." They also had nothing to do with the colors that she had decided to introduce into her wardrobe.

Bonnie now tried on items of clothing in the new colors—and she became noticeably calmer. Her flush disappeared, and she immediately looked more sophisticated.

First, let's identify what is meant by color as "power." Actually the color has no power at all—you either bring the color to life or drain it of life. Specific colors like red and black should not be used to make a powerful statement. Rather, any color that makes you feel protected and secure, that makes you feel your best, *and* that complements your physical characteristics is a color that works for you. You should wear the color; the color should not wear you. When you choose colors that really do work for you, then you are in the power position.

MYTH 4: BLACK MEANS I'M FASHIONABLE

Far from being fashionable, black is often used as a cop-out masquerading as fashion: "I'll wear black—that will be safe." Is black safe? Yes and no: it is not a security blanket unless you know how to wear it well. One reason black remains so popular is that it allows people to avoid thinking about or dealing with color. There's nothing wrong with that. We both love black clothing; we wear it often and rely on it. Black is basic, and it is a backdrop for other clothing colors. But it is important to always be very conscious of how you use it. And while this is true for every color, with black it is even more important.

Believe it or not, there are different shades of black. Just put on a black sweater with a pair of black pants, and lo and behold—outside in the sunlight, you are wearing two different versions of black. The discrepancies between shades of black are usually based on the quality of the garments. Good-quality black is darker, richer, and blacker than lesser-quality. It will not fade, unless it is improperly cared for. Lesser-quality black is grayer and sometimes has a brownish tint to it. It fades quickly, and its appearance soon becomes drab and lifeless.

Another myth about black is that all women should have a "little black dress" and all men should own a black suit. This is simply not true. Some of our clients simply will not wear black—often because it just doesn't look good on them. Black may age one person, while it may cause another to look pale and drawn. It is wrong to include anything black as a "fashion essential" if it doesn't work for you.

MYTH 5: I'VE BEEN IDENTIFIED!

"I'm a Winter." "I wear my 'life' colors." "I wear my feng shui colors." "I wear my aura colors." The popularity of various color therapies has been growing in the last few years. We do not use color as a therapy, and we don't have complex charts for you to "identify" your color palette. People tend to think of "their" colors, once identified, as "forever." This is misleading. A color that may look complementary on a swatch or on a piece of paper may look ghastly next to someone's skin. The colors that you are able to wear well will change through the years. As you grow older, your skin changes color. Changes in your hair color also change the way your skin experiences and reflects color. When you hold on to colors that no longer serve you, you make big mistakes.

People tend to get "color stuck" and refuse to try on colors that they were told long ago they couldn't wear. Perhaps you have disliked dove gray all of your life because someone once told you it looked terrible on you. And then one day you see a beautiful dove-gray sweater and you feel drawn to it, you want to try it on. Do you allow yourself the pleasure? Would you choose to open your eyes and your mind to the color today? You would be surprised at how many people would not.

MYTH 6: NAVY IS NAVY AND GREEN IS GREEN— ALL COLORS ARE THE SAME

There are literally hundreds, maybe thousands of shades of blue. How could you think that out of hundreds, not one of them is appropriate for you? At any given time, we would have suits in four or five different shades of navy blue in the London shop. One navy would have more green in it, another more red, and another more yellow— such is the complexity of color. And not one customer would be able to wear all four shades of navy.

Colors also differ greatly in *quality*. Think again of the spirit of a garment—that same spirit is in the color of the fabric. A rich, deep luxurious red has a great deal more spirit than a red of a lesser quality. The lesser-quality red may have too much yellow in it or be too "thin" looking. It would be unflattering on most people and would lack aliveness.

MYTH 7: MATCHY MATCHY: THE COLORS YOU WEAR MUST BE PERFECTLY MATCHED OR CLEVERLY MISMATCHED

While watching the "talking heads" on television, have you noticed where your attention goes? Unless the speaker is overwhelmingly compelling, your eye will travel to those who wear either extremely complementary colors or else contrasting colors. Probably it will not linger on a slightly tanned woman with blond or honey-toned hair, for example, who wears a beige or tan suit—she will seem blurry or almost disappear. The different shades of the same color rob her of definition. We call it the "matchy matchy" because *everything* matches! Similarly, a man in a gray suit who has gray hair and a light skin tone will project a cloudy day rather than interesting comments. Viewers have to work harder to listen to him and not become distracted when a flash of color appears from somewhere else.

It is difficult to give hard-and-fast rules when it comes to color. You must learn to be your own expert. But here are some bad matches that rarely, if ever, succeed. Pink skin tone hardly works with most shades of pink clothing. Yellow and olive skin tones are not usually flattered by some shades of yellow, green, or orange. The colors you wear should serve you, should *complement* your skin tone, hair color, and eye color—not match them! It is the contrasting colors that are pleasing to the eye and that enable you to focus on the person.

We have heard over and over again from clients and customers, "I just don't know how to put colors together." *Yes, you do!* Unless you are color blind, you do instinctively know how to clothe yourself in the colors that flatter and work for you. One reason many of you don't do it is because you are lazy. Sorry, but it's true! Another reason is that you don't trust yourself and are insecure about trying new colors and color combinations. Open your eyes! Get out there and experiment with color. Put a color next to your skin: does it make you look more yellow, more pink, more beige? Does it bring out your hair color or make your eyes sparkle? You can tell if you can wear blue red, cherry red, orange red, or none of them. Become sensitive to color and fine-tune your eye for it *as it relates to you,* and you will begin to understand your own personal range of color.

MYTH 8: YOU NEED A LOT OF COLORS IN YOUR WARDROBE TO MATCH YOUR MOODS

This is the biggest myth of all. *You don't need a lot of color in your wardrobe period, let alone enough to match every mood you might have.* If you find that statement a little difficult to swallow, rest assured that you are not alone. The concept of a "tight color palette" makes many people nervous because they want to show the world that they are colorful and interesting human beings. How will they do so if they can't wear loud, bright multicolored clothes? But that's the whole point. We want you to tell us who you are by being yourself, not by distracting us with color combinations. Yes, let us see how a certain shade of mauve brings out your green eyes, or how a deep red highlights your fair skin and dark hair, but don't overwhelm us: wear the mauve under a charcoal gray, and use the deep red very carefully.

DIFFICULT AND CHALLENGING COLORS

Some colors are "challenging," and if you purchase them, especially in a poor quality, then you are asking for trouble.

The acid colors—acid yellow, green, and orange—are bright yet weak and shallow. They are extremely hard to wear and are not kind on the eye. They seldom flatter anyone's skin tone or hair color and often give the wearer an almost sour feeling and appearance. Most of them aggravate your sensibilities because they are underdeveloped and not refined. They have a tendency to age you, and they exaggerate any physical imperfections. So buyer beware if you purchase acid color clothing!

Certain pastels—sugary pinks, pale baby blues, lemony yellows, pale corals, and peaches—are female trouble colors. It is not the colors themselves that are difficult but the evolution of their meaning in the modern world.

ETHAN AND BABY BLUE

Ethan is going to a casual Sunday brunch at an outdoor restaurant that overlooks the Pacific. He's tall, in good physical shape, and slightly tanned, and he has a confident yet accessible air. He's traditionally good-looking, in a Hugh Grant way. He wears a very pale ice-blue pure alpaca sweater. The sweater's V-neck sits exactly two inches below the bottom of his neck, and its body fits him like a T-shirt. The square shape of the sweater does not grip him at the waist or at the bottom of the long sleeves. He wears nothing underneath (contrary to the trend of predictably wearing a T-shirt under a sweater). His trousers are navy blue pure cotton gabardine, and he wears a pair of black Italian loafers without socks.

The ice-blue color works on Ethan because of his coloring, his personality, and his body shape. He wears this good-quality sweater as if it were a T-shirt. (It would not work with a pair of jeans—that would push the envelope of its casualness.) The way he wears the unpredictable style communicates a casualness that matches his environment. The iciness of the pale blue hints at masculity, an area in which he is confident. It is a striking color, and just a little surprising, yet easy on the eye.

BARBARA AND BABY BLUE

Barbara is a businesswoman who regularly gives presentations to her peers and clients. She is a short, petite woman with pale, fair skin and blond hair. She wears a baby powder-blue suit in a synthetic crepe-like fabric. The jacket and short skirt are very tailored and fit her like a glove. She wears a white Lycra shell underneath, nude hose, and a pair of darker blue, plain leather, square-toed, high heels. Barbara is a very nice, amiable woman; in fact, her desire to please others and to not offend anyone leads her to behave less maturely. This contributes to her image of someone who is not in charge.

The baby blue does not work for Barbara, because she disappears beneath the sugary color. As a petite woman with pale coloring, she appears weak, ineffectual, and even little-girlish in this color. The powdery blue does nothing to protect her vulnerable personality and even brings attention to it. This color—in this fabric and in the style of a serious business suit—is inappropriate for any woman to wear, especially for someone like Barbara. By purchasing a suit in one of the "difficult" colors, she took a big color risk. She purchased a *color* and not a good item of *clothing*.

So there you have it—two colors, seemingly the same, but as different as they could be. Unpredictably, the pale ice blue works beautifully on the man, but the powder baby blue swallows up the personality of the woman.

On a practical note, pastel and pale colors are more vulnerable to marks, stains, and other damage. But a better-quality pastel will stand up to more washes, more dry cleaning, and more wear and tear.

COLOR CHOOSING – HELP!

Even if you are well aware of your hair color, skin tone, and eye color, it is still very difficult to really see how a particular color looks on you. We all need outside help at times to fully comprehend the effect that certain colors have on the way we look. Although no one else can ever tell us how we *feel* in a color, sometimes an objective eye can enlighten us about how we *look*. Here are some ways to find that objective eye.

1. If you have any photographs of yourself, pay close attention to the colors you are wearing in them. Are they well chosen? Do they flatter you? How does your skin look? Do you look larger or smaller? Could you have chosen a better color?

2. Observe other people whose color sense you admire. Is there anyone—a stranger, a friend, or a co-worker—who wears colors well much of the time? Don't think of how their colors would look on you—but try to figure out why the colors they wear work for them.

3. Enlist the help of someone you trust. Sometimes people can help others with color more easily than they can help themselves. That nonemotional, nonjudgmental eye makes the difference. If they suggest that a color you love is not flattering, ask why. And if they suggest that a color looks outstanding on you and you don't understand it, again find out why.

4. Generally speaking, everyone needs something dark in his or her wardrobe, be it a suit, a jacket, pants, a skirt, or a dress. Your task is to figure out which dark shades are best for you. By experimenting with colors, trying on various hues of navy, dark gray, black, and brown, you will find that you will make an emotional connection with one more than another. You will feel different in charcoal gray than you do in navy blue. (It might be the way you feel that day.) Be very aware of those feelings—they are clear indicators of your emotional and aesthetic relationship with that color. One navy blue may feel different from another. By becoming sensitive to colors and their hues, you will develop a more focused and less fragmented view of colors as they relate to your image.

5. Never dismiss a color just because your initial reaction when looking in the mirror is negative. A similar shade that is warmer or cooler looking might look better.

6. Try to recall any childhood experiences that might be affecting your color decisions today. Vanessa's story is one of many in which color plays a powerful role.

VANESSA: THE EMOTIONALITY OF COLOR

Vanessa is beautiful, tall, and statuesque. Imagine a statue of a Greek goddess; imagine long thick blond hair, very large almond-shaped, bright sea-blue eyes, and smooth skin with a hint of sun-kissed color. Her body is long, lean, and shapely, with well-defined muscles. Her physicality is nothing short of regal; she has a quiet yet strong physical presence. When she smiles, her entire face lights up, and the warmth from it is compelling.

Vanessa's personality is also warm and friendly, and upon first meeting her, you are impressed with her thoughtfulness and her good manners. She owns her own successful interior design business and is on her way to starting a second business as a real estate developer. She works by herself, is single, and is active in several hobbies and charity work. This is the Vanessa that the world sees.

But there is another Vanessa: the one who dresses herself every morning. More often than not, on most mornings when she opens her closet door, she chooses black: a black suit, a black dress, black pants, a black sweater, or maybe a black blouse. She is not trying to be fashionable or trendy, nor is she trying to make some kind of statement. When Vanessa walks into a room you cannot help but look at her. But that is not what she wants, at least not at this time in her life. In fact, she goes out of her way to avoid attention. She is very simply trying desperately to hide.

When Vanessa was a young girl, she was the victim of sexual abuse from a family member. In high school she suffered first from anorexia and then from bulimia. At the age of twenty-one, she nearly suffered a nervous breakdown, and finally at age twenty-five she began to receive the therapy she so desperately needed.

Vanessa's image wounds are great, and she has been deeply affected by the events in her life. One would expect her to wear baggy clothing to cover her body and to keep from sending the wrong messages to men. But Vanessa was hiding in another way as well: she was using color to hide. In fact, she was almost addicted to it.

Vanessa never had a favorite color as a child, but she remembers wearing a green jacket and powder-blue corduroy pants. Her favorite dress when she was five years old had a black velvet bodice with a slight empire waist; the skirt of the dress had a white background with tiny red polka dots. In those years colorful clothing was a natural part of her life.

Then one day in her late teenage years, Vanessa painted her bedroom and her bathroom walls black. She bought a black rug for the floor. She began to wear only black clothing, as she searched for comfort and safety within the confines of one color. The baggy black clothes were her way of deflecting unwanted advances and attention. Rebellion, anger, and defiance were the result of her tumultuous past, and black became the color of her life. It made her feel quiet; psychologically it protected her from being responsible for attracting attention. It covered her in a security blanket of secrecy. Something about black made her feel that her secrets were safe.

Vanessa is in her thirties now and has come far in her healing process. She still wears black often and feels that too many colors or bright colors bring her unwanted attention. She is quite right: loud, bright colors and even certain pale colors would draw too much attention to her. Her physical characteristics already give her more attention than she sometimes wants. Her beauty is equally a source of pain and joy.

Now she has begun to notice that if she wears black for a protracted period of time, she begins to feel depressed. This we see as a healthy sign, for it means black is no longer her source of comfort. A new part of her is ready to come forward and to show itself. She has had the courage to add a few muted tones—neutral colors that can be found in a sophisticate's wardrobe, such as beige, white, dark gray, and dark brown. She must be careful with these particular shades, as some of them tend to wash her out and match her hair color and skin tone too closely.

Finally Vanessa felt ready to introduce small amounts of subdued, good-quality color to her wardrobe. She did it slowly in a scientific and calculated way. Instead of haphazardly choosing an item for its color alone, she found something about it to connect with; the small, pretty flowers in a scarf, or the rich, dark, weathered tones of a pair of wine-colored leather shoes. She would strategically place the scarf under her jacket, with only a small portion visible, or in a pocket as a handkerchief. The shoes are very good quality, subtle with a twist, an easy way to wear a color other than black. They are perfect for leading a roving eye away from other areas of her body.

Vanessa's relationship with color was just beginning. Thinking about it was like opening the door to new image possibilities. It was a fresh start. She had come a long way, and she could now project the image of a more confident woman, a woman who created safety, comfort, and security in her life.

Vanessa's story may seem unusual, but it is not. Everyone has an image story. One man can only now bring himself to wear a pink shirt because his mother told him when he was a young boy that only sissies wore pink. At fifty-five years of age, he is embarrassed, nervous, angry, and finally jubilant about a pink shirt. A woman we know can't wear a certain shade of green because her mother was buried in that color. Tate's drab, lifeless earthy tones spoke of her lack of self-esteem. Color has emotionally affected most people and their images.

- Do you have any emotional attachments to colors?
- Do you avoid certain colors for emotional reasons?
- Are you aware of how and why you choose the colors you do?
- Please write any thoughts you may have in your Personal Style Journal.

THE PRACTICALITY OF COLOR

Many mornings when you are getting dressed, you choose to wear a garment solely because of its color. The color is more important to you than the garment itself. You are actually choosing a color to suit your mood. You may choose a color to lift your spirits. You may try to match your mood, choosing black when you are depressed or red when you want to feel strong. You may choose a color based on some form of "spiritual aspiration," such as white for purity or pink for a chakra. Are you sure you know what you are doing?

More often than not, the results of those decisions are exactly the reverse of what you need. If you are feeling a little down or tired, a dark color will not necessarily make you feel better. Very often it will compound your mood and sometimes set it in stone for the day. Red and royal blue are strong colors, but you cannot hide behind them—they will not protect you if you are feeling vulnerable. Similarly, choosing a bright, happy color in order to feel more "up" can make you feel insecure. For example, thinking of yellow as sunny, warm, and bright is an intellectual experience, not an emotional one. Yellow is a very difficult color for most people to wear well. It drains them of color or makes their skin look yellow, pale, and even sickly. Sickliness does not translate as perky, up, or bright.

When you are feeling down, the last thing you want to do is to bring attention to yourself. In fact, you may want to hide. Up, bright colors will not make you invisible—they will bring you unwanted attention, and you will feel as though your mood is on show for all to see.

We suggest that you think about colors that comfort you.

Instead of thinking about color in relation to your moods—such as up, down, strong, or weak—consider instead the colors that make you feel comfortable.

WHAT ARE YOUR COMFORT COLORS? THE CRITERIA:
1. You know this color flatters you. It looks good on you.
2. You feel good whenever you wear this color.
3. Once you have chosen to wear this color and have put it on, you can forget about it. You don't have to worry about it.
4. If you were to accidentally glance at yourself in the mirror wearing this color, you wouldn't be "shocked" to see it.
5. When you look in the mirror wearing this color, you connect to something familiar and relaxed. You have a "that's me" feeling.
6. The color is in some way related to your Personal Style Statement

Any colors that fit these criteria are *your* power colors.

By following these simple suggestions, you can create a "color mood framework" that will cushion you emotionally, no matter how you may be feeling.

MARY AND COLOR

In many ways Mary has been our Eliza Doolittle. Lying dormant underneath her sober and bland monochromatic exterior was a vivid, glowing, and vibrant woman. Since she started working with us, she had grown as a person in many ways, yet she was still "disappearing" behind her clothes. Where Vanessa used black to hide, Mary used beige, tan, and cream to fade into the background. She was a perfect example of the "matchy matchy." The pale colors dulled her blond hair and made her complexion look sallow, and her pretty green eyes lost their brightness.

Mary's most powerful experience in her search for her personal style came in this session. Ironically, she already had a very specific and defined relationship with color. She had a sophisticated knowledge of the effect that color can have. Her love of floral design was intensely connected to color. Her strong attraction to jewel colors was fascinating given her consistent choice of the pale colors in her wardrobe. The jewel colors evoked passionate emotions, and even the thought of incorporating those colors into her clothing produced a push-pull feeling within her.

When Mary became aware of the huge discrepancy between the colors she used in her image and the colors she used in her life, she had a revelation: One of the things she loved most in her life frightened her. This fear kept her from stepping into a crucial part of her personal style.

Many people, at some point in this work, reach a stage of fear. Sometimes it is merely a nervous excitement about the possibilities for their image, but at other times it is a real fear about the reality that they *can* transform their image. Can they live up to such a change? What will others think of them? Very often the color issue taps into the client's fear of "coming out." They are afraid of any color that highlights their personality and physical assets and instead gravitate to what they perceive as safe.

Emotionally, Mary needed to introduce color into her wardrobe gradually. Just one color would make a big visual splash, because she was so accustomed to her predictable, bland, beige outfits. Vanessa, who was addicted to black, introduced color through items that had less personal contact with her body—the scarf and the shoes. But in

Mary's case, the color would have to sit right next to the skin on her upper body, in the form of a sweater, a blouse, or a finely woven piece of knitwear. A garnet-colored pantsuit would be too much for her both emotionally and physically, as her body would not be complemented by one huge blur of color. But a darker, more subdued-colored jacket or blazer, perhaps in suede or a fine wool, even a carefully chosen jean jacket, could cover the more richly colored items. That would give her a degree of security and would make her feel less vulnerable.

We accompanied Mary on a color exploration trip. She discovered a small clothing boutique where she really felt at home. The store's design, the music, and the fabrics and colors of the clothes—everything about the store resonated with her. It was a new experience for her because she normally shopped in department stores. It was amazing to watch her move toward items that were very different from the clothes she normally wore. It was like night and day. Mary already knew what was right for her—she just needed help acknowledging it.

The staff was very gracious to Mary as she literally played around with the clothing. She played with color, not trying anything on but holding things up to her face. As she did so, she began to form an image in her mind of how she might use color. She saw herself in a black pantsuit, and underneath the jacket, a touch of garnet red would peek out at the neckline in the form of a silk, low-on-the-neck, mock turtleneck. Although the moment took her by surprise, it did not go unnoticed. From a place of raw instinct, self-knowledge, and a little bit of education, Mary was in the process of creating her personal style.

Good quality and well fitting clothing were very important for Mary, but color was the key to bringing her true personality to life. A deep teal blue permitted her green eyes to glisten. Rich black brought out the "cool blonde" sophisticate in her. A very dark garnet flattered her skin tone and kindled a regal, aristocratic air. Mary began to come to life when she explored color possibilities for her new image. Because Mary already had a sophisticated eye in regard to the quality of color, her research was purely about putting color next to her skin and around her face and being sensitive to how she felt emotionally.

WILLIAM AND COLOR

Like many men, William relied heavily upon the tired old staple colors of the male business wardrobe: navy, white, Oxford blue, and a token weekend khaki. His Personal Style Statement, "I make an elegant and sophisticated impression," helped him tremendously to overcome this mental block—after he recovered from a bout of confusion! William had equated traditionalism and conformity with sophistication and elegance. His ability to back himself into an image corner seemed limitless!

In our experience, women are much more comfortable experimenting with color than men. Unless a man is trying to make a "creativity" point, the safety of traditional business colors is the norm. But while they may feel safe, most of the men we have worked with admit that they are not *comfortable* in the drab, predictable colors handed down to them by their fathers and by business icons. And as their eyes wander off to the luscious dark mauve fine cotton shirt on the shelf, you can almost see them wondering, *Could I wear that color?*

In the late 1990s, the tone-on-tone or matching-shirt-and-tie-color combination that became popular was a major shift for men in relation to color. Suddenly even businessmen felt free to wear shades of blue that they had never worn before. Mauve actually became an accepted color for bankers. While all of this "shocking" color was inspirational and liberating, too few men actually took the time out to determine if the colors actually flattered them. One of our clients, the male version of "orange Bonnie," was drawn to a deep pink shirt and tie, but next to his very ruddy complexion, it made his face seem to throb with warmth; we actually felt a little warm ourselves while looking at him

Surprisingly, William felt instinctively that color would play an important role in his personal style. He was attracted to the tone-on-tone look but couldn't see himself wearing it. And he was exactly right. That magazine-cover, overly used, fashion look would have swallowed him. It had absolutely nothing to do with William's wished-for sophistication and elegance, and it was not in harmony with the things and people in his life. In addition, his patients would have been thrown by such a huge contrast in his image—and he did not want that kind of reaction.

William knew that the colors currently in his wardrobe were not complementary to his taste or his developing sophistication. He realized he had given himself no freedom to be creative with color.

So we smothered William with color. We tried to almost overwhelm him with a plethora of different colors and the various shades and tones within those colors. (This immersion into color might not be right for some people. William needed to be woken up, with a cold splash in the face. You must decide yourself how you will introduce new colors into your life.)

We allowed William to feel lost and even a bit uncomfortable, to enable him to shake off old "color eyes" and start fresh with a new relationship with color. We moved around with William in a store-to-store blitz, sailing through shop after shop, just looking at color—not styles, not even all-male clothing, just color. Before we all became too tired, we settled into a made-to-measure shirt specialty shop where there were very few shirts on view but there were bolts and bolts of multicolored shirting fabrics in hundreds of colors. Here it was very easy to experience different qualities of color and different tones of the same color.

William was amazed at the choices that could be considered for a single shirt. Although he did not make any purchases that day, he was introduced, for the first time, to a small but potent selection of colors that he truly loved, colors that would relate to his Personal Style Statement. These flattering colors would spice up his wardrobe:

• Cornflower blue. Having more depth than standard Oxford blue, cornflower blue lent a better balance of color against William's dark suits. When he took his jacket off, this color remained substantial. It didn't weaken him or remind him of his body image wound (his shoulders). In practical terms, it had the potential to complement many basic, classic colors. This blue flattered his hair and skin and highlighted his dark blue eyes.

• Moss green. Very much to his surprise, moss green worked beautifully for him because of the amount of gray that is in it. It is a very soft and sensual color and it is extremely sophisticated, subtle, and even low-key. These factors suggest elegance. It is almost impossible to find in generic retail establishments, which also pleases William's desire to appear sophisticated.

• Cobalt blue. This spirited color is very masculine and secure-making. On William, it was a very sexy color; with his black, slightly graying hair, blue eyes, and fair skin, it gave him almost movie-star glamour. William would not have been comfortable wearing this color for attention's sake; he eventually wore it as a shirt in an understated way. All of the colors William chose are very European, but cobalt blue particularly reminded him of the chic Italian men he had observed on his European vacations.

• Slate gray. This midtone purplish gray is a very unusual color, yet it did not in any way shout or distract from William's personality. The color's subtle luster makes it appear luxurious and tactile. In different lights its mauve hues enabled William to look friendly and approachable. This slate gray demanded that William feel confident, in a "people mood," and his skin and hair had to look good when he wore it. This color made William look approachable, and if he wasn't feeling approachable, he would send the wrong message by wearing it.

When he experienced how color could work for him, William no longer needed to hide behind stubbornness or defensiveness, which had prevented him from looking at himself in a more creative, open fashion.

INVESTING IN A CLOTHING EDUCATION

We could talk about good design, good quality, a great fit, and color all day, but you will not understand these things completely until you have a physical, visual, tactile experience with them. You cannot have an intellectual experience with good food—you have to taste it. You also have to have a garment in your hand to understand both Session 6 and Session 7.

Sadly, generally speaking, retail experts are no longer reliable. In the old days sales consultants' enthusiasm would come from the product, but today their commission generates that enthusiasm. They are not to blame; they are in a results-oriented business where the intensity of the competition is astounding. Gone are the days when a salesperson would guide you to make a wise decision, except in a few owner-driven businesses, where the owner takes delight in steering customers toward ultimate happiness. Seasoned professionals for the most part have relabeled themselves as personal shoppers and image experts, whose agenda is to sell only their store's merchandise. Therefore never has it been more important for you to take your personal style in your own hands. This includes educating yourself about clothing.

Being in charge of your image takes an investment of your time as well as your money.

How much are you willing to invest in the spirit of your clothes?

Before you think about investing any more money in your wardrobe, first consider how much time you are willing to invest, precious as it is. We have worked with many highly intelligent people, people who do very clever and interesting things in their lives. But when it came to clothes, they were lost. They felt insecure and "out of it." They had to be convinced that sacrificing a little time would be a good investment. Without fail, they found that the more time they invested, the better return for their money they received. They created real value for money.

What does investing your time mean? Must you become a clothing expert, spending all of your free time in shops? No, of course not. In fact, you can do it on your lunch hour, or while popping into a store to pick up a shirt, a pair of socks, or a tie, or when you go to the mall to buy your children their next pair of jeans.

EXERCISE: THE HUNT

Please take note:

This is not a shopping expedition.

In this exercise, you will go to a shop or shops and familiarize yourself with clothing that is different from what you might normally be accustomed to. Please do not buy anything while you are doing this exercise. Just follow these instructions.

1. **Decide where to go.** Locate a good-quality clothing shop. If you don't know of any, ask around. Remember, a trendy shop is not necessarily a good-quality clothing shop.

This research cannot be done via the Internet, by looking at magazines, or by paging through clothing catalogues. Here's why. Suppose you read or see photographs, sketches, or fabulous graphics on a Web site that unequivocally state that turtlenecks are the new, hot item for everyone of all ages to have in their coming winter wardrobe and the colors to have are chocolate brown, rust, and mustard yellow. Those photos and explanations cannot answer the following questions:

- How high does the roll sit on your neck?
- Does it fit the circumference of your neck?
- How deep is the roll?
- What does the fabric feel like?
- How does it look under a jacket?
- Is the mustard a deep, dark mustard or a light, thin mustard?
- Does that particular chocolate brown suit your skin tone?
- Is this the right turtleneck for you? Do you need a casual version? A more dressy version? A sporty version?
- Are you a turtleneck person?

2. **Look only at good-quality clothes.** Regardless of whether you ever end up buying them, use them as your template.

3. **Don't be afraid to ask questions.** A young man who used to come into our shop fairly regularly started by just roaming around and looking. He would touch the clothes, taking his time, and pay very careful attention to almost every item. At first we thought he was a researcher, except he looked a little uncomfortable and he never took notes. We left him alone, allowing him to feel comfortable to just be there without any pressure. The next time he came in was during the summer sale. He bought one sale item—a tie. The following autumn he bought another tie and also a shirt, this time at the full retail price. Two more years passed before he was able to afford a suit, but until then he was a loyal tie, sock, and shirt buyer.

This young man had been educating himself as he climbed his professional ladder. How clever he was! Just by dropping by several times a year, he developed his taste and learned about quality, design, and color. As the seasons changed, he watched the changes in fabric and styles, and by the time he was ready to start building his wardrobe, he pretty much knew his direction. And he asked the most wonderful questions! "Why does this jacket feel so good?" "I don't look intimidating, do I? I don't want to intimidate anyone." "Do you think this fabric in this style is good for me?" "How long will these trousers last?" "Where was this manufactured?" On and on he went, but it was very, very good that he asked questions.

4. **If you are made to feel unwelcome, then *leave the store*.** The retail store exists because of you. *You are the customer.* It opens its doors to you, and you have every right to be there—even if you never, ever buy anything. (Of course, if you behave badly, they have the right to ask you to leave.) There *should* be staff in the shop who actually know the product and are able to answer any of your questions about it.

If you feel that you are not being treated well in some way, then we suggest you decide whether you are willing to accept this behavior. If you are, then fine; if not, then move on. There are plenty of clothing stores in the world, and you do not have to be subjected to rudeness, snobbery, or people who don't know what they're doing.

5. **As in the Aesthetic Field Trip, be alert to what you are drawn to.** Notice what your eye responds to. Maybe it's the way the buttons are positioned on a particular jacket, or the shape of a pair of pants, or the depth and angle of a cuff on a blouse. Does its designer "speak" to you? (We don't mean "designer" as in designer label. All clothes have been designed by someone; we literally mean designer in the most commercial sense of the word.) Do you somehow relate to their design vision, the way that they see clothes? Be super aware of your sensibilities and tastes. Look at every detail very carefully; notice how an expensive *simply* designed piece of clothing differs from an expensive *highly* designed piece. What details do you like about the highly designed or simply designed item?

When you are in the inquisitive stage about design, you are most receptive to your sensibilities, so use it to define your aesthetic eye, to educate and cultivate it.

You will know good design when you see it. You just need to be presented with the facts and the relevant information so that you can identify it with more ease and assurance. Then you will be able to make better clothing choices.

There are many, many watered-down versions of good-quality design, and they cost considerably less than the originals. You can find them in department stores, specialty stores, boutiques, and even malls.

Strange as it may seem, these watered-down versions are harder to come by than generic clothing items like T-shirts and jeans. One reason they are scarcer is that they are riskier items for a retailer to carry. They appeal to a smaller audience than cargo pants and T-shirts.

If you want to look and feel special, do not give in to "what's in" for the sake of being seen as "with it." Look for that special, good-quality item, at a price that suits you. Think of it as searching for something that is uniquely for you.

Perhaps in your roaming you are drawn to a certain area of a shop. Maybe one area feels more comfortable or less intimidating. Start there. Let your eyes take everything in, and then follow your eyes. Try not to use your intellect. For example, suppose your eyes are drawn to an item of clothing you would never wear, but the color intrigues you. Don't worry about whether you would wear it. Find something that you are attracted to, and then study it. What does it feel like? What drew you to it? What can you tell about the quality of the fabric, the design, and the color? Don't worry about the fit right now. Is it different from your current clothing? If so, how?

6. **Recall the Ten Easy Tips for Recognizing Good Quality from Session 6 (see pages 156–57). If you need to, write them down and take them with you.**

7. **Look for clarity, purity, and simplicity of form.** Does anything on the garment relate to the list of extraneous additions (see pages 169–170).

8. **Notice the colors and in particularly the quality of the colors.**

9. **Just for fun, if you feel moved to do so, try something on.** It doesn't have to be your size, your taste, or the right color—don't worry about any of that right now. Try something easy and simple—a jacket or a knitwear piece. Get a feeling for the garment. Do not go to a mirror! Just notice what it feels like to wear a garment that is of better quality than you are used to. That's all.

10. **Do not be deflated or upset if you cannot afford anything.** You are using this exercise to develop a frame of reference. It will give you something to aspire to in relation to your image and the way you buy clothes. It may also help you to refrain from buying quantity and buy quality instead.

11. **Color alert!** Are you attracted to the same colors that have grabbed your attention for decades? Most people are. If you are,

steer yourself toward a new color. Make yourself move away from your safe, familiar color choices. Choose a new color to put next to your skin, your face, and your body.

12. **Think of your Personal Style Statement.** Begin to relate your statement to the clothing you are studying. You don't have to understand this now, just plant the seed.

13. **Notice what is current.** As you study the clothes, distinguish between what is current and what is trendy. This will be invaluable when it is time to analyze your closet.

OPTIONAL EXERCISE: ART MUSEUM EXCURSION

Art museums and art galleries have always been inspirations for us. Between us we have covered the art of several continents, and although we are by no means art aficionados, we enjoy the experience because it continues to train our eyes for balance and color.

While we worked together at fashion shows in Europe, we would sometimes skip the glitzy runway shows and pop into a museum or gallery. Often this was much more inspirational than the fashion show. The peaceful, refined atmosphere given to the works of great artists provided both visual and emotional inspiration and fired our imaginations. When it was time to make design decisions, and to choose colors and fabrics, we were more creatively prepared. The same pastime can help you connect with your color sense. Indeed, our clients report back to us too that the Art Museum Excursion is one of their favorite and most rewarding exercises in their style-discovery process.

Looking at an art book or magazine that contains an array of colors is not quite the same. It does not give the essential experience or same results. For one thing, the colors on a printed page are not authentic and therefore cannot provide the vitality, the depth, the dimension, or the quality that you will see in person. For another, the physical experience of relating to a piece of art that is right in front of you requires a completely different sensibility. Its authenticity makes a deeper impact and leaves a more lasting impression.

PLANNING YOUR EXCURSION

The Art Museum Excursion is not the same as the Aesthetic Field Trip. These are two very different and separate excursions. Plan ahead, so you can take the day off without guilt, time pressure, or any other distraction. If you are for some reason museum phobic, we ask you to give it a try, with this mind-set: You are not going to a museum to appreciate art. You are going to appreciate yourself.

We strongly recommend that you go alone, at least the first time. As with the Aesthetic Field Trip, you need the freedom to roam without distractions and without having to feel accountable to anyone else. Give yourself permission to have the experience your own way. If you get hungry or tired, act on those feelings. Make the day a treat and a pleasure. You will be surprised at what you learn.

You will have more success if you choose a museum that has a large, eclectic collection of art from around the world. If you live in a small town, this will mean driving to the nearest large city. Or the next time you have to go to that city for other reasons, try to incorporate a trip to the museum. If spending a whole day is impossible, try to make time for at least half a day.

Put some thought into what you will wear. Dress comfortably but appropriately, as you did for the Aesthetic Field Trip.

Ideally it would be beneficial to take your Personal Style Journal or a pocket tape recorder with you so that you can record your feelings and thoughts. You might use your rest times, a coffee break, or a lunch break to set down your experiences. You might even feel passionately enough to sketch your favorite find.

A word of caution. We do not intend for you to "find your colors" at the museum. Even if you fall in love with a new and special color, that does not necessarily mean it should automatically be included in your wardrobe. Your mission here is simply to become more aware of color.

HAVING A MEANINGFUL EXPERIENCE

As soon as you walk into the museum, be aware of the atmosphere, as it is like no other. The quiet, the reverence, the architecture, and the care that is taken to showcase the art can have an incredible grounding and centering effect. This is very helpful because you are there to focus on yourself. Please do not rent the headphones. You are not there to learn about art—you are there to learn about yourself.

Put no pressure on yourself to see everything. Allow yourself to be drawn into your own personal and private experience. Move around to whatever catches your eye. Move to a certain room or area because you have an urge to do so.

The first time your attention settles on a picture or object that resonates with you, stay there for a while. Notice what attracts you. Either write these things down or stand in silent reflection, enjoying your own thoughts and the experience without interruption.

You may see a piece of art, a painting, or an object that you don't really care for, yet your eye may still be drawn to it. Perhaps the colors draw you in. Try not to discount your attraction because you don't appreciate the entire artwork.

For example, you may have no interest in seventeenth-century French tapestries, but as you walk by, your eye may be drawn to the moss-green border and the rust-colored fringe. Pay attention to that. If you are looking at paintings, you might not like the content of a painting, but you may be very attracted to one or more of its colors.

When you are ready, move to the next item. Notice the items that you moved past; note why they do not arouse your interest. If you haven't already begun to do so, specifically notice the colors in the pieces you like. Notice how they make you feel. Do they arouse passion? Do they produce calm and serenity? Also be aware if you have a strong aversion to certain colors.

Continue until you are ready to stop. Before you leave, you might want to revisit the items you had strong feelings about, either positive or negative. Sometimes gift shops sell postcards: you may be inspired to purchase a postcard of your favorite piece and keep it tucked in your journal as a pleasant reminder.

FOLLOW-UP

If you haven't already begun to record your observations, then please do so after you arrive home. Here are a few questions you may find helpful to answer in your journal.

- What colors were your favorites? Why?
- How did they make you feel?

- Were they colors that you'd never noticed before?
- Were you surprised by any of the colors that you liked?
- Are those colors represented in any area of your life right now? If so, how?
- Are any of those colors in your wardrobe? If so, where? If not, would you like to have them in your wardrobe? Where specifically?

Your answers to the next two questions do not have to be literal; they may relate to a similar feeling or a symbolic meaning.

- Think back for a moment to the things you love and feel passionately about. Is there a relationship between those passions and the colors you love?
- Is there any connection between the colors that resonated with you and your Personal Style Statement? How?

The next questions are about colors you disliked.

- Were there any colors that you strongly disliked? Why?
- How did those colors make you feel?
- Were you surprised by your reaction? If so, why?
- Are those colors represented in any area of your life right now? How?
- Are any of those colors in your current wardrobe? If so, where specifically?
- Are the things you feel passionately against in any way connected to those colors? (This may be a feeling or symbolic.)

Finally:

- If you could have taken one piece home with you, which one would it have been?

Many times our clients enjoy the benefit of the Art Museum Excursion days after the event. Two or three days after visiting a museum, a certain color or a specific color combination may still stay with you. An impression has been made. Be sure to note any impressions you have over the next few days.

Your
Personal Style
Profile

You are in the home stretch now and about to enjoy the rewards of all your work. In this session you will form a distinct Personal Style Profile. You have already been developing and cultivating your profile, and it will become stronger as you continue to define it. This profile is a powerful tool—it will enable you to transcend fashion, handle some of life's challenges, and give you the confidence to be different. Your profile will help you retain what you have learned and discern if your work is accurate and meaningful. And finally, you will always be able to return to your profile and say, "This is what I want for my image. This is who I am and what I want to project."

A few solid truths about who you are right now need to be stamped into your memory: the truths that come from the pages of your journal. It is very important that you be clear about them and be able to use them with ease and effectiveness. In this session you will be certain that your personal style exists and is waiting to be expressed.

In the first half of this book, we encouraged you to delve introspectively into your emotions and feelings. Then we took you through a few sessions of educational and informative material. Now we would like to appeal to your investigative and even scientific capabilities. It is your goal to establish your Personal Style Profile honestly and unemotionally. In order to do this successfully, you will need to adopt a pragmatic attitude. You will need to make practical, mature, and sensible decisions about the clothes you have now and the clothes you may choose to buy. By remaining focused and determined, you will be rewarded with ease and comfort in making your personal style a living reality.

Go back through your material, and highlight the most potent and important aspects of who you are. Think of yourself as a detective who pays close attention to relevant facts. This is a simple procedure and is not time consuming. If you have recorded your thoughts and feelings, the information is there, waiting for you to retrieve it. You will be delighted to find that your unique and personal qualities, values, passions, and even your view on life can be found within the pages of your work.

To show you how to decipher your profile, let's look at how Mary and William did it. In each case, they first identified their thoughts and experiences as they reviewed their work. They then summarized their notes and drew conclusions. These conclusions are what they wished to include in their Personal Style Profiles. Their work is intended as a guideline only. You will have your own insights and revelations, and possibly there will still be things you are still not sure about—that is perfectly normal. Do not worry about whether you are "right"—it is more important to be honest.

Your Personal Style Profile will not tell you that you need a black suit or a crème silk blouse. Your profile, rather, is intended to give you a strong idea of what is most appropriate for you now, in the light of the new things you have revealed about yourself. Then you will be able to reflect the person you really are in your image.

MARY'S PERSONAL STYLE PROFILE

Mary used a highlighter to mark words and phrases as she read through her material. She then organized the material on fresh pages of her journal. Sometimes she used just words and phrases, and other times she would write in sentence form. Most people do this; you should write in any way that is pleasing to you.

Session 1 *Passions*

Travel—ready to take the blinkers off
Travel—to appear and be more sophisticated

Travel—expand my tastes
Figure skating—freedom of physical expression
Figure skating—imagination
Jewel colors—deep luxurious shades
Jewel colors—power and vibrancy
Jewel colors—harmony
Floral design—line, form, color, texture, and balance
Floral design—clarity
Passion for good quality

Session 2 *Personal Style Statement*

I project a substantial and meaningful presence.
Grace, dignity, elegance, substance
Sophistication
A life with meaning
Audrey—always appropriately dressed
No-nonsense; strength and conviction
The meaning of substantial quality

Session 3 *Image Wounds*

I'm definitely an avoider. I avoid the mirror, and I avoid shopping unless it's absolutely necessary.
I would like to be more comfortable with my body. I'd like to move more quickly and be more agile.

Image Wounds—Important Realizations:
Felt lonely and out of place as a child.
I was taunted by my family because I looked and behaved differently from them. I wore clothes I could hide behind or at least be inconspicuous in. I ate for comfort. As I grew taller, I tried to blend in by keeping my head down, slumping, and sitting instead of standing. I found it hard to smile.
When I look in the mirror these days, I think I've stopped seeing myself. I don't really know how I look anymore.

Things I Would Like to Change:
My body talk is all about losing weight. I'd like to work on exercising, my posture, and developing some freedom of movement.

Physical Assets:

The highlight of this session for me was that I discovered that I am really not unattractive.

I like being tall now.

I like my long legs.

I have nice, thick hair.

I still have good skin.

I think my smile is nice and friendly.

People have commented on my hands—they say they are pretty and expressive.

I guess I also like my eyes and eye color.

Acknowledging those things helped me to have an interest in my appearance that just wasn't there before.

Session 4 *Inner Style*

Empathetic, generous, hardworking
Friendly, easygoing
Good listener
Compassionate
Good manners and etiquette
Nice, friendly smile
Good attitude
Patient
Good listener

I guess the highlight of this session was to acknowledge that I have come a long way in my life. I am learning a lot about refinement, sophistication, and elegance and am looking forward to further developing and introducing them into my personal style. I am very attracted to these qualities and am intrigued that they begin "inside." I felt very strongly that I would like to add "refined" to my Personal Style Statement.

Session 5 *Aesthetic Field Trip*

Well, that was great fun. I was absolutely shocked. In the furniture store, the fabric store, and certainly the wonderful clothing store we found, I noticed that my tastes have changed a great deal. I knew immediately the kinds of things I liked. I want to redecorate my house! I can't say enough about this experience.

Favorites:

Colors—*garnet red, amethyst, mulberry, and indigo blue*

Furniture—*Traditional-looking English country furniture, certain antique Japanese pieces, simple bureaus and tables. Some of the seventeenth-century French country home pieces.*

Furnishing fabrics—*I really loved plain, heavy linens and the hand-dyed fabrics. I loved all the traditional damask, canvas bed ticking, and some of the classic checks and plaids.*

Gourmet food shop—*I looked around and noticed the difference in the packaging of the items and the colorful displays. Some of the jars of jam had cloth coverings similar to the checks I liked in the fabric store. I guess the biggest difference between this shop and the local grocery store was the high standard of quality of everything. It was interesting because I was drawn to similar colors in food as in fabrics!*

Session 6 and 7 *Clothes and Color*

[Although Mary did not have the benefit of reading about the spirit of clothes the way you did, we did accompany her on the Hunt field trip. We visited several different shops and stores, all of differing quality, price and styles.]

What an education! They helped me to remain focused on what clothes mean and can say and not to think about purchasing any right now.

Details, details, details! Like the way the clothes were hanging, their quality, and the beautiful colors. The details were really easy to recognize once I just opened my eyes and knew what to look for.

The substantial clothing felt different, and I like the difference and the way I looked in them.

[Mary describes the creative and imaginative color experience on pages 204–5.]

Remember my black suit and garnet turtleneck vision.

I can be creative.

I can wear color safely.

I can trust my intuition.

I felt more confident and able to rely on myself now for new clothing decisions based on my own tastes.

Putting It All Together

I was very surprised to see that everything I desired for my image could be found in my work in the first session. I love what my words said about me, and it is wonderful to recognize the potential they hold. I am grateful for the strong direction my Personal Style Statement gave me. Even though I want creativity, color, and imagination to be present in the creation of my personal style and image—and I think that will come—it is "substantial, meaningful, and refined" that I want to project.

Inner Style—Substantial and Meaningful

Things I can do to enhance or improve it so that it becomes a part of me and I project it in my image:

Learn how to create boundaries and say no—stop being such a pushover.

Trust my intuition.

Don't expect others to have similar values to mine.

Use my opinions to serve my image.

Outer Style—Substantial and Meaningful

For clothes to be meaningful to me, I have to feel really confident and comfortable in them. I want to feel safe in them when I look in the mirror. Hanging on to things that are not substantial and no longer have meaning will not work for me. I should not allow myself to be talked into anything unless I am absolutely sure about it myself.

Small specialty shops, shops with the right atmosphere for me, are vital. I must remember that I'm the customer and it's my money. I'm in control.

My taste is changing. I must pay close attention to what I am drawn to in clothing stores now. I must avoid the old me.

The most important things for me:

Quality not quantity, and fit, fit, fit.

Color in small *amounts that* flatter *me* and suit my skin, hair, eyes, and personality. *Remember the black suit with the garnet turtleneck!*

Body Image and Body Talk Goals:

While I'm working on becoming more comfortable with my body, I'm going to keep reminding myself of my physical assets—especially when I go shopping!

I think I should start researching a new, updated hairstyle that is

more complementary to my hair texture and the shape of my face. I need
more current makeup too.

New Body Talk:
It is safe to look in the mirror.

Every time I think of saying to myself that I'm fat, I tell myself that
I'm doing the best I can.

Something important has happened. I have stopped looking to others
and stopped comparing myself with those other women who used to
make me feel so miserable. When I see other women, I try to remember
to mentally compliment them instead of criticizing myself. I've got
something of my own, and I've created an anchor made up of the things
that are important to me.

OUR COMMENTS ABOUT MARY

Mary is already happier with herself. She has not bought a thing, she
hasn't even analyzed her wardrobe yet, but she is definitely expressing her inner style. This is important because she will need to "show
up" with her inner style when she approaches her wardrobe. The
confidence she has gained and her new tastes and experiences with
refinement will be called upon when she begins to create and merge
her outer style with her inner style. The way she is beginning to
appreciate her body—as it is now—will be important for her when
she goes shopping to replace or add things to her wardrobe.

We were most happy to see her comment about "having an interest
in her appearance that just wasn't there before." This represents an
improvement in her awareness of herself. Even though Mary still
cannot see herself as the beautiful woman she is—as is evident in
her comment, "I discovered that I'm not really unattractive"—we
were confident that in time she would discover that she is much
more than "not unattractive." But most of all, we were delighted that
she has stopped comparing herself to others and continues to be
grounded in the development of her personal style.

WILLIAM'S PERSONAL STYLE PROFILE

William, being a methodical and studious person, had organized his
material on his computer and created a notebook with the printouts

of his pages. The following are William's observations and his most important discoveries relevant to his image.

Session 1 *Passions*

Sincerity and enthusiasm
Old World charm and sophistication
Vulnerability and sensitivity
My tastes are not reflected in my personal style.
I have too many different styles.
I want a strong identity.

Session 2 *Personal Style Statement*

My Personal Style Statement is:
I make an elegant and sophisticated impression.
Great taste without being a snob
William Holden—strength and sophistication
I identify with Holden's vulnerability, Harrison Ford's assuredness, humor, and strong presence.
Elegant and comfortable—jeans or suit
Combining cultures appeals to me.
All of my icons are elegant and sophisticated in their own unique way.
From the definition of elegance, I choose restraint, tasteful opulence, and scientific precision.

Session 3

Physical Assets:
Tall and long-limbed
Good hair
My wife tells me I have really nice teeth.
Clients tell me I have unusually dark blue eyes.
My posture is good considering I don't work at it.

Image Wounds:
Emotional image wound:
Different from everybody else
Made fun of and ostracized
Image wound from physical aspect:
Small-framed, narrow shoulders, physical awkwardness

Fearful of getting and looking older

Session 4 *Inner Style*

Inner Style Assets:
I have an optimistic outlook.
Tiger Woods—go-getter, great attitude, ability to achieve excellence
Patience
Good sense of humor
Honesty
Humility
Mental adroitness

To Work On:
Self-esteem
Empathy
Compassion
Brush up on my manners and etiquette
Get out from behind my desk
Stubbornness

Session 5 *Aesthetic Field Trip*

The Home Exhibition—London
While I was on a business trip in London, Nancy [his wife] persuaded me to attend this event with her. I would rather have spent my time in the museums, but I turned this into my Aesthetic Field Trip. I was surprised that I really enjoyed this visual experience because it was so different from what I normally do.

I came across a room setting that I really related to. It was a home library, combining an old look and a new contemporary look. I realized when I saw this room that I have been completely out of touch with my own surroundings. Nancy has been trying to tell me this, but until the home show, I just didn't get it.

The room I liked was not particularly to my taste, but its aesthetic uniformity drew my attention. It had a nice feeling and an inviting atmosphere—something that, I can now see, is missing from my office space. I appreciated the polished wooden floor, the built-in bookshelves, and the pale leather furniture. The lighting was very soothing and comfortable. Before I left the space, I picked up a business card—even the business card seemed in keeping with the style of the decor. Hmm.

Session 6 and 7 *Clothes and Color*

Highlights:

I'm really pleased that I gave this some attention—because I really didn't want to spend any time doing this. I only go shopping when I have to buy something.

It's weird; I didn't realize that I know so little about what really suits me. I was taking what I thought was the easy road. If it had a designer label, it must be okay. I've now made a promise to look at the garment before the label.

My wardrobe is out of date. Probably not very much in my closet is elegant or sophisticated. Clothes have really changed, and I haven't kept up.

I don't want to look old, because I'm not old and I don't feel it. But I don't want to look as if I'm trying too hard to look young and hip.

As I walked around in the stores and thought of my goals—sophistication and elegance—I was surprised at how easy it was to remain focused. I know I'm still learning, but it was easy to dismiss some of the clothing items I would normally spend time looking at because they didn't meet my new requirements. I loved the fact that I wasn't wasting any time.

Color

Kate and Malcolm took me on a whirlwind tour of color. I wanted to enjoy this experience, but at first I was struggling. I just didn't see the point of taking a risk and going outside my normal choices.

I didn't understand the subtlety of color; it just escaped me. But then they took me to a gray suit area and showed me six different shades of plain gray. When I tried them on, I could see that one gray made me look older, another made my skin look too pale, and another darker one was flattering.

With a little bit of time and effort, I can even do this myself.

Putting It All Together

I want to integrate my tastes into my personal style. My tastes are grounded in sophistication and elegance, and that's what I want.

Sophistication and elegance mean "worldly, informed, and tasteful," to me.

Remain open to starting over slowly.

Be precise about quality and fit.

Pay attention to details.

Practice restraint when I find myself going back to old habits, like pale blue and white shirts.

Look for clothing that says who I am now, not who I was.

I'm tall and slim—be grateful.

Stop worrying about my shoulders—pay attention to an accurate fit. Details!

Smile more often.

Find a form of exercise I really like—maybe try tennis.

Get my hair cut more often.

Use my sense of humor, patience, and optimistic outlook when I go shopping.

Ask Nancy to remind me about my manners and etiquette.

Try to be more aware of my behavior.

Consider if it is viable financially to begin to refurbish my office. Speak to accountant.

Cobalt blue, cornflower blue, moss green, slate gray—my new mantras.

Do three of these things, and I'm fine.

OUR COMMENTS ABOUT WILLIAM

William has surprised himself. He never knew that he could be in control of his image with so much ease and enjoyment. Having a good time with himself is key for William. A world that he considered to be exclusive and closed to him is now a world into which he feels he can enter easily. He realized that he could use his intelligence and creativity, normally reserved for his business, to project something meaningful about his personality.

William is deeply satisfied that his otherwise-hidden sensibilities are going to be reflected in his image. And even if this is something that only he is aware of, it still pleases him enormously. William discovered a place for himself between stodgy business attire and high fashion. He will be looking for all of the details that are pertinent to him regarding color, fit, fabric, and style that enable him to appear sophisticated and unique and to feel confident.

. . .

Please complete your own Personal Style Profile in any way that is comfortable for you. Mary's and William's were unique to them, as yours will be to you. Enjoy it; you can feel proud of completing this experience and confident in your own insights. Experiencing uncertainty and insecurity is normal, but remember that you cannot be wrong. Now you have a view of yourself both from the inside and the outside that is simple, realistic, and congruent with your values, passions, and lifestyle, as well as your unique personality. You are your personal style.

Closet Analysis

None of us knows what we look like unless we really study ourselves. Most people think they look smaller or bigger than they actually look. We've never met anyone who sees themselves as others see them. Other people see you at many different angles as your body moves in all its various ways. Others see how you walk and sit—and how your clothes move on your body when you move. They see how a jacket that is too tight for you restricts your movements, and how sensually a man in a great suit appears to move.

Photographs and videotape can help you gain a more accurate picture of yourself. They often act as a catalyst for a new hairstyle or a source of color information. But learning to trust your own eye is the best way to see yourself. You will need your own vision of yourself as reflected in the mirror when you go shopping.

We would like you to make the rules about what you can and cannot wear by getting to know the truth of your body as it is right now. Find balance and harmony, observe sensitive areas, become used to looking at yourself, and see how others see you from different angles. Then look at yourself as a whole, to see how your inner style and your outer style merge into the person whom the world sees when it sees you.

YOUR PERSONAL BODY MAP

The time has come to take a detailed, unemotional, and nonjudgmental survey of your body. It is very important that you become familiar with and be honest about your body. Otherwise you will not be able to choose clothes that fit well and flatter you. Your Personal Map will help you carry out this survey.

It is not our style to tell you to categorize anything about yourself, including your body. We are not going to ask you to decide whether you are a "pear" or an "apple." And we're certainly not going to tell you that there are certain clothing items that your body shape must never wear. The reason is that we have seen countless people try on an item of clothing that is "not supposed to work for their body type" only to find that it not only works but looks fabulous on them. You just never know when that one really lovely item might look great on you, even though it contradicts the stereotypical do's and don'ts for your body.

You never know until you try it on whether an item of clothing will be appropriate for your body. The rules that tell you what you can and cannot wear are not specific to your personality—only you can decide what is right for you.

When you get to know your body, the task of dressing it becomes much easier.

SEEING YOURSELF AS OTHERS SEE YOU

Don't worry! We're not going to ask you to stand in front of your mirror naked. We're more interested in what you look like with your clothes on.

For this exercise you will need your journal and two full-length mirrors. If you have only one full-length mirror at home, try to borrow a free-standing mirror from a friend or neighbor. You will need to see your whole body from all angles.

Do this exercise alone if you feel confident enough, or enlist the help of a family member or friend—a good friend! He or she can offer you feedback when you ask for it (not before). But do not become dependent on your friend's observations. You just want a sounding board.

Be in the right frame of mind to do this. It will take only a few minutes, but those minutes must be uninterrupted and stress free. Your attitude should be focused and investigative. Remember, you are learning about yourself, not admiring or criticizing yourself. Look at yourself the way you would look at a very good, close friend: someone you care about and whose best interests you have at heart.

For many of you, this will be the first time you have looked at yourself in a long while. Yes, you see your reflection in the mirror every morning, and of course you look in the mirror when you dress. But this is different. You are accustomed to seeing yourself in one way only—selectively. You've trained your eyes to not rest on certain parts of your body; you look for a few specific things each morning or evening and turn away from others. These are your sensitive areas. Let's begin there.

SENSITIVE AREAS

"My stomach is too fat." "My feet are too long." "I'm always aware of my thighs." Many of you, men and women alike, will not need a mirror for this section. If you are uncomfortable with certain parts of your body, you probably think about them often. You may have already written about them in Session 3, but we would ask you to list them again now in your journal.

Underneath your list please write these words:

The sensitive areas of my body do not have to remain as sensitive as they are.

Now we are going to ask you to think about your sensitive areas differently from the way you have been.

Probably your sensitive areas are taking up too much of your attention. You need to learn how to play these areas down, to become more detached from your feelings about them. You need to change your focus and focus your attention on your assets. When you do so, your sensitive areas will be less important and you will be able to accept them and live with them with more ease.

You need not change any part of your body—you can stay exactly as you are for the rest of your life. For example, suppose you are a male with a corpulent stomach and have no interest in changing your lifestyle but are sensitive about that area of your body. In that case, focus on how your shirts fit. Do they give you plenty of room? When you look in the mirror, are the buttons straining to stay on? In the side view, does the shirt have sufficient fabric to divert attention away from your stomach? Or does it have too much fabric, which makes you look as if you're trying to hide that part of your body?

COMMON SENSITIVE AREAS FOR MEN

The following are suggestions of the things a man can do to reduce attention to these sensitive areas and promote a sense of well-being.

Shoulders

Suits and jackets should fit accurately to the shoulder. The shoulder line that flatters best is neither too rigid nor too soft but somewhere in the middle, with sufficient structure to make the shoulders look substantial.

Height

If you consider yourself to be less than average height, short-fitting clothes will not make you look taller. Your trousers should not be too short; nor should the length of your jackets or the sleeves of your shirts. Finally, boots or shoes with heels cannot hide the fact that you are not tall.

To elongate your silhouette, wear your sleeves a fraction longer than is considered accurate. In most cases, this is less than half an inch. Similarly, to elongate the leg, wear your trousers just a fraction longer, again less than half an inch. But be careful—if these lengths are too long, you will appear shorter than you are. Study your silhouette in the mirror to see how the different lengths affect your height. By developing a dispassionate eye, you will be able to trust yourself even more than you trust tailors, for they have their own opinions about how clothes should look.

Stomach

If your stomach is a sensitive area, be aware of how loose or tight the fabric feels around your middle. You might not want your jacket buttoning too low. If you have a penchant for vests (waistcoats), remember that vests need to fit accurately and properly. If they're too tight, they will buckle, and if they're too big, they will flap around. Off-the-peg vests are a difficult fit for men with larger stomachs. But a custom-made vest can be made to fit you accurately.

If your stomach is large and you wear your trousers too low or too high, they are likely to bring attention to your stomach and feel uncomfortable. Wearing them somewhere in between will be more flattering for you.

Clingy, very fine-textured, or very lightweight fabrics will accentuate any part of your body that they touch. If you are sensitive about your stomach, a clingy fabric will intrude upon that area, making too much contact.

Waistline

If you are "thick" in the waist, trousers that are either high in the rise or "fashionably" low will generally look best. A tailored jacket with a slightly suppressed waist and, depending on your height, that is a little longer than average will be more flattering. Short blouson waist-length jackets, sweaters, knitted tops, or anything that "grips" at the waist will not be flattering. A belt that is relatively narrow and simple in design will give the waistline more definition.

Neck

Whether you consider your neck to be too big, too thick, too small, or too thin, your collars should be neither too tight nor too loose. If you have a smaller-than-average neck, keep searching for the right collar size—that is how you will best flatter it. If your neck is larger than average, wearing your collar too tight will only make you look and feel uncomfortable.

Feet

If a man has smaller-than-average feet, then shoes that are too delicate in design and shape will create a visual imbalance. He will look as if he is going to topple over, because his feet do not seem firmly planted on the ground. Generally speaking, men with smaller feet need substantial-looking shoes with sturdy soles. They need to fit highish on the instep, not exposing too much of the sock.

If a man has larger-than-average feet, he should avoid buckles, tassels, and anything extraneous on the shoes, which will make his feet look larger than they are. Stay with a subtle yet interesting style, such as an unusual toe shape. A shoe that you consider elegant or refined will not necessarily make your foot look smaller. Avoid slip-ons made of lightweight leather, which are cut very low in the front and have a delicate toe shape.

COMMON SENSITIVE AREAS FOR WOMEN

If you were to ask ten women to identify their sensitive areas, taken together they would probably cite every single area on the human female form. But here we will list only those that have been historically most common over a period of many years. Remember, these are very general and may not be applicable to your specific body or have anything to do with your personal style.

Hips and Thighs

If you are sensitive about your hips and thighs, you will be more comfortable in pants, skirts, jackets, and dresses that are of better quality and that fit well—not too tight. Keep it simple—no embellishments such as zippers for show or oversized pockets. Avoid clingy or stretchy fabrics. Short shorts or skirts, lightweight fabrics, and very inexpensive clothing will make you look larger than you are. Baggy clothing will not hide your body, especially in these areas. These areas need more of your financial investment. Better-quality clothes will flatter them best and make you feel more confident.

Bottom

Nothing beats a pair of beautifully cut trousers. They are very forgiving and downplay all bumps and bulges. Be very aware of how your skirts and dresses fit. Sometimes women think they can wear only a long full skirt or a baggy dress. This is simply not true. Well-cut, well-designed clothes in good fabrics can actually flatter this area and work visual miracles. Once again, if this is one of your sensitive areas, increase your budget to include better-quality clothing.

Stomach

If you are sensitive in the stomach area, some old clothing habits may make you feel better but actually don't help the way you look. "Tucking in" is one of them. Tucking your blouse into your pants or skirt adds bulk to the stomach area and is invariably uncomfortable. If you are wearing a jacket and never take the jacket off throughout the day, then that's another story.

Elastic or drawstring pants do not flatter this area and in fact make you feel insecure because they do not support that area of your body. Shallow pleats on low-cut pants will not flatter your stomach area.

Deep pleats on a high-waisted pant with a man-cut leg can look very sophisticated.

Overweight Bodies

If you have an overall feeling of sensitivity about your body, we'd like you to know that you do not have to lose weight to feel and look better in your clothes. Here are a few simple tips to help you immediately:

- Avoid layering, which only adds bulk and doesn't hide anything.

- Avoid wearing too many different textures at the same time.

- Avoid wearing too many different colors at the same time.

- Avoid big colorful prints, patterns, and plaids.

- Pay attention to the balance of the clothes between your upper body and your lower body. They should complement each other in fit. If you are smaller above the waist, wearing a tight top doesn't show off that fact—it only shows that you are bigger at the bottom. And vice versa.

- Avoid fabrics that are prone to creasing easily. Creasing brings unwanted attention to sensitive areas and distracts from the visual picture. The neater your clothes stay, the neater your silhouette will appear.

Please be aware that generic do's and don'ts like these can only solve a small part of the problem.

For example, generally speaking, a person with a short neck benefits both in comfort and visually from wearing a lower-necked clothing item. Conversely, a person with a long neck is visually enhanced when wearing a higher-necked clothing item. But this rule fails when a woman with a long neck wears an appropriately proportioned round-neck sweater, which exposes her elegant long neck and makes her look and feel glamorous. When it is proven that a garment with a higher neckline is not her only option, the "rule" goes out the window.

Likewise, a man who has a short neck and wears a low-to-the-neck, very-fine-wool or knitted-cotton mock turtleneck can look very sophisticated. He will have to find the right *height* of turtleneck, in the right *weight* of fabric for his shorter neck, but it will exist. The conventional advice would have been to avoid all turtlenecks. But there is always an exception to the rule—never say never.

PERSONAL BODY MAP CHECKLIST

I don't know what looks good on me, you may be thinking. Yes, you do. You really do. Maybe you have forgotten, maybe your body has changed, or maybe you just need a reminder, but you know.

This part of the exercise is intended to help you to become aware of your proportions. Knowing a few simple, even slightly vague things about your body will give you a strong indication of how clothes look on you.

By answering these next few questions, one female client discovered that her feet would look better in closed shoes than in sandals. Another client used to worry what length her skirts and dresses should be but discovered that the length of her legs made it possible for her to wear any length she desired. A male client discovered that he had a longer-than-average torso and began looking for a longer line in jackets and suits to accommodate it. Another man whose arms are shorter than average realized that all of his shirts and jackets had to be shortened. These people came to these conclusions simply by answering the following questions.

To learn how to try on clothes more efficiently, more effectively, and less emotionally, we have created this fact-finding checklist. It is purely for your information and your awareness. Make no changes in yourself, and pass no judgments. Please try to remain noncritical. Do it quickly, without thinking too much; do not ponder, for no action is required.

CHECKLIST FOR BOTH MEN AND WOMEN

Stand before your two mirrors, and write down the answers to the following questions.

1. Is the length of your neck shorter that average, average, or longer than average?
2. Is the width of your neck narrow, average, or wide?
3. Are your shoulders narrow, average, or wider than average?

4. Is the length of your torso (area from the waist up) shorter than average, average, or longer than average?

5. Is the width of your torso narrow, average, or wide?

6. Is your waist narrow in proportion to the rest of your body? Do you consider it larger for your build or about average for your build? If you are female, how is your waist defined? Is it small and does it curve? Is it small and straight? Is it average or wide, straight or curved?

7. Are your hips narrow, average, or wide?

8. Is your bottom small and narrow? Does it protrude, or is it flat? Does it appear high or low? Is it average and in the middle of the back of your body? Is your bottom wide and flat, or wide and round?

9. Are your legs shorter than average, average, or longer than average?

10. Are your feet narrow, average, or wide?

11. Are your feet shorter than average, average, or longer than average?

12. Now look at yourself at different angles. Notice your posture. How does your side profile look? Do you notice anything you haven't seen before? Use the second mirror to look at your backside, if you haven't already. What do you look like from the back view?

Now spend a moment going over your answers. These physical components are who you are physically. Is there anything about those discoveries that will help you when trying on clothes? Anything at all? It doesn't matter how silly or small it may seem. It is very important that you identify it because it will help you decide what kinds of clothing items will physically work for you and flatter you. These are calculated, unemotional decision-making observations. They help integrate the work you have done in the previous sessions with the work you are about to do now. Your observations will allow you to address anything about your appearance that you feel needs help in creating better visual balance and harmony.

Let's look at Mary's Personal Body Map as an example.

MARY'S PERSONAL BODY MAP

Mary has a medium-to-large neck. Her torso is large and long. She considers herself "big boned," except that her shoulders are narrow, especially in proportion to the rest of her long body. Her arms are longer than average. Her hips are medium to large, and her waist is "thick." Her bottom is wide but not overly so and not out of proportion with her body. Her legs are long and slender, and she is tall. Her feet are average in length and in width. Her shoulders are slightly rounded, but otherwise she has good posture.

Her sensitive areas are her hips, her bottom, and her stomach.

Mary felt she needed to pay particular attention to her waist area and to wear clothes that gave more definition to this part of her body. She can wear almost any length dress or skirt that she chooses. She must be careful about choosing the necklines and the collars of her sweaters and blouses. She will also be picky about exposing her shoulders. Jackets will give her whole silhouette a better proportion, but she mustn't wear big padded shoulders or anything with sloping shoulders.

Her hip, thigh, and bottom areas will receive the most attention. She won't wear anything bulky or fabrics that are thick, lumpy, or too heavily textured. At the same time the fabric must be "substantial" and of good quality.

Feel free to work with the Personal Body Map in as much detail as you wish. Remember, you are doing this to help yourself create balance and security in your clothing choices. Retraining your eye is a very self-empowering thing to do. You may still need to ask, "Does this look good on me?" every so often. But think how good it will feel to know for yourself, to be able to look in the mirror and, with a newly discerning eye, be able to say, "Yes, this is right for me."

CLOSET ANALYSIS

We suggest that you begin this exercise by just sitting quietly and reading through this section before you actually do the exercise. We offer you quite a bit of information and things to think about that will help you before you even open your closet door.

This is not your regular closet clean out—this is very different. All of the work you have done in Sessions 1 to 8 have primed you for this session and, of course, for the last session. What you have learned already has subconsciously given you the tools and awareness about yourself that will make this task seem relatively straightforward. In fact, you will be surprised at how easy this will be.

First, we will give you some general guidelines to make this task as easy as possible, and then we'll share with you some of the tips that our clients discovered for themselves. Our clients become very clear about what is going on inside their closets, as you will! You may then decide to create your own "system," categories, and coping skills. For example, some of you may have a great number of old clothes— clothes that have been in your closet for more years than you probably care to remember! You might find it beneficial to try these things on so that it is very clear to you that it is time to stop hoarding. Others of you may systematically go through your clothing often and therefore will need to concentrate on other things about your clothes, perhaps color, fit, obvious gaps, and relevance to your personal style statement. In any event, each of you will perform this exercise in your own unique way—there is no right way or wrong way. However, we do want to help you get started and guide you along the way.

GETTING STARTED

You will need the following:

A good friend, significant other, or relative

Unless you are perfectly all right being on your own for this, help is a good idea. The physical help will make the event pass by more quickly, and the emotional help is priceless. As you go through each item of clothing, your life will pass before your eyes. Your job is to make decisions—not go through an emotional journey into the past with each sweater or tie or pair of shoes. A friend can keep you on track, be supportive, and lighten up the atmosphere if it becomes too serious. You may ask your friend for an opinion, but the final decision about what to do with each item of clothing is up to you, based on your own knowledge, your own personal style, and your intuition.

Time

Choose a time to do this exercise when you are feeling bright and alert. We strongly recommend starting on a "day off" morning. You may feel a bit daunted at first, but don't let that keep you from getting started. Don't procrastinate! Make an appointment with the person who is helping you. You will be more likely to keep it.

Bags, boxes, or containers of some kind to dispose of clothes

Paper and pen for taking notes and making lists

Tape, pins, or some utensil for attaching notes to clothing items

Your Personal Style Statement and your Personal Style Journal

Some clients have written their Personal Style Statement on a piece of paper and taped it on the wall nearest their closet to refer to it during this process. Although you may know yours by heart, some people find having it visually in front of them keeps them on track.

Your Personal Style Profile pages and your Personal Body Map pages will also be of great help to you. In fact, all of your efforts to this point can be practically used and can offer you an amazing amount of support. The work is a constant reminder to keep you from slipping back into an old view of yourself. As you try on your clothing, you will hear yourself commenting, "This just isn't me anymore" or "This no longer flatters me." You are able to make the comments because of the work you have done. If you had not done the work, your comment would most likely be, "I don't know," and you would feel frustrated, lose interest, and be confused. You might also rely too heavily on your friend to "tell you what to do." So pat yourself on the back for entering this phase well prepared.

KEEP THESE THINGS IN MIND

For many of you, revisiting your clothing will most likely bring up emotional events and lifestyle changes. You will see your history played out in your past clothing choices. Here is a list of other things you will find in your closet in addition to your clothes!

- Weight gain
- Weight loss
- Other change in body shape (as from working out)

- Pregnancy
- Your youth
- Divorce
- New job
- Old job
- Lack of money
- Money
- An old friend
- An old lover
- Your health
- A loved one who has passed on
- Shopping mistakes
- Your former selves (fashion victim, trendy youth, conservative, power era, romantic, eccentric, attention grabbing, creative and theatrical, thrift shop denizen)

When any of these memories arise, bring yourself back to the present. Stay focused on the job at hand. Not only will this help you to make better decisions, it will save time as well. Pondering old flames can be time-consuming and exhausting!

WHERE TO START

How you start is very important. You should begin in what you intuitively feel is the easiest, most comfortable place. Begin slowly—you will develop a rhythm as you work. Do not make any rash decisions initially. Some people begin with their favorite clothes, the ones that make them feel good. This is a good choice. You may want to tell your friend why the particular item makes you feel good and what you love about it. Note whether it relates to your Personal Style Statement. If it doesn't but you still love it, that's all right for now.

You may already feel that a section of your wardrobe is ready to be analyzed. You may almost feel the need for a purging, and you can't wait to get your hands on these items. Start there if you feel strongly about it.

You might also feel overwhelmed in the beginning. You won't know where to start and you might feel fearful or intimidated. You may be a little nervous that your expectations will not be met. We assure you they will. You will create a great deal of physical, mental, and emotional space by completing this exercise. You will find it cathartic and liberating.

If a wave of stubborn procrastination comes over you, then either wait until you feel really ready or ask your friend to get you through this moment. This exercise may seem like a chore, but you will feel differently once you are engaged in it. When you overcome the fear factor, the procrastination factor, and the projecting factor (the internal negative chatter about the project), you will calm down because you will realize that you are taking care of *you*.

HOW TO START

Just put your hand on the first garment. Look at it, and decide whether it represents who you are right now. You may need to try on the item. These are the things you will need to decide about each garment:

- Does it still fit?
- Is it a good fit?
- Is it comfortable against your skin?
- Is it in good shape? (This means it needs no alterations; the fabric isn't worn out; there are no holes, stains, or missing buttons.)
- Does the color still work for you? (Think back to the Color session. Is this color good for your skin and hair color? Does it flatter you?)
- Does it look current?
- Can it be altered to look current?
- Does it suit your lifestyle?
- Does it make any connection to your Personal Style Statement?
- Remember your Personal Body Map and especially your sensitive areas. Does it help or hinder them?

THE FOUR CATEGORIES

There is a place in the world for categories, and this is definitely one of them. Decide which category each garment belongs to.

1. **It's a keeper.** This is a clothing item that you obviously will continue to wear. You can either put it back in the closet or keep it out for a while to categorize it. Some people have already categorized

and organized their clothing in their wardrobe. This is a good opportunity for you to create a system or review how your wardrobe is laid out. We would suggest a way of organizing your clothing to make choices less difficult in the mornings. It would help you emotionally as well as physically.

2. **Needs alterations or cleaning.** Many new outfits have been born from this category. The simple, obvious alterations are lengthening, shortening, taking in, letting out, and repairing. But other alterations can improve an item that you are not currently comfortable wearing but would like to. For these kinds of alterations, you really need to seek out an expert tailor. For example, going up or down a suit size is a bigger job than a simple taking in or letting out—it requires exacting work and is a more complex process. An expert will advise you as to whether it is worth the trouble and money to try to reinvent the shoulders of a jacket that is past its era. The same would apply to any garment that you are trying to make appear more current. It doesn't always work, and the expert must be trustworthy and talented. It is worth your time to discuss your ideas and wishes with an expert. Now that you have gained so much knowledge, you are in a position to make collaborative decisions with a feeling of security. It may be worth your while to seek out an invisible repair expert—often called invisible menders. Is the item worth repairing? A better-quality sweater with a bad snag or a hole, or a good shirt with a small tear, can sometimes be made to look almost perfect.

3. **It's out.** Friends, family members, charity, and the rubbish are the receivers of these items. Take pleasure in giving a gift to someone who needs something. Don't give away stained or torn clothing—it's tacky and belongs in the garbage. Try not to take on the attitude that you're throwing money away—you've probably wasted more money on bad dinners than you will letting go of an expensive suit that no longer fits you.

4. **The undecided.** Having trouble deciding on a garment? Again, go through the list of questions about what you are looking for in your current clothing (see page 242). Your decision will be made for you. If you are still undecided, put the garment aside to rethink later, or create a space in your wardrobe and label it "still not sure" or the equivalent.

TROUBLESHOOTING

How Ruthless Should You Be?

It may be that not one item of clothing in your wardrobe has any relation at all to your Personal Style Statement. Don't worry—you are not alone! Remember, this is a journey, and you have to start somewhere. Even if you build up a new wardrobe one item at a time, it will be worth it. So obviously you will not dispose of every one of your suits—unless you have the kind of budget that would allow for that. Even then you certainly can't be suitless until you can go shopping! So it is basically your budget that will determine how many items you will be able to discard. Some items you won't need to replace because you never needed them in the first place. These are items that you never wear and items that were mistakes.

Quality over Quantity

Do you have many, many pairs of lesser-quality, hardly-ever-worn, or terribly overworn shoes in your closet right now? Or is it T-shirts that you collect? Maybe you have many cheap trousers but not one pair of really nice pants?

After this exercise, you will probably end up with far fewer clothes in your wardrobe than ever before in your life. Don't worry—that's a good thing. What remains and what you will eventually add will be of better quality. The essence of a well-developed wardrobe is quality, not quantity. Now that you can see the forest for the trees, you will be free from physical and emotional clutter and able to carefully create a collection of clothes and accessories that you deserve.

The Fear of an Empty Wardrobe

Almost all of our clients experience an unexpected and surprising amount of fear in this exercise. Getting rid of old clothes, inappropriate clothes, or clothes that don't fit anymore seems to bring out feelings of insecurity. You have become used to seeing a closet full of clothes, even though you wear only half of them. (Most people wear less than half!) Just knowing that those jeans from 1975 are still in your closet makes you feel secure. Or perhaps that expensive silk blouse in the wrong color, bulging with 1980s shoulder pads, is just very difficult to let go. Well, you really must start letting go. Remember what you've said you want for your image in your Personal Style Statement; you can't have it both ways.

Session 6's section on "Being Current" (pages 173–74) and the Hunt exercise in Session 7 have given you firsthand experience of what is current, so you can judge your own wardrobe now accordingly. You may think, "Maybe I can make it work one day" or "Maybe it will be in style again," but these thoughts can be very self-deceptive. Most of the time reinvented trends and fashion items can't be duplicated with the older versions. The business is too smart and savvy for that. Remember, they want to make money, not help you use your existing wardrobe! Every rule has exceptions, but you would have to be very knowledgeable and extremely confident to be able to reinvent your original 1970s Naugahyde maxicoat.

Don't Get Rid of Everything

The wish to purge may become so overwhelming that you actually begin to think about replacing *everything*. Don't. Be careful and thoughtful about this process. Starting over from scratch may actually be an easy way to avoid really thinking about what you're doing. But you will miss opportunities to be creative by reinventing your existing clothing.

Ask yourself the following questions:

- Why is it time to get rid of this?
- Why don't I wear this anymore?
- Why did I buy this?
- Why have I *never* worn this?
- Why didn't I buy two of these?
- Why didn't I return this?
- Did this fit so badly when I bought it?

Be particularly aware of your mistakes and why you made them. The answer may be very simple, but do find out—it's the best way to avoid making the mistake again.

Wardrobe Clean-Out Rules

According to common wisdom, if a clothing item has been in your closet more than one year, then you should get rid of it. But some of our clients have reinvented clothing items that are up to five years old. We say: If an item is six months old and doesn't work—then it doesn't work! If it is three years old and still looks good on you and says something about your personal style—enjoy it, wear it! You are not just "cleaning out your closet."

Reinventing Garments

Trust yourself when it comes to being creative with your existing wardrobe. Reinventing garments is easier on your budget than buying new ones. Before you make a commitment to purchase a new expensive "major" item, take a good look to see if perhaps there is a way to reinvent an existing item. When you absolutely know for sure that you have no alternative but to buy a new suit, pair of trousers, or any other item, then you will feel better about investing the money.

One of our clients who had a huge walk-in closet found that by exercising her creative muscles, she added new outfits to her wardrobe without buying a thing. Her co-workers marveled that she must have gone on a shopping spree. When she told them she had just paired things differently and pulled out long-forgotten but still-well-cared-for items, they couldn't believe it. She could never have created such a wide variety of wearable clothes, she told us, had she not first discovered her personal style.

If you become inspired about a particular clothing item, try it on. The color or shape may appeal to you now in a way that it didn't a few months ago. And because your knowledge of yourself is fresh and current, your ideas will come with more ease. Ask yourself:

- Can I improve the way this looks on me?
- How can I make it more "me"?
- Will this suit be current enough if I wear a different shirt with it?
- Is there a current color in my wardrobe that I can pair with this not-so-current item?

Your eye is more developed now—you know more about what is going on and what you are doing. You are becoming your own expert about what is right for you. So feel free to make decisions confidently.

IN THE THICK OF IT

Once you start taking apart your wardrobe, you will soon be surrounded by your clothes. Spread them around, so that you can see them independently of each other. Your friend may help you move unwanted or alteration items into another room so that you can have ample working space.

Try not to get sidetracked. Stay with what you are doing in the moment, which is to sort your clothes into the four categories. This is a very important step, and it will serve you well to really dive into this project, stay focused, and see it through to the end. Don't labor over anything long enough to keep you from completing it. It is preferable to finish this process in one day, but if the day passes and you would like to continue another day, please do so.

WHAT TO DO WITH THE KEEPERS

When you have decided which clothes belong in category one, it's time to make your wardrobe do what you want it to do for you, by sorting them into new categories.

Rather than using the obvious categories of clothing—business, casual, holiday, dressy, sporty—we suggest that you make your categories more personal and specific to your particular lifestyle and needs. The following category suggestions can allow you to gain emotional and practical support from your wardrobe.

Secure-Making Clothes
Secure-making clothes are those that:

- You enjoy wearing and in some way relate to your personal style.
- Always work for you—dependably.
- Make you feel secure and confident.
- Make you feel more yourself.

If you have any clothes like this, then you are ahead of the game. Please notice specifically what about these items makes you feel this way. If you have no secure-making clothes, then they will be the first items on your shopping list. They will probably be larger, more important purchases, such as business clothes, good-quality social clothing, and first-impression clothing.

Secure-making clothes are those that you feel and look good in regardless of your mood, body image, or environment.

Secure-making clothes are different for everyone. Perhaps you already feel secure in your business clothes and want to feel more secure in your casual clothes. Or maybe you are changing jobs or careers and feel insecure about your business suits. You might even want to feel more secure about your accessories. All of our clients in the business world include their business clothes in their secure-making category.

Secure-making clothes:

- Cover the sensitive areas of your body well.
- Flatter your skin color.
- Always feel comfortable.
- Look current.
- Are easy to accessorize.
- Never attract too much attention.
- Are always appropriate.
- Are always clean, pressed, and well cared for.
- Allow you to move freely and to look good from different angles.

Your secure-making clothes are the heart and soul of your wardrobe. So when you choose them and care for them, they need more attention. Create a section of your wardrobe for your secure-making clothes.

The Loners

"I love this but I don't have anything to wear with it."

This is the definitive statement of a loner. You don't even know whether it was a mistake because you never get a chance to wear it! It just sits in your closet, and sits and sits and sits.

Your Closet Analysis will make your loners stand out even more. You must decide if you want to keep them or let go of them.

Loners teach you about your shopping habits and your state of mind when you go shopping. Try to remember the occassion when you bought the loner, then answer these questions:

- What mood were you in?
- Did you consider your existing wardrobe and its colors?
- Did you buy it with certainty or with doubt?
- Did you just "have to buy something" that day?
- Did someone else talk you into buying it?

First of all, make sure that you really don't have anything to wear with it. Now that you can see the items in your closet more clearly, you may be able to pair it with another item in a satisfying way.

If you decide to keep the loner but don't have anything to wear with it, then include a detailed description of it on your shopping list. Sometimes clients bring a jacket or a pair of trousers along with them while shopping just to make sure that they purchase an item that complements the loner.

Paul: Weekend Clothing

Does your personal style tend to fall apart on the weekends? Our client Paul's did. His story will give you a fresh outlook on your down-time image.

Paul suffered from what we call "weekend syndrome." All during the week he wore his business uniform—a plain dark suit, a light-colored shirt, a conservative tie, black Oxford shoes, and plain dark socks—to please his clients and law partners. He always appeared crisply professional and sartorially in-sync. When it came to his professional image, he didn't have to make many decisions.

But on the weekends Paul became a totally different person. It was as if he were too burned out by the accumulated stresses of the week to care what he looked like. He would show up at neighbors' weekend barbecues wearing T-shirts that were old and faded, jeans or khakis that were either frayed or way past retirement, and old deck shoes. He wore his baseball cap frequently. Even when he went to dinner with friends on a Saturday night and made some effort to dress up, he still was disconnected from his clothes. He would wear an Oxford shirt that was designated as no longer good enough for work, the same pair of khakis he wore every weekend, and sport socks with tennis shoes. In essence, Paul was simply going through the motions.

Paul is a nice-looking man in his thirties, of medium height and build and with short dark hair. He has a great wit and constantly amuses friends and family with his subtle, "sneak-up-on-you" humor. Women find his boyish handsomeness charming, and men admire his wide intelligence. But the way he looked on the weekends didn't correspond to the person we have described.

Paul's wife, Patty, had finally had enough of his neglect of his private and social image. His weekend wardrobe needed some serious attention, she told him. Moreover, he was taking insufficient care of what he did have—he was not replacing missing buttons, or keeping his shoes repaired, or cutting his hair regularly enough. His lack of care was making him look ten years older than he really was. Gently, Patty explained to him that his neglect was sending a powerful message to her, to the children, and to their friends, about how little he valued them; worse, he was giving them all a message that he valued himself very little as well.

That was the day Paul woke up. He was shocked to realize the contrast between his orderly and defined workday image and his image on the weekends. Though Paul laughingly referred to it as his "Jekyll and Hyde" problem, he knew there was more to it than that.

Patty encouraged Paul to meet with us. Paul told us that he wanted to spend as little money as possible on new weekend clothes. Like many men we have worked with, he felt that suits were important "business" investments, and he spent commensurately for them. But he froze when shown a beautiful weekend sweater—as if, like a bad stock, it might not give him a good return on his money.

Many men simply abdicate their style choices to their wives. At every opportunity—Father's Day, his birthday, Christmas—Patty had steadfastly given Paul expensive weekend wear, in a not-so-subtle effort to do for him what he would not. These gifts would lead to a tango of ingratitude and rage. The items would remain in the closet, while Patty fumed, and Paul, resenting her for trying to "manage" him, would turn up wearing those frayed and tired-looking items of yesteryear. Patty needed to understand that Paul had to take responsibility for his own wardrobe. If a man is not interested in choosing his own clothes and is not interested in his own appearance, he won't wear what his wife buys him, no matter how high the quality. Trying to make someone over against his will only leads to power struggles, frustrations, and stresses.

Fortunately, Paul was finally ready to take better care of himself. For a man who admittedly came to us with some reluctance, he turned out to be very good-humored about himself and became very open to the prospect of developing his personal style. He was a good student. Like the well-prepared litigator he is, he put a lot of thought and effort into the homework we gave him, and he really got in touch with the things in his life that were important to him. He created his Personal Style Statement, which helped him tremendously while he was learning: **"I present an image of clarity, confidence, and comfort."**

As we worked with Paul, he gained confidence in his ability to express himself within the framework of his personal tastes. He gave himself the freedom to experiment on the weekends. Instead of always wearing a T-shirt, he wore a good-quality yet casual, crisp, white long-sleeved shirt. He found in the back of his closet a great pair of brown suede lace-up thick-soled shoes that he had forgotten about. He didn't normally wear a belt with his jeans, but when we showed him how it really gave the outfit a sense of completion, he realized it was relevant. The clarity of these simple changes made him feel confident and secure. It also satisfied one of the goals in his Personal Style Statement. This was the first of several simple new outfits that Paul would enjoy wearing on the weekends.

We taught Paul how to reinvent his existing wardrobe by editing and categorizing. He got rid of items in his closet that were not related to his Personal Style Statement and that no longer served him. By editing his wardrobe, Paul was also uncluttering his mind. And by categorizing some of his clothes as "I can always wear this" or "I always feel good in this" or "I can wear this when I'm feeling tired and unimaginative and don't want to think about it," he was giving himself a safety net. More important, he reinvented his existing wardrobe without spending a great deal of money.

The changes in Paul's weekend wardrobe had a ripple effect on his business wardrobe. Once Paul faced who he was at home, he began examining his feelings and attitudes about work, especially for ways to relieve some of the enormous pressure of his caseload. He resolved to try to exercise more, and he also wanted to experience during the week the way he was now feeling about his image on the weekends. His business "uniform" was not based on his own personal style, so he never really felt completely secure in it. Yet he was trying so hard to project the right "lawyer" image that he never considered developing a professional image according to his own personal style. His humor, intelligence, and boyishness did not show up anywhere in his work life visually.

When the time came to analyze his closet, Paul, like many clients, was edgy and apprehensive. He stood before his closet as though we were the closet police about to hand him a search warrant. He was under the misconception that we were going to go through his closet while he sat in a bedroom chair. Instead, we suggested he begin by pulling out his favorite shirt and telling us what he liked about it.

At first Paul had a hard time talking about his clothes. He was intimidated. He said he had no understanding of clothes, no vocabulary for describing fabrics and colors. But he did. He knew what he liked and didn't like; he knew what was wrong for him and what needed to be discarded. He knew which items were just plain old and worn out.

We asked him again what he liked about the shirt. After a little more stalling, Paul told us he liked the way it felt and loved the color (a dark gray). He even said he wished he had more of the same kind of shirt. *Good,* we thought, *he's taking a risk and expressing his opinions and tastes.* After a slow start, he was ready to go forward.

Paul used the words from his Personal Style Statement, *clarity, confidence,* and *comfort,* and combined them with the key words from his Aesthetic Field Trip, which were *elegant, well-proportioned, practical,* and *comfortable.* His favorite shirt represented all those aspects. It was a charcoal-gray, densely woven cotton twill fabric, which is a substantial fabric. It had a soft, relaxed collar that looked elegant even when opened at the neck. The buttons were beautiful mother-of-pearl, slightly larger than a regular dress shirt button, and of a similar color to the shirt. We asked Paul to put the shirt on. It was beautifully cut and the fit was perfect, especially on his shoulders; it made him feel good and gave him confidence. It gave him a look of *clarity* and *comfort.* We asked him to find similar items in his wardrobe, but he could find very few.

We then asked Paul to show us the items that he never wore and to explain why. In some cases, he explained, the colors had faded, they had holes in them, or they were very out of style. Although Paul did not like to "waste" money on clothes, there were brand-new, never-worn items that just needed minor alterations. "Why did I ever purchase this?" turned out to be Paul's most recurring question to himself about his current wardrobe. His closet was full of items that didn't fit into his life. He had shoes he didn't need and ties that no longer reflected his tastes. His business "uniform," with its correct blandness, depressed him and made him uncomfortable.

We cleared the bedroom of all clutter and created clean surfaces everywhere. At this point we always ask everyone living in the house to join in, to be there when the clothes come out of the closet. This energizes the atmosphere and creates an "up" feeling, especially as the retired articles go up for grabs.

Usually the chief beneficiary of this process is the spouse, or a teenage son or daughter who inherits sweaters, shirts, and T-shirts. In Paul's case, involving family helped defuse the emotional problems of getting rid of so many clothes at once. Knowing they were to be recycled reminded him that his original choices were financially not wasteful.

By the time we were halfway through, Paul needed no more encouragement. When we asked, "Are you sure you want to get rid of that?" Paul would always answer, "Absolutely."

With the remaining clothes in Paul's wardrobe, we helped him to create new categories to simplify his life. He found that he needed less than he thought he did and understood that the empty space left from the clean-out did not have to be filled right away or all at one time. He had enough clothes to meet his current needs and a strategy for eventually satisfying each category he created.

Does your weekend clothing help you to feel relaxed and comfortable and still reflect your personal style?

The Casual Friday Dilemma

Casual Friday is just another dictate about how to dress. In most businesses it means trading in one uniform for another: replacing suits, shirts, and ties with polo shirts, khakis, and deck shoes. This new dress code has caused and continues to cause significant discomfort for employees at almost every level. Some who have just been able to afford their first good-quality suit are now unsure of when it is appropriate to wear it. Casual Friday has become very stressful, probably because it has created uncertainty in regard to a person's business image.

The casual Friday category is different from the weekend category. On the weekends you can worry much less about the way you look and dress than you can during the week. Casual Friday is different because you are still being judged—no matter how "relaxed" the atmosphere is supposed to be. Our clients complain about having to bring their "off duty" clothes into the workplace. Their weekend clothes help them to maintain boundaries between work and personal life. On the weekends they wish to totally divorce themselves from work and their weekend clothes are an important part of that psychological process. Maintaining the division between leisure and business clothes is important to them.

If a businessperson does not project an image of reliability and authority, his or her credibility is going to be questioned. A weekend sweater and well-worn chinos do not project reliability or authority.

When you meet people for the first time, they judge you within the first fifteen seconds. Your clothes are included in that judgment. We are not suggesting that every businessperson should wear only serious business suits. We are saying that any businessperson who appears to be in any way unprofessional, or to use the dictionary's definition of *casual,* "not serious or thorough," is taking a great risk with his or her career.

The tried and tested business suit has been a haven of security for businesspeople for aeons. Casual Friday requires a considered and appropriate replacement. It needs more attention than just *any* casual clothes. And now heads of many corporations are saying that casual Fridays will be extended all week. Casual Friday has been called the "new business fashion for the 2000s." It is really not fashion but a cultural shift in our definition of acceptable business attire.

Be alert and aware as to how you interpret casual Friday—you must be careful not to end up as a carbon copy of a co-worker or superior. Your personal style can truly represent you only if you are prepared to be uniquely you, not someone else. But you can create your own unique take on casual wear, be it Friday or any other day of the week.

Before you decide how your wardrobe will accommodate casual Friday, first find out how *you* will accommodate it.

• What is your interpretation of casual for business? What's the difference between casual for business and casual for pleasure?

• Are you comfortable with casual for business?

• Does it affect your work in any way?

• Does casual Friday leave you prepared for unexpected emergencies where your image is at stake, such as an unexpected interview or an unplanned client meeting?

• If you don't want to dress more casually for work, are you comfortable with standing out in the crowd?

• Would you be comfortable with casual Friday if you wore clothes that were more casual but still represented your own personal style?

• If your business has rules about the specifics of casual Friday, how do they affect your choices?

So how do you accommodate this category in your wardrobe? Whether you are male or female, the same advice applies.

It makes no difference whether you are dressing for a regular workday, a casual Friday, or to pick up your children from school; despite the arena, occasion, or environment, you must project one personal style.

Unfortunately, casual clothes tend to be less cared for, less thought out, and of lesser quality than more formal clothes. The attitude of "it's the weekend, it doesn't matter," like our client Paul's, is pervasive. Cheap and cheerful clothes have their place, clothes to garden, paint, and play softball and croquet in—but those clothes are very specific and very different from public casual wear.

Ask yourself if the casual clothes you own now really say something about your personality. Are you really a three-button polo person? Are you really a cargo-pant, T-strap-camisole woman? How do you rate these garments' quality, fit, and design? You probably don't want to spend more money on your casual clothes than on your career clothes, but they must nevertheless represent your Personal Style Statement. Think of it as establishing your own casual trademark.

On one hot Los Angeles summer day, one of our male clients chose a good-quality pair of heavy white cotton drill pants and a dark navy, thick linen, slightly fitted shirt. He wore a pair of beautiful high-front European loafers in soft black leather. He looked crisp, fresh, handsome, and special—and like no one else in his office. He had established his own look.

One chilly fall day in London, a female client traded in her jeans—which she admitted were uncomfortable and never really fit her well—for a more urbane and sophisticated casual appearance. She realized that she had become too reliant on her jeans and that they actually swallowed her personality. She had clung to her jeans for too long because she felt that she could wear them in almost any environment. Now she was determined to search for casual clothes that were unpredictable and would say something more truthful about her. She chose a pair of midweight, very-soft-to-the-hand gray flannel trousers that had the same ease as jeans. The fabric was a pure wool flannel with a little stretch blended in, making the trousers current, comfortable, and casual. Although they did not have the same design details as jeans, they were cut similarly. Our client loved them so much that she also bought them in black.

She also chose a dark chocolate-brown, long-sleeve T-shirt in a tightly woven, dense cotton fiber, which looked interesting with the flannel trousers. It felt and looked as substantial as a sweater, but worn with the trousers it appeared very sporty and contemporary. Her accessories were a brown suede belt that complemented her brown suede, low-heeled, ankle-high boots. The boots had a soft crepe sole that suited this "running around" outfit. Our client was extremely comfortable and found these items to have even more versatility than jeans. She wore this outfit to places where jeans were just a little too casual—namely to work on Friday!

Both of these clients introduced several more items to their repertoire of casual wear that were in keeping with these original new outfits. They went on to develop a strong signature look for themselves.

Casual wear can be as distinctive as business attire or any other category of clothing. Because of the strong movement toward dressing down in Western culture, it is relevant to spend time and money developing your personal casual style. Consider upgrading your casual clothes slowly, a half a step at a time. Take better care of them, and be honest about when they've seen their last days.

Cheap, Cheerful, and Fun

Some of your keepers may feel far away from your image goals. You are in the early stages of redefining your image, and some items that you have now and will purchase in the future do not necessarily have to live up to high quality, fit, and design standards. Hopefully, you will save your money to purchase a few great-quality items for the more important garments.

Some people just have a knack for making lesser-quality, vintage, or downright cheap clothing look like a million bucks. We call this "creating something out of nothing." Anyone can do this by giving it a little time and consideration. The secret is to enjoy it immensely, to get a kick out of "little secrets." For those who do it, it becomes a hobby, a recreational activity that promotes their individuality and creativity. Even very wealthy people derive pleasure from going on "the hunt," finding the clever bargain, and wearing their special purchase.

These goods sometimes have a shorter life than others, but because you have spent considerably less money on them, it is not so painful to witness their demise. A pair of original Pointer farmer's jeans cost only twenty-five dollars at a men's farming supply store, while the trendy ones go for at least triple that. All-American skinny T-shirts that have been designed in the same way for sixty years are found at all of the "mart" stores in a plastic bag three for ten dollars. Men and women from every walk of life wear them. Even the most elitist of designers are still replicating them.

Other items may last as long as you care for them: an antique watch, a flea market silk scarf, or a pair of earrings. Such treasureable finds never date, and although they may not be to everyone's liking or taste, they are solid, reliable, and unique for the right person.

A word of caution. Fun, cheap, and cheerful clothing is not about "costume dressing." In fact, you need to be very careful, selective, and ultrafussy before you purchase clothes from thrift shops and vintage shops.

Some people cringe at the thought of wearing preworn items, but others adore it. If you do get the urge to explore a vintage clothing store, the garment must meet an impeccable standard of cleanliness. It should not need any repairs, and it should look as if it has hardly been worn. A very good vintage clothing store will have vintage clothing that has never been worn.

Be careful about the way you pair lesser-quality items with good-quality items. A very cheap T-shirt with an expensive suit does not work. The quality gap is too large. When in doubt, don't even try it. Always remember to honor your Personal Style Statement, and pay close attention to fit and the design of the garment.

"I Feel Special" Clothing

If you are like most people, you have often felt that you have nothing to wear when invited to a social occasion: a casual party, a dinner with friends, a date, or other nonwork-related event. Maybe you feel as if none of your clothing speaks of who you are outside of your career role, parent role, or any other role that may dominate your life.

"I feel special" clothing can really say something extra about your personal style. Something about it makes you come alive. You feel extra good when you wear it. You receive more complements than the item itself. Someone may comment on how good you look, or refer to the glow on your face, or even how young you look! This happens because the garment makes you feel good—not because it is a stunning piece. Among your category one clothes, the keepers, do you see any that might fit this category? These clothes may be one-of-a-kind or hard-to-find items, perhaps something you picked up on a vacation or business trip.

Clothes for the Unexpected Special Occasion

A real black tie affair that you never thought you would be invited to, a big formal wedding, a special occasion that insists on very formal attire—many sleepless nights are spent because of these occasions. And they do exist; countless people, ourselves included, have received surprising invitations to the most unusual events, sometimes at the last minute.

What do you do? Do you purchase clothing for an event that may never happen, or do you take your chances and wait until you receive an invitation?

Men have all the luck here. A man who already has a good dark suit can get by quite well with only a couple more purchases. A very-good-quality white dress shirt with French cuffs, a plain black bow tie (assuming the suit is black), a pair of plain black dress leather shoes, and plain dark socks will open most doors. If you like unusual cufflinks, here's an excuse to browse around for them!

It's not that easy for women, who have to be resourceful and proactive. First of all, you probably can't believe you are even thinking about formal wear in the 2000s! But you never know—maybe your husband, a family member—or you!—will be nominated for an Academy Award one day.

When you need clothes for a formal occasion, grab a friend or get on the Internet and start searching out information to inspire a few ideas. Stop thinking of it as a chore—make it fun and exciting. Your Personal Style Statement will come in very handy as you start paring down your choices. Do not step outside of what is right for you. Your purchase must be worth the effort and financial commitment.

Be careful of strapless dresses. It is not that you must have a perfect-looking upper body to wear one; it is not that your body is "wrong" or "too" anything. But the fabric of a strapless dress fits over your upper body in a way that can either push your flesh out, making you look fleshier than you actually are, or fit too loosely, which is also unflattering. The generic fit of a strapless dress or top also tends to accentuate the underarm area, which is not exactly where you want people's eyes to be drawn. Even on the thinnest of women, this style, when worn with an imperfect fit, can expose a distracting fold of the skin.

We encourage you to think outside the box, à la Sharon Stone's famous Gap black turtleneck at the Academy Awards a few years ago. Her confidence enabled her to carry that off. Because you are in the process of defining your personal style, you too will be able to take calculated risks and afford yourself the luxury of being different.

A Story from Kate

"Malcolm and I were invited to attend a royal do in the early 1990s in London. The invitation was quite a surprise, and we were both looking forward to the evening. I knew better than to wait until the last minute to prepare for this strictly black-tie event, but it was difficult for me to find a dress that was appropriate for me and for the occasion. In specialty shops where lush carpet-covered floors and deep-cushioned sofas and chairs supported me, I was shown suggestion after suggestion of emerald-green taffeta gowns with larger-than-life bows either on the front or back—it was hard to tell.

"It didn't take long to change my strategy, which was to scrap the specialty shops and try the department stores and designer shops. I actually did try a few things on, but I knew right away that that gold lamé didn't really say anything about my personal style, while the sequined mermaid number must have been meant for this particular shop's thriving, shall we say, cross-dressing-with-a-strong-desire-to-entertain clientele.

"I finally found the solution in my own backyard, so to speak. One evening at home we were in Malcolm's closet deciding what he would wear to this now-bothersome event, when I eyed a beautiful black silk tuxedo. I asked him if he was going to wear it, and he said no. I slipped into it and asked if he thought it could be altered. After he recovered from the theft, he agreed to help me try.

"Designers had been making suits for women inspired by men's traditional suits since the 1930s, so I knew that I would not look completely out of place, yet still be acceptably different.

"Thinking about what to wear underneath, I performed one of those throwing-things-out-of-the-drawers acts and discovered an antique French bustier made of palest-pink-almost-white cotton lace. It had been a gift from my Pilates teacher. It was the feminine touch I would need to feel good about wearing a man's tuxedo to a royal black-tie affair. I bought a pair of knock-out black heels and topped it all off with a blossoming peony in my buttonhole. The whole experience was great fun. And as I sat and listened to the late, great Yehudi Menuhin play his violin in St. James's Palace, my eyes wandered to the bows and ruffles, the chiffons and raw silks, and I felt totally myself."

Many alternatives are perfectly acceptable when you're deciding on special-occasion wear. Men are not the only ones who don't want to spend a large part of their budget on special clothing items that will rarely be worn.

One of our female clients' best friends was being honored, and the dress code was formal evening wear. The last thing our client wanted to wear was an evening gown of any description. She opted for a black organza blouse with an amply cut collar that sat a little higher on her neck than a classic collar. The buttons were handpicked from an antique store and were original art nouveau, as were the ornate silver cufflinks. Underneath she wore a beautiful black Italian-made camisole. The black silk-satin pleated trousers were full cut, and their wide bottoms were stabilized with deep cuffs. A wide soft black suede belt with an oval suede-covered buckle softened the look. The pièce de résistance was a pair of drop-dead Manolo Blahnik high-heeled evening shoes. To complete the ensemble, she draped the lightest-weight black silk, three-dimensional, accordion-creased shawl around her shoulders. All these items could also serve her needs in other ways—formal dinners, cocktail parties, and any other unexpected occasion. Although the items were not inexpensive, they were infinitely wearable and, as perennials, represented very good value for the money.

Your Own Personal Categories

Some of your keepers will go in categories that are personal and specific to you. Here are some of the categories that our clients created according to their specific needs:

- Vacation clothing
- Workout/exercise clothing
- Gardening, washing-the-car, and household-chores clothing
- Business travel clothing
- Weekends-away clothing
- Contradictions—items that shouldn't work but do! (They may contradict your Personal Style Statement but still look good on you and be appropriate for some part of your lifestyle.)
- White shirts (Men feel a strong fondness for this category. Do you need to let go of any of them?)

RETIERING YOUR REMAINING KEEPERS

Some keepers may need to be reassigned a new position—either a promotion or a demotion.

What was once a "special" trouser is now demoted to a jeanlike trouser. You can dress it down with a more casual shirt or top and wear it as you would jeans.

Better quality T-shirt–like tops, which were once perfect for going out for casual dinners, have now lost their luster and are perfect for the gym.

One client found two pairs of trousers and a shirt that were actually too nice for work, so he upgraded them to special-occasion clothing.

WHAT'S MISSING FROM YOUR WARDROBE?

Your closet probably looks quite different now. The next step is to determine which categories need attention. The best way to do this is to create a master list of everything you think you need. Don't worry about the length of your list—you will begin by buying within your budget. But it is important to identify all the gaps in your wardrobe.

After you have made the master list, identify the weak categories. Prioritize them in groups of three: what are the three items that you need the most? Go on down the list until you have prioritized every-thing.

Next decide what your budget will be. Whatever figure you decide upon, always allow for spending an extra 10 percent. This gives you more flexibility, but more important, it's realistic.

Let's say that your number-one priority is a new suit, but right now your budget will just not allow for one of good quality. What will you do?

First, ask yourself: Are you sure that none of your existing suits are salvageable? Could you spruce one up with a good cleaning and a new shirt and tie (for a man), or a blouse or interesting top (for a woman)? Could an expert tailor alter it to make it look more current and improved? If any of these things are possible, then the new suit can wait until your budget can accommodate it.

If the existing suits are not salvageable, then you will have to make a compromise. You will have to spend less money on a new suit than you would like, but you will get the best possible suit for that money. And the suit will represent at least one element of your personal style. And you will not compromise on fit and comfort. In this way you will still honor your values.

This process of reviewing and setting priorities can be applied to all of your potential purchases.

Make sure you have a completed list of your shopping goals. You do not have to buy or even think of buying any or all of these items right now, but even if you wish to buy one item, you should know what it is.

Good luck with your closet! Remember, stay focused and keep a good attitude.

We'll close the door on this session with a few highlights of Mary's and William's Closet Analyses.

MARY'S CLOSET ANALYSIS

Mary was more than ready to face her closet, and she did so with enthusiastic determination. She found many loners that represented her scattered purchasing pattern and ultimately led to her disheveled appearance. She recognized that emotionally she bought clothes to hide in or to blend in with. She could now finally see whom she had been dressing, and she realized that she was no longer that person. Her perception of herself had changed, and it was now time for her clothes to change. She didn't mind letting go of a great number of items.

Mary was left with a substantially reduced wardrobe. The clothes that she most needed did not exist in her wardrobe at all—secure-making clothes. She knew that her first job was to create a secure-making section in her wardrobe. Before she would add to the other categories, she needed "substantial and meaningful clothing." This will be the foundation of her budding wardrobe.

MARY'S CATEGORIES:

- Secure-making clothes for public appearances (casual social events, book club meetings, classes, and charity work)
  - Picking up the children and Mom-related activities
  - Business-related activities with husband
  - Vacation and travel
  - Working out, yoga, and walks
  - Evening and more formal

MARY'S PRIORITY LIST

- Black suit
- A blouse or the garnet mock turtleneck
- A pair of good-quality shoes
- A current-looking casual outfit (possibly a skirt or pants, with a leather or suede jacket)
- Two sweaters in different styles that fit well and can be worn with other new casual clothes
- One dress or dressier skirt and top for dinners, parties, and social occasions
- Goal on first shopping trip—the first three items; anything else is a bonus.

WILLIAM'S CLOSET ANALYSIS

William's experience was completely opposite from Mary's. He had spent a considerable amount of money on his clothes, and as he began to peruse his closet, his shopping experiences came rushing back to him. He found it hard to let go even of obviously dated items and clothes that no longer fit.

For instance, William loved his delicate, hand-woven latticework, Italian slip-on shoes. He actually had four pairs in his closet. For a moment he was confused about what to do with them, because on the one hand they were European, which he equated with sophistication and elegance, but on the other hand, when he tried them on, he could see that they were too delicate for his tall frame. The shoes did not match his physical presence. As sophisticated and elegant as they were, they were not on William. They had to go.

William knew that he must become current, whether that meant making new purchases or reinventing part of his remaining wardrobe. He concentrated on keeping his purchases to the necessary minimum and reinventing as much as possible while still remaining true to his new image goals.

William agreed to augment his wardrobe with a very good-quality, current-looking suit and secure-making, very-good-quality accessories. But his alteration category was large. He would seek the opinion of an experienced tailor to guide him to make wise decisions about his out-of-date but still potentially wearable suits and jackets.

WILLIAM'S PRIORITY LIST

- A suit—current, sophisticated, and good quality
- Shirts that are special in mantra colors
- Shoes—substantial and elegant
- Ties—current
- Something sophisticated for casual wear—to be discovered!

Shopping

You shop for food, you shop for a job, you shop for a car, a house, a vacation—why do so many people dread shopping for clothes? People spend vast amounts of time, energy, and money shopping for important investments, but obtaining clothing somehow becomes an annoying job that they must do in order to cover their bodies.

Now you know that clothes too are an important investment; they are important practically, emotionally, financially, and psychologically. Whether or not you already enjoy clothes shopping, this session will teach you how it is possible to have a better shopping experience. You are now, at this moment, more prepared for successful shopping than you ever have been.

With the skills you have now and your self-knowledge, your clothing choices will be more effective, represent more value for money, and be of better quality. Most important, they will express and enhance your personal style.

LISTS AND NOTEBOOKS

YOUR SHOPPING LIST

Your shopping list is important because it will help you to remain within your budget and make decision-making easier. Before you leave, go over it to make sure that your most needed items are accurately prioritized.

How specific is your shopping list?

Mary had "a black suit" on her list, and William had "a suit." You may not know before you shop exactly what color, fabric, or style you are looking for in any given item. That is certainly all right—and sometimes it is even preferable, since you might miss a wonderful item that would still do the job you wanted because your "mission" to buy one particular color blinded you to it.

But at other times you will want to not compromise on an item. For example, Mary only wanted a black suit. Even though we suggested that she look at dark navy as well, she was adamant. We respected her decision because it was based on her tastes, which she had been cultivating, and all of the things she had learned about her personal style. In other words, her attitude wasn't "Oh, I think I'll have a black suit today because I'm in the mood for one."

William, on the other hand, needed and wanted a suit that was current and of good quality and that was true to his Personal Style Statement, but other than that, he was open to discovering how creative and intuitive he could be.

Both of these approaches are perfectly acceptable. Your list should be as specific as you need it to be. Some people feel more secure with jotting down the color they want or a particular style. The more prepared you are, the more creative you can be.

It's important to remain realistic. If your inner designer begins to create visions of clothes in your head, you might have trouble finding them! But often those visions, if realistic, can motivate you toward something you might otherwise have missed. When creativity emerges in an area that previously was dormant, it is very satisfying.

How many items are on your list?

Be careful here; remember your first three items are top priority for your first shopping trip. If three items seem at all stressful to you, then concentrate on only one or two. If the day goes well, you may want to continue to the others.

YOUR SHOPPING INTENTION LIST

Many of our clients found a shopping intention list to be extremely helpful. It is a list of points to remember while shopping:

- The item must be aesthetically pleasing to you.
- The item must be of a quality that is the best for your budget.
- The item must represent value for money.
- The item must be comfortable and fit well.
- The item must be current, yet have more life than just one season.
- The item must have an element of harmony within the design and must possess some degree of spirit.

This list will support your Personal Style Statement and help you navigate with more ease and confidence in what might be new territory for you.

A NOTEBOOK (OPTIONAL)

You may want to bring a small notebook in which you write down all of the things you want to remember. With all the work you have done, you will probably remember everything—you are superprepared. But, you may want to have back-up security notes on your inner and physical assets, your Personal Body Map, your excursions, clothing information, or color information—anything that you want to be sure to remember. Take any information that will help you to have a better experience; the point is to feel confident and comfortable.

Please use this notebook discreetly. If you have to use it in a shop, do so in the changing room. When sales assistants see you pull out a notebook, they will become a little prickly. That's not your problem, but you will get the best out of the experience if you avoid offending them.

WHERE TO SHOP

We strongly urge you to shop in the best places that your budget allows. This may mean going to new and different places—which is good because you want this shopping experience to be different. Think of it as a shift, not only in your shopping habits but also in your perception of who you are. To go forward with your personal style, you need to resist going backward to the shopping experiences of your past. If you are determined to project a well-defined personal style and a strong identity, you must explore and search for a shopping experience that will satisfy and glorify who you are. If that means going to a remote part of your city to find that special sweater, unusual scarf, or unique shirt, we encourage you to try it, even if you do it just once.

IF YOU DON'T LIVE IN A METROPOLITAN AREA

You will probably have to drive to a city. Significant purchases are certainly worth the time spent in seeking them out. A little research may be required—you may need to explore new territory. Perhaps you already did this to some extent in the Aesthetic Field Trip and the Hunt exercises. Telephoning or going online to research shops can help. Also, whenever you see someone who is wearing clothes that are of a similar quality to what you are looking for, you may very discreetly ask the person where they shop. Obviously, only do this if you feel the circumstances are right and if you feel comfortable.

Don't in any way be intimidated by certain kinds of shops. Shying away may keep you from finding the right shops for you. Give them a chance. You can always leave, but you also might find the shop of your dreams.

Remember, a shopping excursion is not an everyday occurrence. Getting started may seem time-consuming, but once you discover reliable resources and make the all-important connection with shops and staff, your life will be made much easier next time.

Resist the desire for a quick fix. Don't go to the nearest mall—you've been there a dozen times already. Even though you now have new eyes, new information, and new knowledge, it most likely isn't your best choice. Find a new, better place to go.

And please don't to try to do this shopping by catalogue or the Internet. You cannot create your personal style without being physically present in a store. Someday, when you really do have your personal style developed enough to shop with your eyes closed, then—maybe—you can properly buy clothing without seeing it in the flesh.

IF YOU LIVE IN A METROPOLITAN AREA

Your possible selections may be a bit overwhelming! It can be confusing, and you might not know where to start. The most important thing is to start, even if your first choice isn't perfect.

Research is important for you too. If you tend to frequent the same stores over and over, as most of us do, then branch out. Large cities are always developing new areas—try those. Or try an area that you normally avoid—it might be just right for you now. Advertising, magazines, and newspapers may give you an idea about a different area of town to shop in.

On the edge of almost every metropolitan area in the Western world is a "style periphery"—an area that lies just outside the main part of an urban area, where the rents are lower and the freedom to be different is greater. Here your shopping experiences will be a great deal more intimate. Seek these places out by researching and speaking to people and by keeping your ears and eyes open. Usually you can find unique, one-of-a-kind items here, along with more traditional staples.

Atmosphere is important. Suppose you visit a shop in a new area and discover that the music is too loud for you to focus on shopping, or you just don't like the music. If the music makes more of an impact on you than the clothes, then something is not right. But look for other shops in the area. You might find one that surprises and delights you. This has been our experience and that of many of our clients.

DEPARTMENT STORES

Department stores can make shopping easier, but they often do not offer "special" clothing items. They are oriented toward the masses and therefore have a commercial attitude. If you must shop in department stores, be very careful about what you buy. Be extra discerning about quality and fit, and do not be persuaded to buy something because it has a designer label.

Of course there are notable exceptions in most major cities. These exceptional department stores are renowned for offering exclusive, high-priced merchandise of excellent quality and superb service in handsome locations. They do not address the masses and could never be considered commercial. Yet they are neither elitist nor intimidating: they exude taste.

YOUR FAVORITE SHOP

We strongly suggest that for your first shopping trip, you try something new. That doesn't mean never going back to your favorite shop or cutting any ties with your tried and tested regulars. It does, however, mean taking a break from your usual shopping routine. Give yourself the opportunity to see what's out there. Let your eyes feast upon all the alternatives.

You may or may not want salespeople to help you. Make all the decisions for yourself, including whether you want anyone near you right now. It may take you a while to find your feet, and the last thing you need is for a salesperson to guide you or bombard you with questions.

OUTLETS, DISCOUNT STORES, BARGAIN HUNTING, AND SALES

In the beginning, you will be buying mainly the most important pieces: secure-making clothes, and business-related and career-minded clothing. Know what your budget can afford, and allocate the appropriate amounts for quality. You must be very, very careful when choosing these items. Outlet stores and the like generally carry out-of-season merchandise, rejects, and regular retail stores' unsold sale merchandise. They may offer ridiculously low prices on everything from suits to jeans. But retail store rejects may fit badly, be cut badly, have crooked seams, or be of inferior quality. Look for a small cut in the manufacturer's label, which denotes an imperfection—it can sometimes identify these kinds of items. Very often you will not know why a clothing item is on sale. Study it, try it on, and be vigilant about all of the details. Always make sure that its condition is good enough for you.

The very positive aspect about these kinds of stores is that you can always find real bargains there. Shop there just as you would shop in a very up-market, expensive store. Use the same principles that you would employ if you were spending four times as much.

We want to be really honest with you here. A wardrobe full of discount and outlet shop clothing is just not going to be the same as a wardrobe sprinkled with better-quality fabrics, designs, and colors. If your budget does not allow you to make your main purchases in anything but a discount store, then try to reserve a part of your budget to purchase better-quality accessories, perhaps a shirt, a pair of shoes, or a belt.

SEASONAL SHOPPING

Ask yourself if what you have in your wardrobe right now is right for the season. Chances are you need both summer and winter clothing, as well as "mid-season" clothing, for spring and fall. Your needs, of course, also depend on your geographical location.

Don't wait for the snow to fall before you buy your overcoat or wool scarf. And don't wait for sweltering heat before you buy a linen suit. If you do, you are unnecessarily putting pressure on yourself.

These days, as you know, fall and winter goods appear in the shops earlier and earlier. The earlier you can bear the heat, the better, especially if you do not have to depend on markdowns or sales. July through the end of September is the best time to buy for fall. February through April is the best time for spring and summer.

If you have never felt the buzz of being in a better-quality clothing store at the beginning of a new season, try it—it might be a good experience for you. You will see merchandise that won't be there at a later date—the clothes will look fresh and inspiring. They announce the season with their new colors, textures, and designs.

Many of you are not used to preplanning and early shopping. But shopping this way has many positive bonuses. Besides getting the pick of the crop, you will be able to enjoy your accomplishment and also the season itself. You won't have to remind yourself with constant mind chatter that you have to find something to wear!

SELECTING THE RIGHT DAY

After you have decided where you are going, it is very important to carefully choose the right day to go.

You will benefit most from going shopping when you are free of time constraints and pressure and are able to keep a strong focus.

When are you most alert?
Are you a morning person or an afternoon or evening person?

When do you usually feel less stressed—at the beginning of the week or at the end?

What are traditionally your best days of the week? Do you dislike

Mondays? Do you despise Saturdays? Are you always tired on Fridays? Those are not good shopping days for you.

If you can only shop on the weekend or in the evening, decide which weekend day will work best for you.

We normally would not recommend shopping in the evenings, particularly after a day's work; but, if this is your only option, try to choose an evening that is early in the week, when you will fell less weary.

How long will you shop?

The best plan is to reserve a whole day for shopping, then allow yourself to stop the moment you are tired.

WHAT TO TAKE WITH YOU

Your Inner Style

You will need your sense of humor, your patience, and your good manners while shopping. Retail experiences are rarely perfect, and your inner style qualities can soften them. If you have to wait for a dressing room, or if the shop is void of staff, you will need your best behavior to keep your emotions intact and to stay focused. Even if you need to leave a shop because of poor service, do so graciously. You never know—you might want to go back one day.

Your Best Attitude

You need to have a good attitude with yourself. How you feel will have a relevant impact on your shopping experience. If you find yourself moody, grumpy, or just plain tired—don't go.

Your shopping list and your shopping intention list

Your notebook.

A Loner

You may want to bring a loner with you if you are shopping for an item to wear with it. It might seem a bit of a bore, but it really is the most effective way to get a good match for anything. The reason it is a loner is that you probably didn't think it through the first time. Hang it in a nice garment bag—it will feel and look less cumbersome.

WHAT TO WEAR

The clothing you wear while shopping should be both comfortable and appropriate. It should be clothing that you enjoy wearing and that you know you look good in. After trying on new clothes, it's psychologically comforting to put back on something you know works for you.

Dressing appropriately will allow you to go into any shop anywhere and feel comfortable. If there is a disparity between what you are purchasing and what you are wearing, you won't be able to make the best choice. For example, it's harder to try on a suit while wearing trainers, or to try on a silk blouse while wearing sweatpants. The contrast will distract you from seeing the suit or the blouse in its true light. The effect will be inaccurate and will mar your judgment.

Now that you know who you are, it's time to show up. Your respect for yourself and the pride you take in how you present yourself can begin with shop assistants.

HOW TO HAVE A GOOD SHOPPING EXPERIENCE

How you set foot in a shop sets the tone for your shopping experience. It helps to make an appropriate beginning, in which your self-respect, summed up by your inner style, evokes respect from the store's staff. Your self-esteem and level of self-confidence will play a large part in your shopping experience.

HOW TO INTERACT WITH RETAIL STAFF

You know more than any sales staff about what is ultimately right for you. Depending on the type of store, after reading this book you may know more in general about clothes, quality, fit, and style. A staff member with a good eye, knowledge, and a helpful attitude can be of assistance and even inspiring. Ideally he or she will answer your questions and assist you by making your shopping experience as comfortable and successful as possible.

But remember, you are in charge of your experience. Never give your power away or abdicate that responsibility to anyone. If you do, you will diffuse all the work you have done so far. Don't let a pushy or persuasive sales assistant affect or influence your decision-making process. Whenever you feel a staff person compromise your comfort level, it is time to change what you are doing. Communicate what you want clearly, politely, and intelligently by saying: "Thank you, but I am happy to look on my own for now," or "Thank you, but that is not my taste and I prefer to just look around right now."

If they insist on following you around or even "policing" you, then you must make a decision. You can use a different tone of voice and say, "I really would prefer to be on my own right now. I'll call you if I need any help." Or you can leave the shop.

Suppose you need product information, or you are looking for a different color or size, or you need to be directed to a different area. You can ask a staff member, but remember, if you ask a staff member any kind of question, you are inviting him or her into your experience. Make sure you know where your boundaries lie. If you just want information and then to be left alone, thank the person once you have received your answer and excuse yourself. You need to make a verbal and physical disengagement from him or her.

Suppose you want help but there is no one around to help you. Are you being ignored? Cutbacks in the larger stores have left them devoid of proper staff. Some of you may relish the freedom, but others regret the feel a lack of energy and professionalism.

It sounds as if we want the best of both worlds, doesn't it? A sales assistant should be there and somehow also not be there. Well, yes—exactly. You are entitled to the best of both worlds, equally balanced. This is what good service is all about—being there for the customer when it is appropriate and seeming not to be present so as not to disturb them.

When you leave a good shop, you should feel that you had a great time, whether you bought anything or not, and that you just can't wait to go back.

YOUR ENERGY LEVEL

Be aware of your energy level. Rest when you need to. Shopping can be physically and mentally wearing, and you need to listen to your body. If you suddenly become exhausted after a few hours, it is time to go home. You cannot be inspired, creative, or even wise when you are too tired. But you are not a wimp. The reason many people get tired "just shopping" is that you are using a different part of your brain. You may work an eight-hour day at your demanding job and feel less tired than you will after a few hours of shopping.

EATING AND DRINKING

If you are caffeine sensitive, don't have too much caffeine before you start out in the morning. The jitters and an adrenaline high are not a good place to start. We have seen many mistakes made by people who were overstimulated by caffeine.

Eat when you are hungry, but don't eat a heavy, boozy lunch. Any food that makes you feel bloated or heavy will affect the way you feel when you try on clothes. Feeling heavy affects you emotionally, and then your confidence level will drop. Instead, eat a light lunch or stop and snack throughout the day. You're eating for energy.

PARTNER OR SPOUSE SHOPPING

Be ultrasensitive about bringing a significant other shopping with you, especially on this first trip. Everyone is highly influenced by emotional ties to a partner: some are too dependent on the partner, while others are defiant of them or unconsciously stubborn. Maybe in this particular area you don't entirely trust your partner's judgment. Be sensitive about who you take with you. Be aware of their tastes. This is a relatively "new you." Explain before you go that your tastes may have changed quite a bit. And communicate that your relationship with clothes is much more positive than it used to be.

TIPS FOR YOUR PARTNER ON HOW HE OR SHE CAN HELP:
- Be unconditionally supportive.
- Don't impose your taste or opinions—be selfless.
- Be nonjudgmental.
- Help to create an "up" atmosphere.
- Be 100 percent present, but not intrusive.
- If there are no sales assistants around, you can help by retrieving sizes and keeping the dressing area uncluttered.
- Do not allow yourself to be distracted.
- Be patient.
- Do not shop for yourself.

Don't bring your children with you on your shopping trip. Enough said.

IS THIS GARMENT RIGHT FOR YOU?

SELECTING CLOTHES TO TRY ON

When you are visually drawn to a garment, you may have moments of confusion, doubt, and even disorientation about whether the garment is right for you. After all, this is the first time you are going shopping with so much information about yourself. When in doubt, ask yourself these questions:

- Is this item on my priority list?
- Is it the old me or the new me?
- Does it suit my taste for the present or from the past?
- Does it suit my budget?

Think of a word to identify how you might look in this garment. If the word or words do not resemble your Personal Style Statement, then it is not right for you.

If a garment that catches your eye does meet all these requirements, then touch and feel the fabric. Do you like the way it feels? If you do, try it on.

Sometimes you might be attracted to a particular color, but you find the fabric unappealing. Do not try this garment on, but make a note of the color. It will probably be available in other garments in that store and others.

IN THE DRESSING ROOM

Bring at least three items of a similar type—three suits, three jackets—to the dressing room.

Try each item on carefully and relatively slowly.

Notice how it feels. Does it slip on easily?

Check yourself in the mirror.

Does the feeling, whatever that may be, match the visual? You are looking for that match—a good visual and a good feeling.

Does it fit you well? Sometimes two garments, in the same fabric, design, and size will fit differently. If you like a garment, try it on as many times as it takes to see if one fits and looks better on you than another.

Now ask yourself:

- How does this garment look from the back?
- How does my profile look?
- Can I move freely in it?
- What does this color look like against my skin?
- Do I need to see this in better light?
- What part of my Personal Style Statement does it represent?
- Does this garment hide me, attract attention, or flatter me?
- Do I feel secure and confident in it?
- Is this garment comfortable on my sensitive areas?
- Would this be a loner, or will it easily work with my other clothes?

If you still don't know if the garment is right for you, then it is not.

Moving right along.

TEMPTATIONS AND OLD HABITS

You will probably be tempted to gravitate toward items that resemble the ones you were accustomed to wearing. This is quite normal. If it happens, try to adopt a more positive attitude about what you are there to do. Do not be distracted—stay focused on the feelings of satisfaction that you will derive from finding what is right for you now.

Items that have nothing to do with your Personal Style Statement, or that are not priorities on your shopping list, will also tempt you. Suppose you find an item of clothing that is not on your shopping priority list but you cannot drag yourself away from it. You try it on and it looks fabulous. Don't panic. First establish whether it really is right for you. Are you having a "love it, got to have it" moment, soon to be followed by a "regret it" moment? In the event that you feel strongly that this item should eventually be included in your wardrobe, ask the store to put it on hold for you for at least twenty-four hours. That way it will still be available after you have found all the priority items on your list. It will also give you time to review whether it is a loner and to see whether you still feel the same about it the next day.

In fact, it is always a good idea to ask about the shop's return policy. You may want to take an item home to try on with your other clothes. Before you leave with it, make sure that you can return it for a full refund. An exchange-only policy might be too limiting for you, especially if the piece is relatively expensive or represents a large part of your budget.

Suppose you find an item that fits one of your sensitive areas perfectly but doesn't satisfy any other aspect of your shopping list or your Personal Style Statement. You are so pleased with the way it fits and it makes you feel so secure, you are prepared to let all of your other requirements slide. Leave it! Although the temptation may be overwhelming, don't give in—you'll end up regretting it.

Suppose you are overwhelmed by the amount of the season's "hot numbers" in a shop, and initially those are all you can see. Unless those clothes are congruent with your priorities and personal requirements, you will need to do one of two things: either see what else is on offer, or leave the shop. The importance of doing this must not be underestimated. When people decide to steer away from trends for the first time in their lives, negative and critical chatter often begins to take place in the mind: "Will I still be current if I don't buy a sheer, clingy top with a 1960s pattern on it?" "Am I going to be boring if I stick to *substantial, unique,* or *sophisticated*?" "What if I can't find anything else?" Some current-looking clothes will be less trendy than others; you will not be boring; and you will always be able to find other items. The world is full of clothes.

MARY'S SHOPPING TRIP

Toward the end of Mary's shopping day, she still had not bought anything and was starting to feel a little panicky. But she finally found the black suit of her vision. The shade was perfect; it was a good-quality, deep rich black. The design was exquisite, as was the fabric. She loved the way it looked and the way she hoped it could look when she lost the weight she wanted. But the fit was not good enough—it was just a little too tight in her sensitive areas. Mary was uncertain what to do. The suit was expensive, and if she were to have it altered, she would not be able to return it. She was committed to losing a little weight, but what if she didn't?

A chorus of reed-thin sales assistants surrounded her, urging her to buy it because they thought it looked "so good" on her. But she knew it didn't by the way it felt. Mary almost allowed her negative body talk to tell her it was her fault that the suit didn't fit, but she brought herself back to a good attitude by telling herself that the style of the suit was just not right for her body shape—and that was okay.

If Mary had bought the suit, she would have violated three fundamental shopping rules:

- Buy for who you are in the present, not for who you were or who you think you are going to be.
- Don't buy anything that doesn't fit.
- Never buy under pressure, whether it comes from the outside or is self-induced.

Mary literally took a deep breath, thanked everyone for their help, and took a walk around the block. She emotionally detached herself from the experience and then was able to make the right decision. She did not buy the suit. It took maturity to walk away from the suit and an ability to make the right kind of sacrifice. It was a good decision.

Mary then took stock of how she was feeling emotionally and physically. Her energy level was good, and after only a few minutes, she was relieved that she had not bought the suit. She remembered that there is no shortage of clothing. There would another black suit somewhere that would work for her. So she continued the hunt. After her "close call" experience, she was even more certain of exactly what she wanted.

Mary eventually did find her suit that day. To her surprise, it was more current looking than the one that didn't fit. The fabric was pure midweight wool, with a small percentage of silk woven into it, giving the suit a smooth appearance and a little drape. The fit was just right for Mary. It did not pinch in places that she is self-conscious about. And it was so well designed and made that when she tried it on, she knew immediately that it was the one.

As Mary's shopping day was ending, she decided to go into one more shop. She was thrilled about her suit and felt satisfied that if she found nothing else that day, her shopping trip still would have been very successful. Immediately her eye was drawn to the deep garnet red that had been occupying her mind for weeks. It was a blouse. It was made of 100 percent pure cotton damask. It reminded her of some of the home furnishing fabrics she had seen and liked so much. The collar had an Edwardian look to it, while the French cuffs were a little deeper than average, and she knew she would enjoy finding cufflinks for them. Although she couldn't put her finger on what, the blouse touched something meaningful and nostalgic within her. When she tried it on, the fit was fine. It would be a special complement to her new suit.

Mary was very surprised to find this unique blouse because she had a preconceived notion that underneath her black suit she would wear a garnet mock turtleneck. But when she saw the blouse, she knew that it would look beautiful under her suit, and she had no doubt that it matched her Personal Style Statement perfectly.

Mary made only two purchases that day. Both items strongly represented her Personal Style Statement—they were both substantial and meaningful to Mary. They were of good quality, fit, and design, and they carried plenty of spirit. Most important of all, when Mary wore them, she felt confident, secure, and substantial. Mary was well on her way.

Mary's relentless pursuit for the right suit was a first for her. In the past, shopping had been a chore and often led to disappointment and what she called "after-shopping blues." But she had never been so focused and determined to fulfill a strong image desire. Her successful shopping day had much to do with her attitudes, behavior, and the way she communicated. She felt very good about herself, and she was not emotionally attached to an outcome. She was in charge of her shopping experience. Taking charge and being responsible for her image were very empowering for her.

Mary continued to slowly build her wardrobe a few pieces at a time. Soon she found that with great ease she was able to go to her closet and put her hands on clothing items that she was pleased to wear to her floral design class or while picking her children up from school. For the first time in her adult life, Mary felt comfortable, secure, and confident about her image.

REMAIN FOCUSED

If you remain focused and keep your eye on the ball, you can create a strong foundation for your wardrobe that will enable you to appear and feel strong, grounded, and substantial. Once you have achieved this backbone for your personal style, you will be freer to sprinkle your collection of clothes with any "fun" items you may come across. It might take you several shopping trips to reach this point, because you want to make sure that you have purchased *all* of your priority items, not just the first three on your list.

In one of Mary's later shopping trips, she caught a glimpse of an indigo blue garment hanging in the back of a store. She made her way over to it and discovered that it was a very contemporary, almost trendy blouse. She would not normally have been attracted to this blouse, but her new color awareness inspired her. The blouse was almost foppish looking. It was made of a luxurious nonshiny silk and was covered with the most amazing randomly placed polka dots of all sizes. The polka dots were in the striking indigo blue, while the background color was black. This blouse constituted an element of fun in Mary's wardrobe because it was fashionable and young looking. And because she already had enough basics, she could afford to add something that would be right for her on days when she was "out of hiding" and comfortable being seen.

Only you will know when you have reached a sufficient comfort level with your image to be able to play and be a bit more creative. For some people the item might be a T-shirt in one of the fashion colors of the season, while for others it could be a wild 1960s printed shirt or blouse. Only you can judge to what degree you wish to add that sprinkle to your wardrobe.

Even in this arena, though, the clothing items must relate to your Personal Style Statement and be congruent with the rest of your clothing. Mary's fun item was still of great quality; it worked beautifully with her black suit; it was in two of her new colors; and it was a substantial piece of clothing. A leopard print spandex tube top would not have been a choice for a fun item for Mary.

WILLIAM'S SHOPPING EXCURSION

When it was time for William to go shopping, he preferred that his wife, Nancy, not come with him. This was a mature and well-thought-out decision on William's part. He knew that he was highly influenced by her opinions and taste, and even though he did appreciate her help, he felt that on this occasion he needed to go it alone. At first Nancy was a little disappointed, but realizing how hard he had worked to come to this place, she supported his decision.

William had learned a great deal about himself and the clothing industry when he completed the Hunt exercise in Session 7. Prices were much higher than he thought they would be. Although he could afford the things he was attracted to, it was still a leap from what he had last spent on a suit to what it cost now. He made a decision based on his budget and what he would be comfortable with.

William was quite enamored of the made-to-measure shirt store that he had visited previously. It carried the perfect colors for him, and he knew whatever they made would be special and unique to him. Therefore he allocated a substantial amount of his budget to made-to-measure shirts. He would also buy a suit, but instead of searching for the very best-quality suit, he would concentrate on a current, mid- to better-quality suit, without compromising fit, comfort, or quality of fabric.

When we questioned William about these decisions, he explained that the shirts would play a very important role in the projection of his Personal Style Statement. He often takes his jacket off at work, and sometimes he wears his doctor's coat over a shirt and tie. He thought that on most occasions his shirts and ties would say more about him than a suit. But he did need a current-looking suit to wear with his new shirts. He felt confident that the right shirts and ties would allow him to appear elegant and sophisticated. He did plan to eventually purchase a very good-quality suit and was even thinking of having one made to measure sometime, but not now.

William chose a contemporary-looking three-button suit. It was single breasted, Italian made, and the fabric was a Super 100s pure wool—a durable, very-good-quality midweight fabric. If, by the way, you don't have a current-looking suit in your wardrobe, the kind that William selected is a great place to start.

Because William was tall and slender, his suits had to be long in the body and in the sleeves. He managed to find a fit that was perfect for his frame.

Creating his new shirts would be a real treat for William, since he would be able to select the specific elements that matched his personality. He decided to have a new shirt made in each of his four new secure-making colors (cobalt blue, moss green, cornflower blue, and slate gray). Each of these colors was an excellent match for his new suit and for his existing suits, jacket, and trousers. They would give his existing clothes a new lease on life until William was ready to upgrade further.

Working closely with the shirtmaker, William collaborated in the styling of his shirts. Each one would be a little different: one would have French cuffs; another, deep single cuffs with an extra button; another, an Italian-shaped collar; and the last one, gray mother-of-pearl buttons to go with the slate-gray fabric. Needless to say, the shirts fit him beautifully.

William had disposed of every tie in his closet, so ties were another priority for him. He didn't have to go too far: his shirtmaker carried a very unique, small, one-off selection of ties that he had handpicked while in Europe. This was a boon for William because he would not have been happy with traditional-looking or classic American ties.

William also wanted to make a start on secure-making casual and weekend items (which also affected his suit budget). After trying a few different items for his upper body, he came to some interesting conclusions. For one, open-neck shirts made him feel insecure. For another, a beautiful soft brushed cotton shirt with a slightly larger collar made him feel too "dressed up." He was very pleased to find a merino wool mock turtleneck in a gunmetal gray, with a tiny blue fleck almost hidden within the gray base. He wore it with a high-waisted, deep-pleated, almost-black, whipcord-design cotton-and-wool-mix trouser. Because of his lean frame and the fineness of the wool sweater, he was able to tuck it in without any bulkiness. He wore a wide black saddle leather belt with a chunky stainless-steel buckle.

His contemporary and elegant shoes were of black-grained leather. The grained look made then appear less formal. They could be worn with both his suit and his new casual attire. His socks were a fine wool with a small blue and black geometric design.

William's image journey was one of continuing creativity. He gradually learned to trust his intuition and continued cultivating his personal style. Looking current, elegant, and sophisticated seemed not as foreign to him as it once had. He continued to allow his passions and his love of culture to touch him and reveal themselves in his personal style.

SHOPPING AFTERCARE: WHAT TO DO WHEN YOU RETURN HOME

TAKING CARE OF YOURSELF

Congratulations! No matter what the outcome of your shopping trip was, we know that you went shopping for the first time for who you are. Many people come home after their first shopping experience on a high note. It may last for days or weeks, and they feel inspired and motivated to continue to make significant changes. Many times their desires branch out into other areas of their lives. They start renovating their homes or planning the vacation they always wanted, or suddenly they get "dressed up" and go to nice restaurants or to the theater to celebrate their new image.

Some of you may not have experienced this "shopping high." It's also not unusual—in fact, it's often a very good thing. If you didn't buy anything, you probably saved yourself an inappropriate spending spree and learned a great deal as well. No doubt you have thoughts and observations about your experience. The following questions can help you highlight aspects of the experience that will be useful when you next go shopping.

- **Do you know exactly why you didn't buy anything?** If you didn't find anything, you learned something about your taste and benefited from the process of elimination. You gained an even more defined picture of what you want. Maybe your specific requirements will not always be met. But with your new clarity and determination about what you want, you can go out shopping again and again. This is not the end—this is the beginning.
- **Did anyone influence your decisions that day?** If so, who and why?
- **Were you aware of any emotional tugs and pulls?** If so, what were they? Did you do anything about them?
- **Did you give yourself enough time?**
- **Do you feel disappointed?** Was your trip less successful than

you had hoped? Was it the experience that disappointed you, or the number of items you bought or didn't buy?

- **Were you frustrated by expensive items that you couldn't afford?** Most people fall in love with an item or two that they just cannot afford—this is true for clothing and in many areas of consumerism. Did you move on to items that were in your budget, or did your frustration affect the rest of your day?

- **Did you have difficulties finding the right size and fit?** If so, next time go to shops and stores that have ample choices for your particular size.

- **Were you too late in the season to get the best selection of styles, colors, and sizes?**

Whatever your feelings and thoughts from the day, you have learned a great deal about yourself and about shopping successfully. Perhaps you learned that staying focused saved you time and money, or that you had previously been sacrificing too much in regard to fit and comfort. Maybe now you perceive clothes in a new way, with a broader vision and more defined tastes.

Your personal style is still unfolding—there is no time limit on achieving it. Each of your small victories on this journey will bring you closer to it. One shopping day is a minor detail in the process of merging your inner and outer style.

TAKING CARE OF YOUR CLOTHES

When you arrive home, whether you are tired, elated, or somewhere in the middle, you will need to do a couple of things. Here is how to enjoy, integrate, and take care of your purchases.

- Hang up your new clothes right away. Start out on the right foot with their care. Respect them and take care of them, and they will live a longer life.

- Don't try on your clothes again as soon as you get home. It's too close to the experience. Wait until the next day. If you immediately try on your clothes for family or friends to give a fashion show, you are opening up yourself to their judgment and criticism. You might not want that right now, especially if your new clothes are very different from what you normally buy. We suggest that you kindly ask others to wait until you are ready to be seen in the new clothes.

- When you do begin trying on your new clothes—after the shopping high wears off—do so at different times of the day, in different kinds of light. Take the time you need to rediscover how you feel about each item. See if the colors are as you thought they were. Judge whether the new pants really do go with that jacket or sweater.

- Avoid the Sunday Best Syndrome. If an item is a keeper, don't hold it as a personal treasure for your eyes only. The longer you wait, the more of an impact or impression you'll feel it needs to make when you finally do wear it—which only adds pressure. Integrate the garment into your wardrobe quickly.

- Invest in identical hangers for your suits, jackets, and trousers. This will create visual harmony and show respect for your clothes and for yourself.

- Allow enough space between your hanging garments that they can easily recover after wear.

- For your better-quality clothes, choose a good dry cleaner. The better the cleaning and pressing, the better your clothes will look, and the longer they will last.

- Try not to wear the same clothing item two days running.

- Once in a while, "air" clothing items that are usually folded on shelves, and refold them so that the new fold creases are in new places.

- If you turn your jacket, shirt, or sweater cuffs back when you wear them, turn them back down when you put them back in your wardrobe.

- Hang your trousers with the front and back creases in line with each other on the hanger.

- Occasionally brush the shoulders of your jackets, coats, and suits.

- Avoid any laundry that uses a starch-only finish for shirts and blouses, as it will reduce the life of the garment.

- Use shoe trees in your shoes—they will look better longer.

- If you must fold your shirts or blouses, because of the lack of space, insert tissue paper in between the folds. It will prevent the shirt from looking too creased.

FINISHING TOUCHES

Shopping for your image doesn't stop with clothes. A few more very important elements also affect your image: hair and, for women, makeup. Achieving correct balance and harmony for your image will be easier when your hair and makeup are congruent with it.

The following practical information will help you make these very important decisions. The information comes from well-informed, highly experienced, and talented experts. We have asked them to guide you toward having the best experience possible in these arenas.

SHOPPING FOR YOUR HAIRSTYLE

Your hairstyle is the crowning glory to your overall image. In essence, it is a frame for your face that, like a picture frame, can create the essential finishing touch.

Hair that is in any way inappropriately styled or disheveled will create a distraction. You may wear clothing that is current, of good taste, and congruent with your personal style; you may have a graceful physicality that exudes confidence and charisma; but a hairstyle that is not connected visually to your overall style will cast doubt upon your image.

To help our clients achieve this necessary finishing touch, we first ask them for their thoughts and feelings about their current hairstyle, their practical needs, and how their hair affects them emotionally. Since hair is a sensitive topic for both men and women, the discussion is often intimate. It brings up image wounds that have not previously been discussed, as well as issues of confidence and self-esteem.

Both men and women form strong attachments to a particular hair length or hairstyle. But this attachment keeps them from looking current and is usually less flattering now than it was years ago. Even after a man or woman's personal style has evolved and matured, often their hairstyle has not. Although we are not hairstylists and depend on the expertise of others to execute their magic upon our clients' hair, we work very closely with our clients to ensure that they make wise decisions about their hair, be it color, cut, or style.

For hairstyling and its complex and multifaceted aspects, John Barrett's philosophy and extensive knowledge are a perfect complement to our own beliefs about the psychology of image. New York's Bergdorf Goodman's store plays host to the John Barrett Salon. We asked him a few questions about how anyone, anywhere can achieve happiness with their hairstyle.

KATE AND MALCOLM: We fully understand why having a good hairstyle and haircut is vital to one's image. It can make or break a whole look, either bringing someone's personal style to life or acting as a negative distraction. Could you expand on the importance of "good hair"?

JOHN BARRETT: "Good hair" is any hair—having it is like "being comfortable in your own skin." Hair is a certain texture, color, and thickness. These are finite boundaries. Anyone who carefully evaluates maintenance needs, day-to-day styling requirements, and their basic hair type can come up with a comfortable, workable look that equals "good hair." Certainly some hair is a bigger challenge than others, especially when working against hair type to achieve a trendy look. Trendy hair is really about being comfortable with your own hair and realistic about the time and cost associated with the style, color, and maintenance you choose. If someone is not at ease with their hair, a "bad hair day" can really affect mood, self-presentation, or overall projection. You've got to feel together to look together.

K&M: What are the biggest mistakes people commonly make in choosing a hairstyle? Many people don't understand that having a current (but not trendy) hairstyle is vital to a polished image. Why do you think it *is* important?

JB: The most common mistake people make is making a drastic change without really thinking it over. This usually happens when a hairdresser overinterprets what the client wants—or doesn't take the time to talk it through with the client. At my salon we listen carefully and generally underinterpret. Clients who say "Cut it all off" rarely mean it. We have very few complaints regarding "too short," yet "too short" is the number-one complaint from hairstyling salons. Looking current (as opposed to being stuck in the mud or looking "too trendy") is important and is usually accomplished by making subtle changes to a basic look as fashion evolves.

K&M: By the time our clients are ready to think about a new hairstyle, they have learned a great deal about their image. But hair is hard. Both men and women have blind spots about how their hair really looks. We often call this being "visually stuck." How can a person really see if they need a change?

JB: Many people are stuck, but a small evolution with a trend will bring them to "current." A drastic change to "trendy" is the one they may regret. One suggestion is to review a variety of photos of yourself—see if one style pops out as user-friendly or comfortable, or evokes a positive response. Another is to ask someone whose opinion you value, or your hairdresser. Or consider visiting a new hairdresser for a consultation only, just to compare options and ideas. Finally, review recent photos of yourself, and think about what will be comfortable and current.

K&M: We suggest that clients begin by researching a new hairstyle through magazines, paying particular attention to styles they like that are close in color, hair type, and face shape to their own. (We remind them that magazine hair is pampered by stylists with product—not always realistic.) For more inspiration, we also suggest that they look at real people whose hair they admire, so they can see texture and color in person. The point is not to copy the other person's hairstyle but to let it be a guide, a place to begin. Would you agree? And do you have any further suggestions about how to begin?

JB: Magazines are great. I actually like it when clients bring in a picture—it's a good starting point for a discussion about their hair's texture, color, type, and any ideas to evolve their style a bit. But your clients should be realistic. They might bring in a picture of Cameron Diaz, but they shouldn't expect to look just like her.

K&M: If someone likes the hairdresser but is not entirely happy with the cut, what should they do—move on or try again?

JB: If your client really likes the hairdresser, they could ask him or her whether they'd like to try again or would like to recommend someone else. All hairdressers admire each other's work, and they may have seen just the look or the cut on someone else's client. This way your client can maintain the friendship and can be comfortable about returning to the salon or hairdresser. It may help the hairdresser see that you are serious and listen more carefully.

K&M: For people who do not live in a metropolitan area and cannot always travel to one for a top-notch professional haircut, how do you suggest they find a good stylist? Should they make a special effort to travel?

JB: For those who travel frequently on business or for personal reasons, going out of town is an option. For most people it is not. We suggest that your client ask people whose cut, style, and color they admire where they go for hair styling. People are always flattered that you noticed and are willing to answer this question. Those who opt for going out of town may still need or want local options for styling and maintaining. Most colorists will write down formulas and instructions. Also, if you've opted for out of town, take photos of your look—it may be easier to show your local hairdresser than to tell them.

K&M: We tell people to take an active responsibility for communicating and participating about their hair. We encourage them to maintain an open conversation with the stylist and be willing to ask questions, as many as it takes to become clear about what the stylist recommends and why. Do you have any specific questions or comments from clients that help you to create the best results?

JB: All hairdressers like to hear the question "What would you do if you could do anything?" But the hairdresser should return the gesture by asking the client what they want. If you can't blow dry at home, you need to ask, "Apart from anything that involves blow drying, what would you do if you could do anything?"

K&M: If fashion says to wear hair short but the client loves long hair are they stuck and inflexible or are they right?

JB: To be fashionable, you must be comfortable. In other words, are you wearing the hairstyle, or is it wearing you? We want clients to receive general compliments like "You look great" as much as or more than specifics like "What a great color." General compliments are your way of knowing it's current and right—not too trendy.

K&M: What do you do, as a professional and an expert, when the hairstyle that a client desires is not really the best one for him or her?

JB: I suggest a slight evolution or modification that will update the look or be more flattering.

K&M: What should the client do if he or she feels that the cut is going the wrong way and you are in the middle of the process?

JB: The client should ask, "Could you remind me how short this will be when dry?" "Did we talk about how long the bangs will be?" Just ask a question that reminds the hairdresser of the consultation discussion.

K&M: When the client, at the end of the session, doesn't see the end result being the same as what was described at the beginning, what went wrong?

JB: Obviously, poor communication. What "one inch" means to me may not be "one inch" to someone else. Maybe the description wasn't specific enough, or maybe you or the hairdresser needed more focus. Or possibly the idea was unrealistic and the hairdresser should have told you.

K&M: We tell people to find out how to take care of and style their hair before they leave the salon. They do, but they still tell us that they can't duplicate the look at home. Can you offer any suggestions here?

JB: A salon styling experience can be a "how to" session if the client pays attention to the tools and techniques. Discussing maintenance with the stylist is vital. If you don't want to style the hair every day and aren't really skilled in this area, make sure your stylist knows this. A good haircut should be wearable both with a blow dry and without. Longer hair adds options—up or down. Bangs forward or bangs back.

Quick photos taken after the styling for later reference can help. Use the same products your stylist used. Buy them there, or write down the names for purchase elsewhere. Make notes during styling to remind yourself of the hairdresser's tips. If it's really out of control, go back for a blow dry or for a consultation on styling options.

Your haircut should be your friend—ready to go with your mood and your total look, which requires some variety.

SHOPPING FOR HAIR COLOR

In Session 7 we demonstrated the important role that color plays in clothes and accessories. Hair color is a crucial part of your overall visual image. Even the slightest change in hair color informs that way your skin reflects color and therefore can have a significant effect on the clothing colors you need. For example, before you highlight your dark brown hair with red tones, think first how the addition would affect your ability to wear the colors you now wear. Some of our clients have been disappointed to discover that a new hair color choice limits the use of their existing wardrobe.

It has become culturally acceptable for both men and women to color their hair. Covering the gray, trying a new color for a specific reason or just because you want to no longer has a stigma. Many relatively safe hair-coloring products are available, so people are less concerned about harmful side effects.

Hair colorist Diane Hosie, co-owner of the Piero Salon in Santa Monica, California, has fifteen years of experience coloring the hair of men and women. Her clients are a wide, varied, and eclectic group, from bankers to movie stars. She respects her clients' lifestyle, careers, and their practical needs and works with them to achieve the best results.

The following are Diane's recommendations, tips, and philosophy about achieving the best hair color for your personal style.

KATE AND MALCOLM: What are the biggest mistakes clients commonly make when choosing a hair color?

DIANE HOSIE: When a client chooses a color from a color chart, sometimes they don't realize how a whole head of, let's say, bright red hair would look on them. I prefer clients to choose a color from a photograph in a magazine. This gives them an overall feel for the light and dark tones of the color. I always have the client show me pictures of *colors* they would like, and then we choose the one best suited for them.

K&M: What do you do when a client wants a hair color that just doesn't suit them?

DH: Usually I go to the color room and bring out a hair swatch of that particular color and hold it against their face. This usually helps them to see that the color is unsuitable. If they still want a particular color even after I tell them it might not suit them, I will do it, as long as their hair is strong enough to take the process.

K&M: How do you recommend the clients choose a hair color? Should they stay close to their own original color? Should they include thoughts about their lifestyle? For example, if a man is an artist, maybe it is fine for him to bleach his hair blond, but would this be right for a banker? How can a client get a handle on what really suits their look, skin tone, type of hair, *and* lifestyle?

DH: The majority of clients, regardless of their occupation, choose natural shades. For the most part, I would recommend choosing a color that flatters your eyes and your skin tone. If you don't know exactly what that color is, then communicate at least this much to the colorist. People whose lifestyles might affect what color they can wear their hair usually stay with natural colors.

Wearing a daring hair color is not for everyone, but neither are trendy clothes and body piercing! I find that age is not really a factor when choosing color. I have more women over fifty with avant-garde hair color than those under fifty! Maybe this is because women and men feel freer to express themselves after forty, without worrying about what other people think of them.

K&M: What are your recommendations for choosing a colorist?

DH: Choose a colorist who listens to your ideas and has some of his or her own ideas too. If a colorist disagrees with your choices, he or she should give you good reason.

K&M: What might be going on psychologically with clients who choose colors that don't flatter them? Are they trying too hard to look younger or to be trendy, or are they just not able to see themselves accurately?

DH: Self-image is subjective; you need a color expert to guide you. I can ask three women to show me a picture of dark golden blond, and I will get three different colors. This is normal.

Some women choose a hair color that is unsuitable for them at an emotional time in their life. Maybe they're getting a divorce, or they've lost a loved one. Some women use this time to pamper themselves and truly are determined to look and feel better. But others react differently. Their self-worth is at a low point, and they feel they don't deserve to look good. They may then choose a severe color like boot-polish black, a color that is obviously unnatural and would actually damage the client's naturally blond, fine hair. It is as if they want to punish themselves. If I can ascertain what is really going on without intruding, I won't make the change, especially if I feel it will damage their hair. Men don't do this; it is definitely a female thing. I would advise every woman to think very carefully about making such a significant change in her hair color when she is feeling vulnerable.

K&M: Speaking of men, has it become totally acceptable now for men to color their hair?

DH: Yes, we get more and more men every day. Many are definitely looking to hide the gray, but others of all ages are leaning toward more trendy shades such as bleached out or jet black.

K&M: Many men don't color because they think it looks false. But aren't the products very sophisticated now, and don't they look natural if applied well?

DH: Colors are improving every day, but there is still the awkward regrowth period. Sometimes this bothers men who want to look natural.

K&M: So how do you recommend that men and women maintain their hair color? When should they color again? When they see regrowth or before?

DH: Part of your commitment to good hair color is maintenance. It's really up to you. Recolor when you think it looks like it needs it. It's different for everyone. Some people with gray can't stand to see a fraction of regrowth, while others will wait until they feel self-conscious about it.

K&M: There seems to be a "rule" for women that states that the older you get, the lighter the color should be. Do you believe this is true? Please explain.

DH: People put too much emphasis on age and rules. Can you imagine Jackie Onassis with blond hair? It's still all about eye and skin color and also hair length.

K&M: What do you think of the "blond phenomenon," especially with women? We keep expecting it to die down, but it still seems very popular.

DH: I consider myself a blonde, yet my natural color is brown. I've been trying to be a blonde since high school. Most people think it's my natural color now. When I try to go darker, I can only stand it for a short while. Blond hair makes me feel good. Different colors make you feel different ways. Everyone should try blond, red, or brown or whatever color they want at least once! Or maybe even wig it one night!

K&M: Any tips for coloring your hair at home? What are the positives and negatives of doing this?

DH: Most colorists will give advice for do-it-yourself touch-ups in between visits. If you are going it alone, use permanent colors that are close to your natural shade. Experiment with tones such as medium golden brown or medium ash brown or medium auburn. Some of the semipermanent colors will suffice. Just steer clear of five-minute shampoo-in color. You have very little control of the darkness with progressive colors, and you could end up with a bad result. Then you'd have to visit me!

SHOPPING FOR MAKEUP

Sensitive, defensive, nervous, intimidated, and reluctant—these are some of our female clients' reactions to the very idea of addressing their makeup. We can understand and respect their feelings. They often fear wearing what they describe as "a mask" and being false. One did not want to be thought of as being "all dolled up," and one with slightly feminist views thought makeup might weaken her image. Many didn't wear makeup because they had seen too many other women wearing it badly and were afraid of "looking like that."

Many women consider makeup to be some kind of manipulative tool. For thousands of years, derogatory stereotypes of the seductress, the tart, the glamour-puss, and even the clown have been used to describe the art of makeup. Think of movies you've seen—we're sure you can recall several contrasting images of heavily made-up "bad girls" and natural-looking "good girls."

What has evolved as culturally acceptable these days is a visual balance in makeup. In business, in the media, socially, in almost any arena, good makeup provides a comfort level for both the individual who is wearing it and for the viewer. Conversely, when we see a woman in the business arena wearing "bad" makeup or no makeup, we feel some visual discomfort. In the real world, makeup is as important as the clothes you wear and the style of your hair. It is an essential part of your grooming.

Our many clients, in their busy careers and family life, were simply uninformed and needed an introduction to the positive aspects of good makeup. When they were educated by professionals, purchased good-quality makeup, and learned how to integrate it into their routine, they were absolutely thrilled. Each and every one of them who had never given makeup much thought felt much better about themselves and the way they looked.

We're talking about makeup that relates to your personal style, makeup that is influenced but not dictated by a fashion trend or a media promotion. This is about making makeup work for *you*.

Lisa Casino and Michael Rey III are makeup artists and co-owners of Chroma Makeup Studio in Beverly Hills. They are known for their individualistic approach to what they call "makeup with awareness." They were kind enough to sit down and talk with us so that we could convey their ideas to you.

"Makeup is an invaluable tool on the road to discovering one's unique and individual beauty," Lisa and Michael explained. "This personal beauty exists within each of us. Makeup is either going to enhance that beauty or detract from it. When chosen well and properly applied, makeup is truly an enhancer.

"Each person should decide what makeup means to her—a little lipstick, a coat of mascara, or more. With the help of a professional, each woman will find out what is right for her. When you have an understanding of your own look, you can vary your makeup depending on your mood.

"The road to discovery involves understanding your needs and desires. You want makeup to work with your own unique facial structure and allow you to present your desired image to the world.

"We all have some facial features that we like and others that we don't like. We use makeup to enhance our best features and play down those we like less. It is our job as makeup artists to show you how to do that. You can actually change the way your features look with makeup; you can look in the mirror and see the differences. For example, we often hear, 'My lips are too small.' Well, you don't have to feel that way. There are several things you can do to enhance your lips.

"You must also be realistic and learn to accept certain things about yourself. If you feel your nose is too big, you can shade it—or you can learn to accept it. We have worked with many very beautiful women who can't see their beauty, while others who are not as beautiful have a very healthy appreciation for their looks.

"We are effective as artists only insofar as we can teach our clients to create the look and simplify it enough that they are comfortable with it. If you feel the makeup artist you are working with is unclear or not informative enough, then ask questions. Ask him or her to watch you apply the makeup, ask questions about why he or she chose a certain color. To help you simplify, we have the 'three W's':

"What—What is it?

"Why—Why am I using it?

"Where—Where do I place it?

"For example, 'It is a concealer. I use it to neutralize discoloration. I place it on the darkness under my eyes.'

"A desire to learn and practice will help make even clients who feel they have absolutely no talent capable of applying makeup acceptably well.

"As makeup artists we must honor the client's wishes and at the same time direct her toward what in our opinion is flattering and right for her. If a client has a strong desire for a color or procedure that we feel will create a distracting effect, then we do strongly state that opinion, and give our reasons.

"If it is at all possible, the best thing your readers can do for themselves is to locate a makeup studio that employs professional makeup artists and carries its own makeup line. Try to get a recommendation for a particular artist, or ask for a consultation to see how you feel about the artist. Any makeup artist can apply makeup, but a good one really listens to the client's individual needs. What is her lifestyle? What does she want? What is her history with makeup? A good makeup artist will listen well and then try to understand and interpret what the client wants. It is a process that unfolds.

"If you don't live in or can't get to a city that has a makeup studio and must rely on department store makeup, this information will help you.

"First of all, take control of your experience. Don't hand yourself over to someone. Carefully choose the makeup brand and the makeup artist.

"One way to choose the artist is to notice if you like the artist's own makeup. (If, of course, the artist is a woman!) Is it natural enough for you? Are the colors flattering? Is the style what you want? Or perhaps a talented male artist at a particular counter has a great reputation. Even though a man will not be wearing makeup, use your judgment about how he presents himself visually. Does he look as though he might relate to your sensibilities?

"Many department stores carry brands of makeup that can be custom-blended to your skin tone. This is the ideal choice when choosing which counter to consider.

"Prepare questions in advance if you need to, and make sure they are answered to your satisfaction during your consultation or application. Bring a notebook if you wish to take notes.

"Remember that the bottom line for department-store makeup-counter personnel is that they are there to sell to you. Do not allow yourself to be pressured, and say no if you are not sure.

"Go outside into the daylight with a mirror to ensure that you are happy with the result even in the brightest light.

" 'Designer name' makeup is not always the best quality. You are often buying the name and the packaging. Be careful that you are not drawn to the name only.

"Trends and seasons are also important to consider. After your makeup artist has worked with you to create a palette that works for your everyday needs and that contains your essentials, you can build on that little by little each season.

"Fashion plays a big part in what seasonal makeup colors will be. There is a natural evolution in the development of each season's colors. Fashion, architecture, and art are some of the influences that affect it. Our makeup colors also come from our own maturity and experience. Between us, we have twenty-six years of experience participating in and observing the trends. The difference from season to season may be the small addition of only a few elements, but there will be something notable each time.

"Nature's change also affects makeup. The sunlight is extremely different in the summer, and the clothing is lighter not only in color but in fabric, so the colors of makeup are lighter and sheerer. In the winter, the light will withstand deeper and warmer shades.

"The biggest mistakes are made in choosing colors. That's why it's so important to have an expert's eye to help you. An expert will help you to determine your skin's undertone. This is a vital step in the makeup-selection process. Some skin tones are naturally pinker and rosier while others are warm and golden. If you remember to stay within the warm or cool palettes, your makeup becomes an extension of your natural coloring.

"Another mistake is the amount of makeup people apply. Look for sheer products when first starting out, because they are easier to apply. You can build on them and are less likely to apply too much.

"The eyebrow is essential to the overall facial structure. We really urge you to have your eyebrows professionally shaped. And please go to someone who tweezes rather than waxes. Waxing does not afford the control that tweezing does. Tweezing puts the artist in complete control. The hair is removed one at a time. You are truly sculpting the brow, and you can see the shape unfold. Waxing can damage the skin in what is already a sensitive area. The wax can be too hot, and when it is removed, it can take your skin off with it. In the waxing process, the wax and muslin are placed on broad areas of the skin, obstructing the overall view of the brow. You do not know what you are left with until the removal of the hair. It is now, in many cases, too late to make a change.

"Makeup is truly magical. Do not be afraid of it or hide behind it. You should use it to its greatest potential and take advantage of its magical qualities."

A FINAL WORD

You have reached not the end but the beginning of a very personal and often intimate image journey. Your diligence, commitment, and discipline in completing the work in this book are highly commendable, to say the least. You have given yourself the opportunity to be the best that you can be from the inside out. Any transformation that takes place in this area of your life is an achievement on your part. May this transformation be as life-changing for you as it has been for so many of our clients.

We encourage you to continue taking field trips to refine you tastes and aesthetic eye. Return to your journal regularly to witness how far you have come and to refresh your memory about what you continue to move toward. Review your Personal Style Statement and continue to record all experiences that relate to your image journey.

Your journey has been paved with your own hard work. Questions and uncertainty are normal, and you will probably still make a few shopping mistakes—everyone does. But you now have a guide that will help you to eliminate those mistakes, and they will be fewer and farther between. Rely on your inner assets, and acknowledge that they are an equal and important part of your personal style.

Mary, our homemaker whose progress you have followed throughout this book, shared with us the most powerful thing she had learned from her work: she said that she had learned to trust herself. The magic of her style lay not in the style pages or in a fashion statement but in her. Her personal style was something that she owned, and it was like no one else's. She said it was an astonishing feeling.

You may be a teacher or a lawyer, you may be a parent or a scientist, but whoever you are, you aim to be successful in a way that has meaning for you. It is said that success is a choice. We firmly believe that the mix of success contains many disparate elements, and image is one of them. There are many things in your life that you are not responsible for. But taking responsibility for your image and the way your personal style evolves both inwardly and outwardly will bring you closer to the success you desire. This is one of the areas in your life that you have the ability to change. Use that ability and direct it toward a more fulfilling, inspiring, and creative life experience.

INDEX

acid colors, 197
Aesthetic Field Trip, 22, 51, 139–47, 214, 268
   evaluation of, 146–47
   guidelines for, 143–45
   Personal Style Profile and, 220–21
   planning of, 140–43
   what to look for, 145–46
aggressive behavior, 16
aging, fear of, 83–84
angora, 160
Aniston, Jennifer, 53
Anna (client)
   image wounds, 71–74
   inner style, 131–32
   Personal Style Statement, 42, 132
   physical assets, 78–79
anorexia nervosa, 66
antique shops, 142
armoring, 113
Art Museum Excursion, 213–16
assertive behavior, 16, 95
assets
   inner style, 129–30, 225, 299
   Personal Style Profile and, 220, 224–25
   physical, 77–84, 91, 220, 224–25
Atlas, Charles, 87
attitude
   as behavior factor, 103, 108–9
   shopping and, 272
   as style element, 7, 98, 99, 103–8

Attitude Inventory, 105–8
avoider (behavior style), 63, 88–89

bad taste, 174–75
Barbara (client), 198
bargain hunting, 270
Barrett, John, 287–91
behavior
   assertive vs. aggressive, 16, 95
   attitude as factor in, 103, 108–9
   effect of body image on, 62–64, 88–90
   emotional, 118
   good vs. stylish, 109
   as style element, 7, 98, 99, 108–23
Behavior Inventory, 117, 120–23
Biella, Italy, 190, 191
black clothing, myths about, 194
blaming, need to stop, 91–92
blond hair, 294
body image, 22
   actions for change, 88–96
   as behavior factor, 62–64, 88–90
   body talk and, 75–76, 90–91, 95–96
   compassion's importance to, 65–66, 95–96
   contributing factors to, 67–68
   definition of, 61–62
   dissatisfaction as universal, 64–65
   image wounds and, 68–75
   media influences on, 67, 84–88
   Personal Style Profile and, 222–23

body image (*cont.*)
  physical asset identification and,
    77–78
  physical communication and, 127
  sensitivity areas, 234–36
  visual history exercise, 76–77
  See also Personal Body Map
body language, 106, 121, 123
body talk, 75–76, 90–91, 95–96,
  222–23
Bonnie (client), 192, 193
bottom, sensitivity about, 234
Boyer, Charles, 55
breathing exercises, 93–94
budget, 261–62, 285
  price of clothing and, 169–70
  shopping list as guide, 265
  store return policies and, 278
  where to shop, 267, 270
Burke, Edmund, 115
business attire, casual, 119, 253–56
buttons, quality of, 152, 157

cashmere, 158, 159
Cash, Thomas, 67
Casino, Lisa, 295–98
casual Fridays, 119, 253–56
catalogue shopping, 268
categorization
  of clothes, 242–43, 247–61
  of style, 6–9
celebrities, media images of, 85–86
change, impact of, 5–6
charisma, 103–5
cheap and cheerful clothes, 255–57
checker (behavior style), 63–64,
  88–89
children, shopping with, 276
civility, 119, 123
clarity, of design, 164, 166–67, 212
client profiles, 11–12
Closet Analysis, 18, 23, 238–64
  filling in of wardrobe, 261–62
  garment categories, 242–43
  keepers category, 242–43, 247–61
  memories and, 240–41
  preparation for, 239–40
  troubleshooting tips, 244–46
  where and how to start, 241–42

closets
  garment care, 286
  organization of, 18, 107, 243
clothing, 16–18, 22, 148–89
  being current, 170, 173–74, 213,
    245, 278
  budget issues, 261–62, 265, 267,
    270, 278, 285
  care and maintenance, 18, 285–86
  casual business attire, 119, 253–56
  cheap and cheerful, 255–57
  Closet Analysis, 238–64
  color and, 17, 22, 189–216, 221,
    226, 276
  communication and, 123
  designer, 7, 162, 167–69, 269
  design of, 155, 157, 162–69, 174,
    212
  educating oneself about, 208–13
  elegance in, 58
  extraneous additions to, 163,
    168–69, 212
  fabrics, 149–52, 157–60, 174, 212,
    276
  fashionable, 171–73
  fit of, 17–18, 151–53, 155, 160–62,
    174, 269, 277, 285
  fun items, 256–57, 281
  high-fashion, 172–73
  Hunt exercise, 209–13, 245, 268
  "I feel special" garments, 257–58
  image wounds and, 74–75
  as investment, 154–55
  loner category, 173, 248–49, 272,
    277, 278
  messages conveyed by, 178–89
  overcoming dressing dilemmas, 107
  Personal Style Profile and, 221, 226
  price of, 169–70
  quality of, 17, 19, 151–60, 169–70,
    174, 212, 269, 270
  reinventing garments, 246
  seasonal, 271, 285
  secure-making, 107, 154–55,
    247–48, 270
  shopping for, 18, 23, 92–93, 265–98
  special-occasion wear, 258–60
  Sunday Best Syndrome, 286
  taste and, 174–78

trendy, 19, 170–71, 278
weekend, 249–53
color, 17, 22, 189–216
    Art Museum Excursion, 213–16
    challenging shades, 197–98
    emotionality of, 200–202
    of hair, 290, 291–94
    of makeup, 298
    myths about, 191–97
    Personal Style Profile and, 221, 226
    practicality of, 202–3
    selection tips, 199–200
    shopping considerations, 276
coloring hair, 290, 291–94
comfort, of fabric, 158
comfort colors, 203
communication, 5
    body language, 106, 121, 123
    with hairstylist, 290–91
    importance of listening in, 114–15,
        121
    physical, 127–28
    as style element, 7, 98, 99, 123–28
    verbal, 124–26
compassion, 65–66, 95–96, 106, 114,
    120–21
compliments, 62, 95
Cooper, Gary, 85
cosmetic surgery, 48–49, 70, 85–86, 87
cotton, 157, 159–60
Cousteau, Jacques, 54
creativity, 140, 144, 177–78
cuffs, of shirts, 157
cultural heritage, 77, 78
current
    in clothing, 170, 173–74, 213, 245,
        278
    in hairstyles, 288–90

Daphne (client), 68
department stores, 269
depression, 186
design, of clothing, 155, 157, 162–69,
    174, 212
designer clothing, 7, 162, 167–69, 269
designer makeup, 297
desire, charisma and, 104
details, elegance and, 57–58
determination, charisma and, 104

Dhani (client), 78–79
Diana, Princess, 10–11, 54
dieting, 94
dimensionality, of fabric, 159
discipline, charisma and, 104
discount stores, 270
Donegal tweed, 158
dry cleaners, 286
durability, of fabric, 158–59

eating, shopping trips and, 275
editing, as taste key, 176
elegance, 56–58
emotionality, of color, 200–202
emotions, 107, 127
    hair color choices and, 293
    management of, 117–18, 122–23
    trying on clothing and, 153
empathy, 114, 115, 120–21
energy level, when shopping, 274–75
Eric (client), 27–28, 30
essence, personal, 128–29
Ethan (client), 197–98
ethnic neighborhoods, 141
etiquette, 119, 123
Eve (client), 48–52, 54, 56
exercise, 87, 94
eyebrows, 298

fabrics, 149–52, 157–60, 174, 212, 276
fabric stores, 143
fashionable clothing, 171–73
Fawcett, Farrah, 53
fear, 83–84, 204, 244
feet, sensitivity about, 233
Feldenkrais method, 65
Finney, Albert, 9
first impressions, 3, 10, 24, 98
fit, of clothing, 17–18, 151–53, 155,
    174
    body area sensitivity and, 234–35
    good fit identification, 160–61
    shopping considerations, 269, 277,
        285
    weight concerns, 161–62, 235
fluidity, of fabric, 158
Ford, Harrison, 55
fun clothing, 256–57, 281
furniture shops, 143

galleries, art/photography, 142–43, 213
Gandhi, Mahatma, 104–5
Garbo, Greta, 85
glamour, 52–54
Gordon (client), 46
graceful assertiveness, 16
Gretchen (client), 178–81
grooming
    body image concerns and, 64
    communication and, 123
    elegance and, 57

hairstyles, 15–16, 23, 53, 123
    color and, 290, 291–94
    new image and, 287–91
    trendy, 288, 289
Harry (client), 28–29
health and fitness
    actions for change, 94
    excessive exercise, 87
height, sensitivity about, 232
Hepburn, Audrey, 44, 80, 135
Hepburn, Katharine, 17, 85, 183
high fashion, 172–73
hips, sensitivity about, 234
Holden, William, 55
home furnishings stores, 143
Hosie, Diane, 292–94
humor, 116–17, 121–22
Hunt exercise, 209–13, 245, 268
Hutton, Lauren, 177

icons, personal, 43–45, 55, 80, 85
identity, 3, 9, 87, 267
"I feel special" clothing, 257–58
image, personal, 2–10
    attitude and, 107–8
    body image vs., 62
    clothing as source of, 153, 154
    as success factor, 300
image experts, 6, 209
image goals, 21, 43, 48–54, 57, 61,
    87–88
image wounds, 14, 22, 61–96
    actions for change, 88–96
    behavioral effects of body image and,
        63–64
    body image definition and, 61–62
    body image dissatisfaction and,
        64–65

body talk and, 75–76, 90–91, 95–96
    clothing-related, 74–75
    compassion for, 65–66, 95–96
    hairstyles and, 287
    identification of, 68–69
    media body image and, 67, 84–88
    negative body images and, 67–68
    Personal Style Profile and, 219–20
    physical asset identification, 77–78,
        220, 224–25
    visual history exercise, 76–77
impatience, 115, 121
impressions, first, 3, 10, 24, 98
inner style, 97–138
    assets, 129–30, 225, 299
    personal essence, 128–29
    Personal Style Profile and, 220, 222,
        223
    Personal Style Statement and,
        130–31
    shopping and, 272, 273
Inner Style Inventory, 14, 22,
    100–128
    attitude and, 7, 98, 99, 103–8
    behavior and, 7, 98, 99, 108–23
    communication and, 7, 98, 99,
        123–28
inspiration, 140
Internet, 141, 268
investment clothing, 154–55
invisible repair experts, 243
Isle of Lewis, Scotland, 149–50

Jackie (client), 181–84
John (client), 100–102
Julia (client)
    Inner Style Inventory, 14, 16, 111,
        113, 114, 116
    Personal Style Statement, 14, 42
    profile of, 12–19

Keaton, Diane, 17
keepers (clothing category), 242–43,
    247–61
Keller, Helen, 105
Kelly, Grace, 44, 55, 80, 135
Kennedy, John F., Jr., 59–60
Kevin (client), 130–31
King, Martin Luther, Jr., 104–5
knitwear, quality of, 156

linen fabrics, 157, 160
Linklater, Kristin, 125
listening, importance of, 114–15, 121
logos, designer. *See* designer clothing
loners (clothing category), 173,
    248–49, 272, 277, 278
Lovett, Lyle, 164

makeovers, 8–9
makeup, 14–15, 23, 294–98
manners, 119, 123
Martha (client), 70–71, 111–13, 120
Mary (client), 299
    Aesthetic Field Trip, 143, 220–21
    Closet Analysis, 262–63
    color issues, 204–5, 221
    image wounds, 80, 219–20
    inner style, 134–38, 220, 222
    passions, 31–35, 218–19
    Personal Body Map, 237–38
    personal icons, 44–45, 80
    Personal Style Profile, 218–23
    Personal Style Statement, 42, 46–47,
        137, 219, 280
    physical assets, 79–81, 220
    shopping list and trip, 266, 278–81
"matchy matchy" color, 195–96, 204
maturity
    emotional, 118
    taste and, 175
media, body images and, 67, 84–88
Menuhin, Yehudi, 260
Michaelis, David, 59
mirrors, avoidance of, 89
mohair, 160
Monroe, Marilyn, 86
mood
    as body image factor, 93
    color and, 196–97, 202–3
    exercise's impact on, 94
museums, 141, 145
    Art Museum Excursion, 213–16

Nancy (William's wife), 282
neck, sensitivity about, 233

Onassis, Jacqueline, 11, 294
opinions, personal, 36–39
Oscar (client), 184–86
outlet stores, 270

Paltrow, Gwyneth, 160
passion
    charismatic people and, 104
    emotion vs., 118
passions, personal style and, 21, 25–41
    discovery of, 32–35
    identification exercise, 26–28
    opinions and, 36–39
    Personal Style Profile and, 218–19,
        224
    risk taking, 37–38
    things disliked intensely, 36–37
    tools to help determine, 28–31
pastel colors, 197–98
patience, 115–16, 121
Patty (Paul's wife), 249–50
Paul (client), 42, 249–53
Personal Body Map, 89, 229–38, 240
    checklist, 236–37
    sensitivity areas, 231–36
personality, good design and, 164
personal shoppers, 6, 209
personal style, 2–4, 300
    discovery of, 6, 10
    identity and, 9
    inner style and, 7, 22, 97–138
    passions and, 21, 25–41
    self-reference as key, 75, 84
    sense of self and, 98
    shopping issues, 267–68, 285
    See also image, personal
Personal Style Journal, 20–21, 217–18,
    299
    Aesthetic Field Trip and, 143, 144,
        146–47
    Art Museum Excursion and, 214,
        215
    Closet Analysis and, 240
    Inner Style Inventory, 97, 105, 120,
        124
    Personal Body Map and, 230
Personal Style Profile, 23, 217–28, 240
Personal Style Statement, 14, 21–22,
    42–60, 140, 299
    Aesthetic Field Trip and, 143
    casual Friday attire and, 255
    changes to, 48, 51–52, 54
    Closet Analysis and, 240, 241, 244
    clothing's messages and, 178
    color issues, 192, 203, 216

Personal Style Statement (*cont.*)
  dictionary as tool for, 47
  elegance's reality in, 56–58
  glamour's reality in, 52–54
  Hunt exercise and, 213
  Icon exercise and, 43–45
  identification of qualities, 45–47
  Inner Style Inventory and, 130–31
  Personal Style Profile and, 219, 224
  shopping and, 267, 276, 277, 281
  sophistication's reality in, 56, 59–60
  special-occasion wear and, 258
  unrealistic vs. realistic goals, 48–54
physical assets. *See* assets, physical
physical communication, 127–28
  body language as, 106, 121, 123
physical fitness. *See* health and fitness
power colors, 193–94, 203
practicality
  of color, 202–3
  as design hallmark, 163
price, of clothing, 169–70
purity, of design, 164, 166–67, 212

quality
  Closet Analysis issues, 244
  of clothing, 17, 19, 151–60, 169–70,
    174, 212
  of color, 193, 194, 195, 212
  elegance and, 57
  shopping concerns, 269, 270

Rainier, Prince (Monaco), 55
recovery, of fabric, 158
red, as power color, 193–94
Reeve, Christopher, 104–5
relaxation exercises, 93–94
respect, 113, 114, 120. *See also* self-
  respect
restraint, personal style and, 118
Rey, Michael III, 295–98
risk taking, 37–38
Rob (client), 70
Rory (client), 36–37

salespeople, 270, 273–74, 297
sales, shopping at, 270
Savile Row suits, 151–52
seasonal shopping, 271, 285

seasons, makeup and, 297–98
secure-making clothes, 107, 154–55,
  247–48, 270
selective attention phenomenon, 91
self, sense of, 6, 9, 98, 110
self-confidence, 4, 103, 106, 144
  clothing as source of, 153, 154
  hairstyle and, 287
  shopping and, 273
self-esteem
  assertiveness and, 95
  body image and, 22, 62, 87, 88
  clothing as source of, 153
  hairstyle and, 287
  inner style and, 103, 109–14, 120
  shopping and, 273
self-reference, personal style and, 75,
  84
self-respect, 110, 113–14, 120, 175
sensitivity area, of body, 234–36
shirting cotton, 157
shirts
  care and maintenance, 286
  quality of, 156–57
shoes, 233, 286
shopping, 18, 23, 265–98
  experience maximization, 273–76
  for filling in of wardrobe, 261–62
  for finishing touches. *See* hairstyles;
    makeup
  garment selection, 276–77
  importance of focus in, 281
  key rules, 279
  lists for, 265–67, 272, 277–78, 281
  notebook for, 267, 272
  postponement of, 92–93
  post-trip considerations, 284–86
  right day for, 271–72
  seasonal, 271, 285
  store return policies, 278
  temptations and old habits, 277–78
  trying clothes on, 276–77
  up-market, high-end areas for, 142
  what to bring, 272
  what to wear, 273
  where to go, 267–70
shopping intention list, 266–67, 272
shoulders, sensitivity about, 232
silk, 157, 158, 159

simplicity, of design, 164, 166–67, 212
skin tone
    clothing color and, 196
    hair color and, 291, 292, 294
    makeup considerations, 298
sophistication, 56, 59–60, 130–31
special-occasion wear, 258–60
spouses/partners, shopping with, 275
steroid abuse, 87
Steven (client), 100–102
stomach, sensitivity about, 232–35
Stone, Sharon, 259
strapless dresses, 258
Streep, Meryl, 54
stress, 93–94
stretch fabrics, 159
style
    elements of, 98, 99
    verbal, 124–25
    See also inner style; personal style
style periphery, 269
Sunday Best Syndrome, 286
synthetic fabrics, 159

taste, personal, 174–78, 299
    Aesthetic Field Trip and, 139–47
Tate (client), 186–89, 202
techno fabrics, 157
Teresa, Mother, 44, 105, 135
thighs, sensitivity about, 234
Thompson, Emma, 98
thrift shops, 257
Tony (client), 165–66
trendy clothing, 19, 170–71, 278
trendy hairstyles, 288, 289
tweed fabrics, 157, 158

Ueland, Brenda, 123
understatement, in clothing, 163

Vanessa (client), 200–202, 204
verbal communication, 124–26
vests, 232
vicuña, 159
vintage clothing shops, 257
visual harmony, 41
voice, assessment of, 125–26
Vuitton, Louis, 167

waistline, sensitivity about, 233
weekend clothing, 249–53
weight (body)
    benefits of exercise and, 94
    fit of clothing and, 161–62, 235
    image wounds concerning, 70–71
    media images and, 86
    sensitivity about, 235
    shopping postponement and, 92–93
William (client)
    Aesthetic Field Trip, 225
    Closet Analysis, 263–64
    color issues, 206–8, 226
    image wounds, 224–25
    inner style, 132–34, 225
    passions, 39–41, 224
    personal icons, 55
    Personal Style Profile, 218, 223–28
    Personal Style Statement, 42, 55–56,
        59–60, 132, 134, 206, 224, 282
    physical assets, 81–84, 224–25
    shopping list and trip, 266, 282–84
Woods, Tiger, 133
wools, 157, 159–60

ABOUT THE AUTHORS

MALCOLM LEVENE has been designing clothes for more than twenty years. He was trained on Savile Row in London and consulted for numerous fashion companies before opening the renowned Malcolm Levene shop and designer label in London in 1982, which played host to business executives, politicians such as Tony Blair, and celebrities such as Kenneth Branagh, Tom Cruise, and Lyle Lovett. He is the cofounder of the Personal Style and Image Development Consultancy, which caters to corporate, private, and business clients internationally.

KATE MAYFIELD is a graduate of the American Academy of Dramatic Arts and has performed onstage in New York, London, and Los Angeles. She has trained extensively in body and movement awareness methods, including Pilates, the Feldenkrais Method, and the Kristin Linklater method of freeing the natural voice. She has worked with Malcolm for the last twelve years and is the cofounder of the Personal Style and Image Development Consultancy.